MW01628075

J. W.

"Alive As Long As He Lived"

"Alive As Long As He Lived"

THE STORY OF

JOHN WILLIAM FANNING

GEORGIA AGRICULTURAL AND

COMMUNITY DEVELOPMENT LEADER

Gene Younts

with Contributions on Leadership Georgia

by Dink NeSmith

Published in association with

The J. W. Fanning Institute for Leadership

The University of Georgia

STRATFORD PRESS, ATHENS, GEORGIA

Published in association
with the Fanning Institute for Leadership

Set in 10.5 on 15 Sabon
Printed and bound by Thompson-Shore, Inc.
The paper in this book meets the guidelines for
permanence and durability of the Committee on
Production Guidelines for Book Longevity of the
Council on Library Resources.

Printed in the United States of America
06 05 04 03 02 C 5 4 3 2 1

Library of Congress Cataloging-in-Publication Data available

ISBN 0-9671886-4-4

Front endpapers: "Yesterday's Cotton" as remembered and painted
by artist Jack C. DeLoney, Ozark, Alabama.
Back endpapers: "Celebrating America's Cotton" as depicted in a painting
by Jack C. DeLoney, Ozark, Alabama.

Family tree (pages xx and xxi) prepared by Suzanne Smalley,
The J. W. Fanning Institute for Leadership

For all whose lives have been enriched
by the words and work
of Dr. J. W. Fanning
as an educator
with the University of Georgia for 43 years
and as the co-founder
of Leadership Georgia

Contents

Acknowledgments

John William Fanning was one of the great Georgians of the twentieth century. For all practical purposes, his life spanned the century. He was born in 1905 and lived for almost ninety-two years. J. W., as he was fondly and respectfully called, left behind a legacy of accomplishments that should be described and documented as information for generations to come. We agree that Dr. Fanning was one of the most widely accepted, admired, and loved persons in Georgia, and in this book we are presenting his life's story for the reader to have a clearer understanding of what this unusual man did, the lives he touched, and the impact he had on our heritage.

Shortly after J. W.'s death, the decision to write the book was made in consultation with his two children, Sibyle Fanning Jenks and John William Fanning Jr. We knew the task would be awesome; yet our resolve was strengthened by the encouragement from them and scores of other people.

The notion of producing a history of J. W.'s life had been suggested as early as twenty-six years before his death. Dr. Fred C. Davison was serving as president of the University of Georgia at the time of J. W.'s retirement in 1971. In a communication to a campus editor, dated December 10, 1971, President Davison wrote, "J. W. Fanning is the most remarkable single individual it has been my good fortune to know. In his quiet way he affected the lives of more people and the direction of more institutions in Georgia, through his service to the university, than any other person. . . . It is my hope that some day someone will write a definitive biography of Mr. Fanning."

Many persons have contributed to this book. They have conducted numerous personal interviews, completed scores of questionnaires, contributed personal observations, and made available mementos representing experiences with Dr. Fanning. Our list of materials, though not exhaustive, has provided a wealth of information. Without the full cooperation of hundreds of people, this book would have been less than complete.

Sherry LaBoon, a graduate student in the College of Education, University of Georgia, spent many hours conducting audiotaped interviews with Dr. Fanning during the last four months of his life. She generously provided the authors the tapes, which were a rich source of information about his thoughts on all stages of his life. Without that information many details of his early and professional life never would have been learned.

Jeanette Stroer has served as a special assistant to the authors from the beginning of the project. Her skills in researching the libraries and photographic archives, her patience in making inquiries to hundreds of people over the telephone, and her total commitment and determination to see the book completed has been a major factor in making it happen.

Sibyle Fanning Jenks provided insights into her father's life that only a loving daughter possesses. She made available her family photo album, from which historical pictures were selected.

We are indebted to Bill Fanning, J. W.'s son, for providing information forthrightly about the relationship he had with his father and his perception of the professional and community achievements of his dad. Bill was also a rich resource for family photographs.

John Greene, J. W.'s nephew, was reared in Wilkes County, and his knowledge of family history added much to the details of the lives of the Fannings. His propensity to tell human-interest stories replete with humor transformed the mundane into the authentically alive.

Sam Nunn agreed to write the foreword, an excellent gesture since he and J. W. were close personal friends for decades. They knew and respected each other in ways only they understood and appreciated. We are grateful to Senator Nunn for this invaluable contribution.

Good photographs and illustrations energize the ability of the reader to remember people, places, and things dear to the heart. Jack C. DeLoney, a renowned artist from Ozark, Alabama, is in a class by himself when it comes to painting scenes of the Old South. He graciously gave permission for us to use images of three paintings that appear in the book. Printed on the inside front cover is his "Yesterday's Cotton," which portrays cotton being picked by hand in the field the same way it was done when Dr. Fanning was growing up in Wilkes County. On the inside of the back cover is DeLoney's "Celebrating America's Cotton," depicting a cotton harvest as it is done on large southern farms in the twenty-first century. These two harvesting scenes bracket the nearly ninety-two years that J. W. Fanning was on this earth. The reader also will enjoy a printing of DeLoney's "Dinner on the Grounds," probably a scene close to what J. W. enjoyed as a young man attending August church revivals.

The typing and retyping of the manuscript has been an arduous task requiring hours of tenacious labor over the keyboard of a computer. Our appreciation is expressed to Vicki NeSmith as well as to Jeanette Stroer for assuring that deadlines were met and quality was preserved.

A long list of individuals made numerous types of contributions that deserve special recognition: Gene A. Bramlett, Auburn University, a former colleague of J. W., for a number of written materials and his general comments about the life and accomplishments of the subject; Howard A. Schretter, a close-working associate of J. W., for comments about the man, especially his work in community and area development; Ruth Younts, the wife of author Gene Younts, for reading of the manuscript and offering many suggestions for improvements; Robert Newcomb, Nancy Evelyn, and Heidi Hensley of the photography group of the Georgia Center for Continuing Education, for digitizing all of the photographs and illustrations; Carol and Bob Leavell of Washington, who made arrangements for the author to conduct meaningful interviews in Wilkes County; Robert E. "Skeet" Willingham Jr., of Washington, who gave insights into the lifestyle in Wilkes County during the first half of the twentieth century and provided photographs; David Mills and Bobbe Nelson, Houston County, for locating persons who had worked with J. W. when he was a county agent in their county; Russell and Betty Slaton, Washington, who provided excellent background information on the history of Wilkes County; Gilbert Head and Venus Jackson, who were invaluable in our searches in the Main Library on the University of Georgia campus; Ed Chin, Marine Sciences Program, for his advice and suggestions about the formation of the Marine Extension Service and his comments about J. W.'s life; retired director Melba Cooper, interim director Norma Reed, and the staff of the Fanning Institute for Leadership—Suzanne Smalley, Diane Little, Niki Easterwood, and Amy Sumerlin; the curator of the Berry College archives; Douglas Bachtel of the College of Family and Consumer Sciences, University of Georgia, for providing useful demographic and historical data; Emily NeSmith Wilson, who collated all of J. W.'s personal papers; Dorothy Elkins of the Webb School, Bell Buckle, Tennessee, who made arrangements for a meaningful visitation to the school and town; Phil Hudgins of Community Newspapers Inc., for his many editorial suggestions and constant encouragement; the Office of the Vice President for Public Service and Outreach, for its support; the many friends, former colleagues, and family members who responded to surveys and special requests (their thoughts appear throughout this book).

We express our gratitude also to our editors. Melinda D. Hawley, with professional care and painstaking work, has assured that the text of the story conveys to the reader the true life and accomplishments of Dr. J. W. Fanning.

Foreword

If anybody's life story is a book waiting to be written, it is Dr. J. W. Fanning's. J. W. left an indelible imprint on Georgia and our nation.

This biography is special because of J. W.'s commitment to serving his fellow human beings in many ways. He was, among other things, a student leader in high school and at his university, an agricultural extension agent at county and state levels, a university teacher and student adviser, an agricultural extension specialist, a university administrator, a leader in his church and community, and a living legend in community and individual leadership development.

J. W. loved the state of Georgia, and he possessed a burning desire to help make it better. His life span traversed an amazing century. His mode of transportation changed from the horse and buggy to the train and automobile to jet aircraft. During his boyhood, Georgia was still straining to shake the ravages of the Civil War. There was the devastation to Georgia's one-crop agriculture by the ravenous boll weevil in the early 1920s, only to be followed by the Great Depression. These setbacks fortified J. W.'s resolve: he would dedicate himself to leaving his beloved Georgia a much better place than he found it.

It was J. W. who built bridges from agriculture to business, to government, to academia.

It was J. W. who saw a need for greater understanding of the economics of agriculture and built one of the most productive economic research and service institutions in the nation.

It was J. W. who saw rural communities withering away because of a lack of money and management expertise and developed programs to help hundreds of communities, thereby delivering more than six million hours of service to Georgians each year.

It was J. W. who saw Georgia's 159 counties and hundreds of cities often struggling in isolation and proposed area planning and development commissions so that small governments could pool their planning resources.

It was J. W. who developed Leadership Georgia, a program that allows young people from small communities to understand the problems of Atlanta's inner city while helping young urbanites see the challenges of making ends meet in the state's rural areas.

One of J. W.'s earliest professional assignments was in 1933 in Houston County, where he served as a county agent for several years before moving to the University of Georgia campus in Athens. His arrival in Houston County, where I grew up, was a few years before my birth, but he and my father soon became good friends. J. W. often visited the farm, and my father served under J. W.'s leadership on a number of county agricultural committees. Cotton was bringing Houston County farmers about five cents a pound in those days. J. W. and my father worked together in implementing one element of the Agricultural Adjustment Act, which encouraged farmers to reduce their cotton acreage in favor of other farm enterprises.

I became particularly close to J. W. during the early days of Leadership Georgia. I was a member of the first class in 1972, and I fondly recall the early organizational meetings. I can testify to the benefits from that experience throughout my career. I called on J. W. for advice and counsel through the years. He supported my decision to run for the U.S. Senate in 1972 and often guided me through rough waters while I served as senator. J. W.'s advice was always as good as gold. He had a profound effect on my life and the lives of thousands. He has departed this life, but his vision and influence have multiplied many times and will be passed on from generation to generation.

The authors of this tribute have an excellent background of experiences with J. W. to present his story objectively and meaningfully. Gene

Younts was first hired by the University of Georgia under J. W.'s tutelage as director of the Rural Development Center at Tifton in 1969. Later, Gene was to follow J. W. as university vice president for services, a position he held for twenty-eight years. His position afforded Gene the unique opportunity for a close insight into J. W.'s accomplishments. Gene traveled the same roads around the state and became acquainted with many of the people who had known J. W.

Dink NeSmith first met J. W. when selected as a participant in the Leadership Georgia Class of 1983. The bond of friendship and a mutual admiration began immediately, and Dink was soon to occupy a strategic leadership role in the organization itself. The two of them worked closely in boosting this wonderful enterprise, and like most others, Dink was absorbed by J. W.'s demeanor.

Abraham Lincoln asked that he be remembered as one who always plucked a thistle and planted a flower where a flower would grow. John William Fanning plucked thistles and planted flowers his entire life. And now, thanks to this book, J. W.'s flowers can be seen by all.

Sam Nunn
Atlanta, Georgia
March 2001

Prologue

When I look back at the last century, outside of public office, there were some real giants in Georgia. Four people come to mind: Robert W. Woodruff, John Sibley, Martin Luther King Jr., and J. W. Fanning. Those four sum up the verse, "Where there's no vision, the people will perish." Vision was Dr. Fanning's real contribution to Georgia. He could almost see around corners and expect what was going to happen.

JAMES LEE ADAMS,
Leadership Georgia 1986

Life is in session. Are you present?

J. W. FANNING

The year 1905 came and went. There were no cataclysmic events at home or around the world that commanded the attention of the populace or the press. It was, however, a year that produced a few threats of global conflicts and skirmishes, and it saw a number of advances in the sciences and the arts. In a sense, America was coming of age following the devastation of the Civil War. The South, in particular, was putting the pieces back in place.

Theodore Roosevelt, the twenty-sixth president of the United States, began his second term in January. His fifth cousin, Franklin Delano Roosevelt, married Theodore's niece, Anna Eleanor, and their partnership would generate a tremendous flow of legislation to take the United States through the Great Depression and World War II. The Panama Canal was on its way to becoming a reality. Albert Einstein proposed his special theory of relativity, and Sigmund Freud published his *Three Essays on the Theory of Sexuality*.[1]

Events of August 1905 were unremarkable yet significant. In Washington, D.C., Teddy Roosevelt met with Russian and Japanese representatives to seek a solution to their Far Eastern conflict. Immigration in the U.S. was booming. More than one million U.S. immigrants arrived in 1904, principally from Italy, Austria-Hungary, Great Britain, Ireland, and Germany. The Chinese government halted the boycott of goods flowing from the United States.[2]

The Georgia House of Representatives passed a controversial child labor bill "providing that no child under the age of 12 years shall be employed at labor in or about any factory or manufacturing establishment within the state unless a widowed mother or disabled father is totally dependent upon the labor of such child."[3]

"Cotton in Need of More Rain," read a headline in the *Gazette-Chronicle*, a weekly newspaper in Washington, Ga. In a related story, the Atlanta Chamber of Commerce and local cotton men voted to send a commission of southern businessmen to China to establish better relations.

Another story with more local flavor in the *Gazette-Chronicle* on Wednesday, August 2, 1805, told the story of a farmer, Oliver Carter, and two mules that ended up in the Savannah River after the animals became frightened and backed Carter's wagon off Hester's Ferry. Two hours later, the wagon, mules and driver were back on land and ready to roll.[4]

On August 14, 1905, President Theodore Roosevelt's train was diverted on a trip from Chautauqua, New York, to Jersey City to ensure the president's safety following a bomb threat.[5]

In rural Georgia, John William Fanning drew his first breath.

The Fanning family, according to ancestral records, immigrated from Ireland in the late seventeenth century, first stopping in Virginia, where they farmed, mostly tobacco. From Virginia the first Fanning came to Wilkes County, Georgia, around 1787. In 1799, the year George Washington died, one of the first babies born in Wilkes was Welcome Fanning, J. W. Fanning's great-great-grandfather.

Welcome Fanning became a prominent citizen, accumulating nearly three thousand acres of land, most of which was in Wilkes County. The tax digest of 1857 showed him owning fifty slaves, as well as a number of mules and horses and cattle. His estate value was placed at $36,721, a tidy sum for those days.[6]

In another tax digest of that period, a clerk wrote the word "teacher" after the name Welcome Fanning. Records show him teaching for about ten years. Among his students was Robert Toombs, who later became a prominent political figure in the state. On one occasion, the story goes, Welcome disciplined young Toombs rather sternly, and Toombs later told a fellow student, "I'm going to beat the hell out of Fanning when I get big." Years later, when asked about his promise to whip Fanning, Toombs remarked, "No, I never did get THAT big."[7] Coincidentally, the state house of Georgia adopted a bill creating Toombs County on August 14, 1905, the day Welcome's great-great-grandson was born.[8]

John William Fanning would grow to be revered, a son of the South who envisioned its rebirth. He has been described as a visionary and a leader of unparalleled integrity and humility. But his private wish was simple: to guide a mule named Buck and to hold in his palm a warm clump of red Georgia clay.

Fanning Family Tree

08/02/01

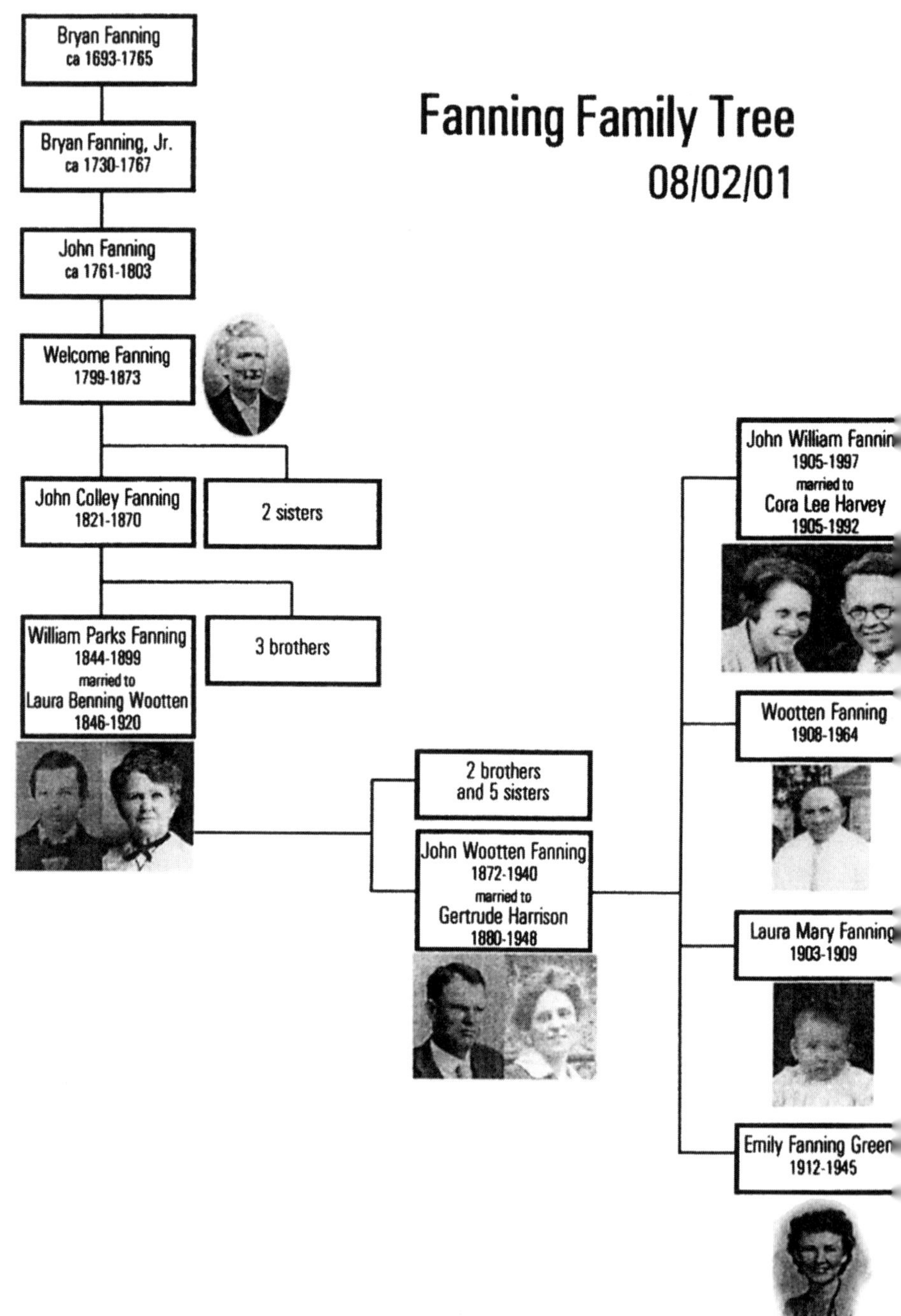

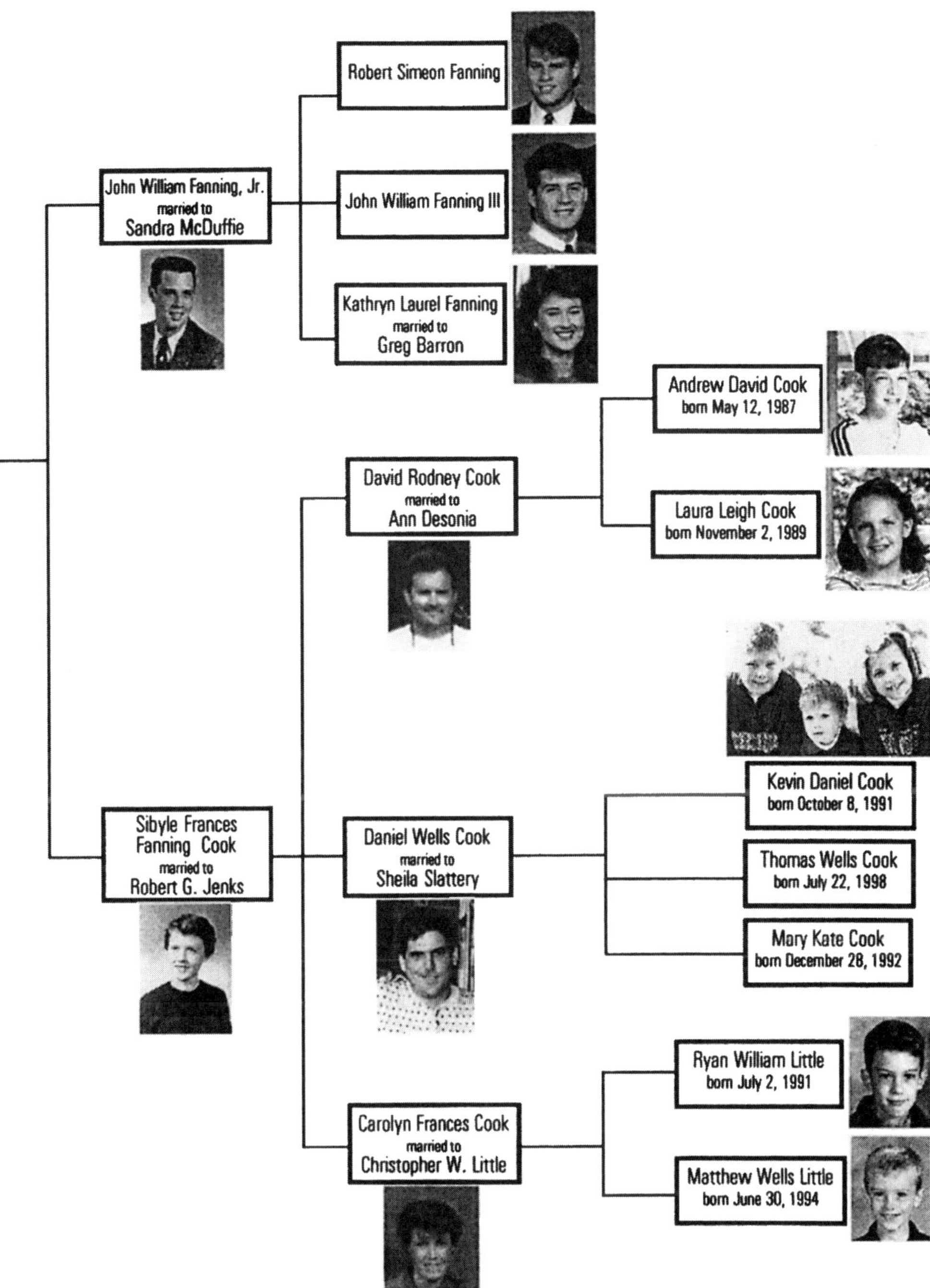
John William Fanning, Jr.
married to
Sandra McDuffie
Robert Simeon Fanning
John William Fanning III
Kathryn Laurel Fanning
married to
Greg Barron
Sibyle Frances Fanning Cook
married to
Robert G. Jenks
David Rodney Cook
married to
Ann Desonia
Andrew David Cook
born May 12, 1987
Laura Leigh Cook
born November 2, 1989
Daniel Wells Cook
married to
Sheila Slattery
Kevin Daniel Cook
born October 8, 1991
Thomas Wells Cook
born July 22, 1998
Mary Kate Cook
born December 28, 1992
Carolyn Frances Cook
married to
Christopher W. Little
Ryan William Little
born July 2, 1991
Matthew Wells Little
born June 30, 1994

There is no doubt that J. W. lived a complete life,
witnessing everything from the
horse and buggy to putting men on the moon.
He had his problems but rose above them,
taking life as it came.
It is difficult to describe his personality
because it contained so few flaws, but it would be great to
have it done using the right words so those who never
knew him would understand that he was indeed
a great individual through and through.

FRED C. DAVISON,
University of Georgia colleague

You can take a day off but you cannot put it back.

J. W.

CHAPTER ONE

The Formative Years, 1905–1923

J. W. Fanning got much of his grit and determination from his father, John Wootten Fanning. John Wooten didn't have much when he married Gertrude Harrison on June 4, 1902. The story is, he carried his bride home to a borrowed house in a borrowed horse and buggy.[1]

John Wootten was a man driven to provide for his family a better lifestyle than he had as a child. He was born into poverty, but he was determined to escape it. After laboring on his farm all day, he worked a second job managing the local general store. Despite his absences, the family was close-knit. Father, mother, and children managed the many tasks of growing crops and raising livestock.

J. W. had two sisters and a brother. Mary, born in 1903, was the firstborn in the family, two years J. W.'s elder. J. W. was the first son, born in 1905, followed by brother Wootten in 1908, and sister Emily in 1912. Mary died of diphtheria in 1909. She was six years old. She wasted away to practically nothing before she died. Her obituary appeared in the *Augusta Chronicle* on August 8, 1909: "A sad gloom settled over the home of John Wootten Fanning. It was the king of terrors as we call death who visited his home and tore away little Mary to the land of sunshine and smiles. For many months, this little girl suffered untold damage that puzzled the most skilled physicians. When the last breath left her body, she was nothing but a skeleton."[2]

About one month after J. W. was born, the Fannings moved to rural Tyrone, eleven miles southwest of Washington toward Greensboro.

They first lived in a small wooden shanty while the father built the permanent house on land that would soon be the family farm. John Wootten had bought a handsome piece of property with considerable frontage on Sandy Cross Road, stretching from Wilkes County across Little River into Taliaferro County. The size of the initial tract of land is not known, but it grew to more than one thousand acres.[3]

The home was positioned at the corner of Quaker Spring Road and Sandy Cross Road, on a spot from which John Wootten could view almost his entire farm. It was here J. W. became immersed in a rich and happy farm environment for the first eleven years of his life. The values he learned in both the pleasures and the drudgeries of farm work affected his thinking and demeanor throughout his nearly ninety-two years.

All his life J. W. longed to be a "dirt farmer"—one who makes a living working the land. As an adult, far removed from tilling the red Georgia clay, he would recall the good feeling of plowing. The sights and smells lingered: the slow, steady motion of the big red mule named Buck, the pleasant odor of freshly turned soil, and the grunts and clangs of feeding and milking the cows.

Growing up in the Tyrone community was secure. Families were neither desperately poor nor independently wealthy. You did for yourself, or you did without. And you normally worked from sunup until sundown, five days a week—sometimes on Saturday but never on Sunday, which was always reserved for church and rest.

Fathers took their sons to the fields as soon as they were big enough to help with planting, hoeing, cultivating, and harvesting. In early twentieth-century Georgia, this usually meant only one crop: cotton. J. W. reveled in every task, despite the sweat and toil. He learned the value of hard work by watching his father, who drove himself almost relentlessly to produce a decent cotton crop.

Nothing compares with waking up on a farm, when the sun has yet to break the darkness. The family arose early because most of the morning chores could be accomplished without full sunlight. The rest of the day then could be devoted to field work. Once the roosters crow, night on the farm is over.

J. W. loved milking and working with livestock. He took great pride in owning animals. He bought his first brood sow with money earned from working his own one-acre patch of cotton.[4]

J. W. milked the cows every morning. Pail in hand, he walked through morning darkness to the barn, ladled a tin cup or two of ground corn and wheat into a wooden trough and watched the cows nose their way to the food. Sitting on a box or his haunches, he would place the pail under a cow's udder from the right side and begin a gentle squeeze that yields fresh, warm milk. The cow was not fooled, but she was content to allow the boy to fill his pail.

The evening milking would offer more of a challenge. Flies would torment the cows in the summertime, and they would switch their tails to shoo them away. Rain could make the barnyard muddy, and a wet, dirty cow's tail can be an awesome weapon against the milker.

If more than one cow was milked, each had her turn in a sequence that never varied, morning or night. The smell of warm milk, mixed with barnyard odors, is one a farm boy has fixed in his senses forever.

When the chores were done, then came breakfast, one of the great treats of farm life. The cook, or sometimes the wife and mother, prepared country ham in a heavy iron skillet. She also made grits, buttermilk biscuits, and eggs—sometimes scrambled, sometimes over-easy. Everyone's appetite was strong following morning chores, and a big meal was needed to sustain them through the hard work ahead.

After breakfast J. W. returned to the barn to get his mule, harnessed and hitched by his father to a cultivator. Before him lay a field of cotton with weeds that seemed to have sprung up as if by magic. They had to be removed if cotton was to be harvested in the fall.

A farm boy learned, by trial and error, how to hold the handles of the cultivator and guide the mule between the cotton rows. Sometimes the cultivator would drift too far to the left or right, plowing up cotton plants along with the weeds and testing his father's patience. The more he plowed, though, the better he guided the mule.

Plowing a team of mules to break ground also was a learning experience. If the moisture in the soil was right and if the mules or horses were well-disciplined—two big ifs—the plowing went well. The plow would glide and the soil would slide over the moldboard, turning itself bottom-side up. Soil buried the surface debris, which eventually rotted away.

A boy plowing in a hot field out of sight of the farmhouse often was independent. Sometimes he was lonely. But he did not stop except to rest his team or to take a drink of water from a jug of cool water from the well. By midmorning the water had lost much of its coolness, even though it was shaded by the wagon the team pulled to the field. By the end of the day, it was as warm as the late spring air, but it still quenched the boy's thirst and washed down lunch his mother had packed for him.

J. W. had plenty of time for thinking, and his background music was free: an off-key chorus of horseflies swarming around the mules and june bugs buzzing overhead and grasshoppers fluttering underfoot. The hotter the day, the louder the music. There was little to distract him as he wondered about the rest of the world.

The sticky nights that followed the hot, midsummer days brought fitful sleep. A farm boy would look for a cool breeze in the night so he could get his rest for the next day's work. But the heat would persist. Bed sheets would stick to his sweaty body as he turned, restless, in the bed, finally falling asleep just before the first rooster signaled daybreak. The saga would repeat itself until the cotton crop headed for the fall season, when the days shortened and the nights breathed cool winds through open windows.

J. W.'s earliest recollection was of the day his father brought home a surrey with a fringed roof. J. W. was four or five years old. John Wootten yelled for the family to come out into the yard to see the surrey pulled by a mule named Emma. Father was proud, and everyone in the family shouted at the sight. The surrey, unlike the old buggy, afforded room for everybody. The Fannings were making progress.[5]

Before long, another sign of progress graced the Fannings' yard. It was a little two-seated, red automobile—a Maxwell, without a top—one of the first cars in Wilkes County. The power of the two-cylinder engine was not impressive, but its putt-putt-putt drew attention as the Maxwell chugged through the countryside. J. W. remembered riding propped up on his knees in the seat, wind in his hair, filled with the excitement of a first visit to a circus, his father at the wheel. On one father-and-son trip, they rode to a Catholic school in Washington to deliver eggs from the store his father managed.[6]

The family's second automobile was a Buick passenger car, considerably more powerful than the little Maxwell. The Buick was speedier, but the Fannings loved the little red Maxwell. When it was driven away for the last time, they planted a good-bye kiss on its fender.[7] This was during World War I, and the family had plenty of money.

J. W. was now twelve years old, and it was time to learn to drive the Buick. His father taught him. Little supervision was needed, though, because few automobiles traveled the unpaved and rutted, dusty roads. J. W. would drive his mother to the doctor at a place called Hillman and to Athens and elsewhere—wherever she wanted to go. Driving was a rite of passage for J. W. Nobody said so, but he was now an adult.

Some Saturday afternoons as a young boy, J. W. would go to his father's store and watch John Wootten at work. "I am my father's son, and he is in charge here," he remembered thinking.[8] Many of the old men who came in to make purchases or just to loaf would greet J. W. and call him "Mr. William."

John Wootten was always looking for new ways to increase the family's income. Not all of his ventures were successful. He sometimes invested without much thought, and his quest for more land to farm increased his debt beyond his ability to pay. But he pushed on.

John Wootten missed opportunities to make it rich. He once snubbed a friend who tried to sell him $12,000 of stock in a company known as Coca-Cola. John Wootten didn't refuse because he couldn't lay his hands on the money. "I know farming," he said, "and that is where I should put my extra dollars." If he had invested in Coca-Cola stock in 1919, it would have grown in value to $46,088 by 1925 and to $253,800 by 1940, the year of his death.[9]

John Wootten could have used more money. High medical costs plagued the family, because Gertrude was sickly most of her life. Her medical bills often exceeded $500 a year, a daunting sum in the early 1900s.[10] Once, when Gertrude was in the University Hospital in Augusta, John Wootten and J. W. took the train to visit her.

J. W. was a small boy at that time, and was all eyes and ears. It was his first train ride. The noise of the train as it sat at the station in Washington frightened him so much that his father had to carry him on board. The conductor helped to calm J. W. once the train left the station. Now and then, when the engineer would blow the whistle, J. W.'s father asked the conductor to explain the source of the noise to his son. J. W. long remembered the conductor's story: "There is a big black horse pulling this train, and every time they hit him, he hollers."

Father and son arrived in Augusta and made their way to the hospital, where J. W. encountered his first elevator. Fear took over again, and his father once more took him in his arms and carried him on the elevator. J. W. never forgot those two frights. Yet pleasant memories accompanied them. After visiting his mother, J. W. and his father had an unusual afternoon. His father took him to harness races at a horse track in Augusta. J. W. remembered a famous horse named Dan Patch that was entered in the races. All in all, the day was magical for young J. W.[11]

Perhaps the most precious memory of his mother was the loving care she gave him when he suffered from recurring malaria, usually around the middle of September. J. W. lay in a hammock in the hall where the breezes blew, and his mother fanned him when his fever peaked. She made sure he had the right medicine, and read books to him and talked about her early life.[12]

The family's doctor, Dr. Amonson, commonly made house calls, and since Gertrude was sick most of her life, the doctor came often to the Fanning home. He charged three dollars for each visit; the Fannings paid what they could.[13] When no money was available, the doctor often accepted in-kind payments such as hams, fresh vegetables, or whatever was available. Dr. Amonson lived across the road from the Fanning family, and his son, Ed, was a playmate of J. W.'s. Once, during a hush-hush conversation, Ed left J. W. limp by destroying his belief in Santa Claus.

One day, while working at the sawmill, John Wootten suffered a serious injury that caused a large blood clot in the calf of his leg. Dr. Amonson came to the house and asked J. W. to hold a light above his father's leg so the doctor could see as he cut out the clot. While no anesthesia was used, John Wootten showed little discomfort during the operation. He gritted his teeth but didn't make a sound. J. W. was impressed by his father's courage.[14]

The two most dreaded diseases at that time were diphtheria and smallpox, both of which were killers; no vaccinations were available for either illness.[15] Visits to a dentist were rare. If you had a bad tooth, you went to the dentist and had it pulled. Only occasionally would the dentist fill a cavity. When he did, he used a foot treadle to grind the tooth in starts and jerks. Dentists did not use novocaine, and J. W. remembered having one of his teeth pulled without any painkiller.[16]

Complications from measles eventually claimed the life of J. W.'s paternal grandfather, William Parks Fanning, in 1899.[17] His widow, Laura Wootten Fanning, never remarried and lived a good part of her remaining years with John Wootten and his family. The Fanning house was not imposing, even for its day. It had only four rooms, which required some doubling up at bedtime. When J. W. was a small boy, he slept in the same room with Grandmother. She didn't like sleeping in total darkness, so an oil lamp kept them company during the night. He remembered being glad she was a live-in part of the household.[18]

Their bond was strong. Funny and amicable, Grandmother was a beautiful woman and a great storyteller, J. W. remembered. At times she spoke of her husband and their post-Civil War days. She was fifteen when the war began. Shortly after the war she married William Parks Fanning. Times were hard; survival was the only goal. She told stories of plundering by Union soldiers. She detested Yankees.

Wilkes County had supplied many able-bodied men for combat in the war. Grandfather Fanning was a member of the Wilkes Volunteers, a unit dispatched to defend Atlanta against General Sherman's army in the spring of 1864. William Parks, twenty years old at the time, wrote of the war in a letter to his Aunt Martha, dated less than a month before the Battle of Atlanta:

> Camp Randolph near Decatur, June 25th 1864
> Dear Aunt Martha,
>
> As I am idle now I will drop you a few lines. I arrived at this glorious place last Tuesday. I find the officers unpopular, overbearing & c. We have a great deal of guard duty to do. Drill one hour & half twice a day. I guarded the prisoners all day yesterday & last night. I just woke up. I have been sleeping ever since dinner.
>
> I went to Decatur this morning. I am so tired and sore I can hardly walk. Wyley Bryant [Wiley Bryant had been wounded at Sharpsburg with Hill's Wilkes Guards, was discharged, and reenlisted as a private in the Wilkes Volunteers] & some more of the boys went to Atlanta today.

> They say John Hood & Sherman are fighting like forty. They say General Robert Toombs said we would know the results by Monday evening. He said the hardest fighting will be tomorrow & next day . . .
> Signed,
> *W. P. Fanning*[19]

The family often heard Grandmother's stories on the front porch, an important part of the Fanning home. The family would sit there together, often with visitors, and relax in rocking chairs or lounge under a large magnolia tree that provided shade nearby in the yard. Most of the visiting took place at these two spots. J. W. remembered one visitor in particular, an old veteran of the Civil War who had fought alongside his grandfather. His tales of the horrors of war captivated his listeners. He spoke of unmerciful treatment meted out in Sherman's march to the sea from Atlanta to Savannah.[20]

Later in life, J. W. was asked what the South was fighting for. He replied:

> We were fighting for the South. Slavery was not the big issue, but it did become an issue when President Lincoln signed the Emancipation Proclamation a couple of years after the beginning of the war. Slavery was wrong, but the South was freeing its slaves already and probably would have freed them all eventually. The Northern states had imposed a tariff on England that was hurting the South's cotton crop and the economy of the entire region.
>
> We, the South, made the mistake of firing the first shot of the war at Fort Sumter, South Carolina. This gave the North the excuse to invade, and they came, disturbing the entire South. It was a terrible conflict, with a total of six hundred thousand young men being killed. My grandfather fought in the war because he was

> convinced that the South was going to become an independent nation, which he believed important for economic prosperity.
>
> The South was wrong, but it fought.[21]

Tales of Rebels and Yankees piqued the curiosity of young J. W. Fanning. He wanted to learn, and his hunger for learning deepened when he began school. His formal schooling started in a two-room, two-story building three miles from Tyrone. J. W. remembered the walks well. White and black students attended separate schools, but they walked together because the schools were in the same direction from home. The school for the black students came first, and they would drop off while the white students walked on. At the end of the school day, the blacks joined the whites on the return home. If it was raining, John Wootten arrived in the surrey to pick up his children.[22]

Like all of the students, J. W. carried a bucket lunch, which was placed in a small room at the school until recess. Students in grades one through eight attended the two-room school; one teacher taught in each room. Combining grades had some disadvantages, but J. W. thrived, listening to the older students and learning things in advance. J. W. soon was reading books. *Sinking of the Titanic* was one of his first.

J. W.'s first teacher was eighteen-year-old Addie Sue Griffin, who taught him for five years. She taught reading, writing, and arithmetic, plus English grammar and spelling. She taught him how to think, J. W. said, and he found all of the courses interesting. Schoolchildren in the lower grades liked and respected the teacher. J. W. was proud to be Miss Griffin's pupil.[23]

It was common in those days for a teacher to spend nights at the homes of the students so that she and the families could know each other better. Miss Griffin stayed with the Fannings two or three times a year. She also saw her pupils in their home environment and how they interacted with other family members. As J. W. said, "It was a special moment when Miss Griffin came to spend the night at our house."[24] He was proud that his family was singled out.

Even though the house was small, the Fannings found space for Miss Griffin to sleep comfortably. Most likely she retired to the parlor, because this was the room used only for special occasions and special guests. Miss Griffin always showed a genuine interest in J. W., he remembered. She had a great influence on him as he was beginning to understand the surrounding world.

In the early 1920s Wilkes County was approximately 75 percent black, a population that reflected the one-crop cotton economy.[25] Most black families were involved in the manual production and harvesting of cotton and lived on land owned by whites. Cotton undergirded the entire economy of the Tyrone community, and many of J. W.'s neighbors and friends were black.

J. W. developed a deep concern for all people regardless of race or status in life. He valued their contributions. When he was born, his mother was so weak and sickly she was not able to produce enough milk to feed him properly. As was a common practice in those days, a black woman in the community came to the rescue, providing him sustenance and serving as nanny during J. W.'s infancy.[26]

When he was about five years old, J. W. made friends with a black child named Joe Lee and two other black boys. He remembered riding with Joe Lee in the pan of a road grader, when suddenly the operator of the pan dumped them to the ground, bumping J. W.'s head and almost severing Joe Lee's finger. J. W.'s Aunt Lil was visiting at the time, and she ministered to both boys.[27] Joe Lee became a good friend, and J. W. knew him all his life. They visited each other's homes and often ate together. On October 30, 1985, the city of Washington proclaimed "J. W. Fanning Day," and Joe Lee was among the participants. "Joe was my friend," J. W. told the crowd.[28]

John Wootten was a model for his son, enjoying close relationships with blacks. He was more than an employer; he also had black partners in business and farming. Before John Wootten married, he found his first job plowing mules in the field for five dollars a month, or sixty dollars a year. Working next to him was a black man named Duncan Sherrar, who was making seventy-five dollars a year. Later, in 1910, John Wootten bought his first sizeable acreage, which joined the land where the family home sat. Duncan soon came to call, and the two men formed a partnership in farming that lasted the rest of their lives. John Wootten always referred to Duncan as his partner, never as a sharecropper. When Duncan died, J. W. and his father attended the funeral. J. W. remembered watching his father stand at the edge of Duncan's grave with tears rolling down his cheeks.[29]

He who cannot lie does not know what the truth is.

J. W.

As a young man living in Washington, Georgia, however, J. W. was exposed to racial conflict. Some experiences affected his thinking and philosophy. One was a mob scene near the Washington city jail. J. W., then about thirteen, had walked into town on a Sunday afternoon. A mob of white men, several on horseback and carrying guns, gathered in front of the jail. A black man accused of assaulting a white woman in Lincoln County had been brought to Wilkes County for protection, an impossible task for the county sheriff. The mob quickly dragged the prisoner from jail and lynched him.

J. W. was horrified. He thought the reality of all those men using pistols and shotguns to get one man out of jail was inhumane and unbearable. Strange sensations ran through his mind and body. He slowly walked the several blocks back to his home on Spring Street, thinking about what he had just witnessed. Later, after telling his story, his parents told him to stay clear of unruly mobs in the future.[30]

A short time later, no more than a few weeks, J. W. stumbled upon evidence of an equally heinous act by a mob. He had visited a friend in Stephens, about thirty-five miles from home. On his return home, in the sparsely settled countryside, he saw the remains of a man recently burned at the stake. Again, a mob had taken the law into its own hands; the man also had been accused of assault.[31]

Several black people were considered to be close to the family. One good male friend was called, coincidentally, Bill Fanning. J. W. remembered riding with Bill in a two-horse wagon filled with cotton. One day, the boys traveled into town in the wagon to pick up goods for the Tyrone store. After buying the supplies, J. W. and Bill went to a bakery where fresh bread had just been removed from a stone oven; and on the way home they ate the bread, johnnycakes, and cheese, and washed them down with soda pop.[32] He remembered those days with Bill as good ones.

Even the serious Gertrude, J. W.'s mother, laughed with little restraint in another incident that involved the family buggy, pulled by a small mule. During a ride downhill one day, J. W. and his mother noticed the buggy repeatedly bumped the back legs of the mule; the breeching of the harness was too loose. The mule responded by jumping and kicking, and ceased his frustrated dance only when he reached level ground. Greatly amused by the sight, Gertrude laughed uncontrollably all the way down the hill.[33]

J. W.'s maternal grandparents were William and Mary Harrison, both of whom lived until the late 1930s. Grandpa Harrison was a jovial live wire who didn't seem to take life too seriously. He took time to get to know his grandchildren. He played baseball with them, hiked in the woods, and talked about the things that interested them. J. W. also enjoyed his visits with Grandpa Harrison's brother, Uncle Wiley Harrison, and his wife, Aunt Ida. They had two daughters who were a few years older than him. The girls always gave him special attention. They told him stories, took him on long walks, and played all types of games with him. Uncle Wiley, a real character, told of stealing a rifle from a moonshiner who was defying the sheriff, daring the moonshiner to come and get him. The moonshiner never came, and Uncle Wiley later gave the rifle to Wootten.

Horse and mule riding was a favorite pastime for J. W. and his friends. The boys rode along, whooping and hollering as they played cowboys and Indians. J. W. loved the togetherness with other boys; but he often enjoyed the solitude of riding solo on his pretty bay mare, Billy, distinctive because of her slick, shiny hair and striking mane. His father bought Billy when J. W. was fourteen years old. J. W. often climbed on Billy's back and rode across the green countryside, jumping ditches and fording streams. Horse and rider trusted each other. J. W. rode the mare with an almost religious fervor until he left home for good. Later, when money was tight, his father sold Billy and two mules, Buck and Tag, to a man in Hartwell, Georgia. Many years later, when J. W. was invited to speak at a church in Hart County, he told the audience that some of his ancestors—Billy, Buck and Tag—were buried in Hart County.[34]

J. W. also liked buggy riding. He remembered taking a girl named Peggy Barker on a ten-mile ride into the country in an "open top." A heavy thunderstorm came up, but neither J. W. nor Peggy minded the rain as they huddled together on the way home. Two of his buddies had horses and so did three girls in town. So the six young people often went riding together. "One day we did not come home for lunch, and we got a good spanking when we reached home," J. W. recalled. "We were not supposed to be out in the woods with girls by ourselves because it was wrong."[35]

A favorite gathering spot was on Little River at Smith's farm, where cornmeal was made in large quantities during the Civil War and served to the Confederate Army. J. W. and his friends would go riding down there on Sunday afternoons. Often, one of the friends' mothers would cook a chicken supper for everyone. On one occasion, the group stayed overnight in the woods. When J. W. arrived home the next morning, his father was waiting for him. J. W. got a whipping, and was told never to stay out that late in the woods again with a group of boys and girls. J. W. later said the punishment was necessary to make him understand how wrong he was.[36]

A clear conscience makes a restful pillow.

J. W.

Most parents in those days spanked their children on occasions, and J. W. received his share of whippings because he often misbehaved. "When I shirked responsibility," he said, "I paid for it."[37] At times when his parents were away from home, they would leave him in the care of a black woman who was instructed to whip him if he got out of line. She did, several times. J. W. did not remember ever getting a spanking from his mother, but his father made up for her benevolence.

He remembered one episode in particular. He had attended a picture show in Washington starring Charlie Chaplin, and he became so engrossed in the movie that he stayed to see it three times. Suddenly, he felt a sharp rap on the shoulder and recognized his father's silhouetted image, even in the darkness. His father said, "Do you realize it is dark outside? Come on, let's go home." When they arrived home, his father walked over to a bush at the edge of the yard, removed a switch, and proceeded to give him a good thrashing.[38] As he was making his licks, J. W.'s father said, "I want you to remember I am not going to milk those five cows again. That's your job, and so is bringing in the wood to fill the boxes in the kitchen and elsewhere. Tonight you made me do it, and from now on you will do it. Remember that!" J. W. remembered.

Children learn a lot of things early on the farm. One of them is responsibility. They learned responsibility by doing daily chores. J. W.'s first chore was to feed the horses; as he grew older, the list also included feeding the chickens and cows. Milking the cows was next, when he got old enough to handle it. In the summer he worked in the garden, raising tomatoes, corn, cabbage, beans, cucumbers, onions, and other vegetables. Turnips were planted in the fall. Most of J. W.'s chores were outside, and at least one was a Southern ritual: sweeping the yard with a brush broom. Southerners didn't have lawns; they had bare dirt that needed sweeping, especially when the leaves fell in the fall. Brooms were fashioned from small trees in the woods, often the dogwood because its limbs were tough and stiff—just right for good clean sweeping.

Later in life, when J. W. talked about his childhood exploits on the farm and his responsibility for milking, he liked to tell a story about an old, devout Quaker man who was troubled by his cantankerous milk cow. After he would finish milking her, J. W. would say, she would invariably kick over the pail or even step in it, which would raise the farmer's ire above the level permissible for a Quaker. One morning when he had reached the end of his patience, he lectured the cow. "Thou surely knows that I cannot strike thee with my hand or kick thee with my foot," he said. "Thou knows that I cannot curse thee. But what I can do is trade thee to the Baptist preacher on the other side of the county, and he will beat the hell out of thee."[39]

People raised on a farm always looked forward to Saturdays when they skipped the drudgery of farming. Everybody, black and white, went to town, sometimes to the local Griffin Store in Tyrone, other times to the city of Washington. Saturdays were filled with relaxation and barbecues and people and wagons from all over the countryside. A Saturday feature at the Griffin Store was a game of marbles, which often became competitive and noisy. The contest was staged on bare ground inside a circle about a yard in diameter. Each contestant placed a specified number of marbles in the center of the circle. Players would get on their knees and try to knock the marbles outside the circle by propelling a shooter—a taw—into the group at the center.

On Sundays, everybody in the community went to church, usually to a worship service in the morning and Sunday school in the afternoon. The Fannings attended Phillips Mill Baptist Church. Established in 1785, it was one of the oldest churches in the county.[40] The family chose this church because it was close to home. John Wootten had been raised in the Methodist church, but Gertrude grew up a Baptist.

Their young son, curious and eager, would marvel each Sunday at the large number of horses and mules tied to wagons and buggies in front of the church. The animals stood quietly, as though they were meant to be there. Inside the church, the seating arrangement placed women and young children on the right and men and older boys on the left. J. W. sat on the right side with his mother until he was about ten years old. One Sunday, his father unexpectedly took him by the hand, saying he was old enough to sit with him. It was a moment without ceremony, but it was a symbolic rite of passage, another stage in life.[41]

The worship service consisted of hymn singing by the congregation, preaching by the minister, and soul-saving at the end. A man named John Key Griffin led the congregation in singing, and J. W. learned to sing. His two favorite hymns were "When the Roll Is Called Up Yonder" and "Shall We Gather at the River." These traditional hymns were sung frequently throughout the rural sections of the Bible Belt because they contained messages of promise, beauty, rest, and plenty in the hereafter. Hard-working folks of modest means yearned for a better day, free from the toil and heartaches that spanned generations on cotton farms of the Georgia Piedmont.

After church, the family returned home for Sunday dinner, prepared by the family's black cook and often enjoyed by ten to fifteen friends—the exact number was never known in advance. Sunday was the one day in the week when meat, usually pork or chicken, was on the table. Beef was a rarity because there was no refrigeration; the icebox would come later. Pork could be cured with salt and kept for long periods of time, and chickens were caught, killed on the spot, and readied for cooking or frying.

Most farm families had yard chickens that roamed free, scavenging for food among the grass and debris to add to the nightly handful of grain they were fed. Their diet produced a meat with a distinctive flavor appreciated only by those who have tasted chicken from the rough. Yard chickens sometimes required special care. A hen would "steal her nest"—hide it well—and hatch a batch of chicks that would instantly be at risk for survival. This was particularly true when hatching occurred in the cold of winter, when the hen and her biddies had to be sheltered in some way. On the Fanning farm, John Wootten would secure the hen and her brood in a wire cage near the wood stove in the kitchen. Once, J. W. was heckling a hen and she pecked him. Two weeks later, he broke out with a serious case of chicken pox, which he always attributed to the sharp peck.[42]

To make an extra-special Sunday meal, Gertrude occasionally would buy a piece of beef from a man in Tyrone who slaughtered a cow nearly every Saturday and sold the meat from his buggy, which he drove from house to house.

In the afternoon, the Fannings—minus the head of the family—returned to church for Sunday school and Bible study. J. W.'s teacher was Mrs. Ashbury, whom J. W. remembered mainly because of her beautiful surrey, pulled by a handsome gray horse. Mrs. Ashbury required her students to commit to memory many verses in the Bible. She called on students to recite the verses, providing proof they had learned their assignments. Sunday church experiences formed a strong foundation for J. W.'s adult religious sense and self. His mother believed children should be grounded in the Scriptures and spent a lot of time teaching J. W. to pray.

A rooster isn't unpopular because he wakes up early. It is because he has so much to say.

J. W.

Protracted two-week revival meetings at Phillips Mill Baptist Church came as regular as the cotton seasons, and they were always held in late August, when heat shimmered visibly above the green fields and dusty roads. There was a lull in farm work then: the cotton crop was "laid-by" and on its way to full maturity. A laid-by crop no longer required cultivation or hoeing, and farm implements were set aside for the next season.

A revival meant that an invited preacher from another church, usually some distance away, would lead the main part of the service amid intense preaching, praying, and singing. The rafters in the old Phillips Mill Church would reverberate from fervent messages from the pulpit and exultant, high-volume singing. Rural folks who worked daily in the fields had strong lungs, and having another crop in its final stages was reason enough to sing without inhibition.

An anticipated part of revival meetings was dinner on the grounds—twice during the two weeks for the Phillips Mill congregation. Dinner on the grounds was a sumptuous meal prepared by the ladies of the congregation—or their cooks—and brought to the church in cloth-covered baskets. The food was held until the morning service concluded, then carried to tables set up outdoors under the thickest shade trees in the churchyard. All worshipers in the church knew a feast awaited them, and at times they were certain—especially the young folks—that the preacher was speaking much longer than usual.

As the dishes were set out on the long tables, the feast was a sight to behold. There was fried chicken, cured ham, clabber-milk biscuits, corn bread, vegetables of all kinds, cabbage slaw, sliced tomatoes, pickles, cakes, and pies of all descriptions. The tables literally creaked under the weight of the dishes. On one table sat a large tub filled with sweet lemonade or cool water readied by the men; an aluminum dipper hung next to the tub for filling drinking glasses. Watermelons were in season, heaped and ready for slicing.

At last, it was time: adults went to the tables—first men, then women. Children were last. Plates were heaped with a selection of the most delectable choices available. Flies were a constant nuisance, hovering too close and lighting on the food. Men would break branches from a nearby tree or bush to shoo them away, but it was useless. People just fanned them away while they filled their stomachs. Any edible leftovers at the end were returned to baskets and carried home for supper.

In later life J. W. liked to tell a story about a South Georgia church that held its two-week revivals and dinner on the grounds in August. This church would always invite some preacher from Alabama to lead the services. One year, as always, the church had preaching and dinner on the grounds, preaching and dinner on the grounds, preaching and dinner on the grounds. By the end of the two weeks, the preacher had almost lost his voice. As he walked toward the tables where the last of all the dinners on the grounds would be enjoyed, the hoarse preacher asked a rather stout woman what she thought of the services.

She said, "Preacher this is the best revival I have ever attended. I don't believe I can eat another bite." Well, the preacher, a little miffed, turned to her son, Willie.

"Willie," he asked, "what did you think of the revival?"

And Willie replied, "Just like momma, I had a belly full, too."[43]

Holidays came and went with little celebration because farming required daily diligence, especially when animals were involved. Christmas, however, was special. It was more of a celebration at church than at home. The family would go to a morning service and then return in the evening for a program that often focused on children. A large tree covered with decorations was placed in the center of the church, and at the appropriate moment Santa Claus would enter carrying gifts for the children, especially the little ones. The preacher would close the program with a Christmas message, and everyone went home.

J. W.'s father would buy oranges and apples, which he hid all over the house, and the children were challenged to find them. No stockings hung on their mantel, but they did at church.

New Year's Day was not a major holiday, but folks gathered at the Griffin Store in Tyrone to watch a fireworks display, just as they did on the Fourth of July. Easter was special only at church, where the minister preached, the song leader focused on the Resurrection, and the children occasionally performed a short skit.

People celebrated the history of the region on Memorial Days. The town filled with people from the countryside. Eloquent speakers stirred the crowds, delivering lengthy orations that paid homage to the South and the loyalty of southern people "to the cause." All the students and teachers from the local school went to the courthouse to hear the speakers.

J. W. was absorbed by the speakers' skills. He listened from the balcony. He studied the speakers' modulated voices and easy tones that could hold the crowd spellbound. Later in life, when J. W. was invited to make speeches himself, he would remember those Memorial Day orators when rehearsing his own style of delivery.

Many of the speakers were almost heroes to the young J. W., but not one came close to William "Bill" Hart. Hart was a cowboy actor who rode a pinto pony. J. W. never missed his movies when they were shown in town. Cowboy Bill Hart rode hard and did a lot of shooting, and he and the pinto had a show of their own in the circus that visited Washington. J. W. was thrilled to see his hero in person. He admired the man throughout his whole life; and on a trip out West many years later, he visited Hart's gravesite in Denver, Colorado.[44]

Another hero was a Washington resident, William H. Slaton, a lawyer. As a boy, J. W. would visit Slaton, and the two of them would talk about current events and other topics. J. W. admired Slaton for his wisdom as Slaton advised him on a variety of issues.[45] Slaton and other men filled some of the gaps J. W. felt throughout his youth, gaps caused by lack of time with his busy father.

From time to time, the Washington community would hold a "Chautauqua," a popular educational event of the early twentieth century. A person of note would deliver a lecture, and people would come to listen. The Chautauqua speakers were mayors, governors, members of the legislature, university presidents, and distinguished learned people. J. W. thought the presentations were too deep for him, but he did remember one humorous lecturer who held the rapt attention of all of his listeners. The talk impressed J. W., and humor became a trademark of speeches of the adult J. W. Fanning.[46]

J. W. also enjoyed acting in the plays the school put on in the Masonic Lodge across the road from the schoolhouse. Children never figured out the real purpose of the lodge building, and one day they asked a man about it. He replied, in a peculiar manner, that there was a billy goat on the top floor of the building, and everyone initiated in the Masonic Order had to ride that goat all the way down to the ground floor. J. W. and the other children thought this was funny, and they always wondered where the goat was kept when not being ridden. They never did get an explanation.[47]

The annual arrival of the circus was another memorable event of childhood. The circus train would pull into the Washington station, disgorging animals, circus performers, and workers carrying the big tent and support gear. The animals were unloaded and a parade was held down the main street, lined by people young and old who would later assemble under the circus tent. Children would sit in awe of the performers on the high wire and swings, imagining one day they themselves would be up there.

Wilkes County fairs were held each year, usually around October, to coincide with agricultural harvests. The men exhibited farm commodities and animals of all types, and the homemakers competed in food preservation, sewing, and knitting. The fair even held horse races.

Gypsies—a band of gaudily dressed people—made their way to Washington once or twice a year to trade mules and horses and to try to steal items from the people. They camped just outside of town. Georgians seldom swapped horses or mules with the gypsies; the gypsies couldn't be outdone.

One day J. W. and two of his buddies rode on their horses to see them. One of his friends was riding a spotted pony, another a Texas pony, and J. W. had an old gray horse. The gypsy boys challenged J. W. and his friends to a race. The boys accepted. It was just plain fun, J. W. recalled. Another incident wasn't fun at all: J. W. was driving his mother home from Athens one day, and gypsies stopped the car. One of the gypsy women climbed into the car, presumably hoping to steal something. J. W.'s mother ordered her to get out. She did, reluctantly.[48]

The best adventures, however, always involved J. W.'s father. Family vacations were rare but memorable. Usually his father took the family to the North Georgia mountains. Spending one night away from home was an adventure in itself. The cool mountain air was a relief from the heat and humidity of Wilkes County, and the sights were spectacular. J. W. never forgot the thrill of sliding down Neels Gap. His father would stop the car, cut off a sapling branch and place it in the spokes of the wheels. The contraption would slow the sliding vehicle enough to ensure a safe trip to the bottom.

Wilkes County seldom got snow, but it was plentiful the winter of

1919. It stayed on the ground for weeks. J. W. recalled the snowfall not so much for its depth and longevity, but because that was the time he went sledding. His father made a sled to which J. W. hitched a beautiful horse, Prince Albert. J. W. took his brother, Wootten, sledding across the countryside—through the harvested cotton fields, along wooded trails, and down the main roads. It was an unforgettable experience, the type that triggered all of the winter fantasies that small minds could conjure. J. W. loved the stillness of the ride as the sled made its way across the snow. The horse's hooves and the sled runners would make crunching sounds as they broke through the frost heave that was so common on the frozen red soil of the Piedmont.[49]

Around 1917, the family moved from rural Tyrone to the city—a house at 506 Spring Street in Washington—so J. W. could attend what was recognized as a better school.[50] His parents, especially his mother, thought the change to in-town life would be good for the entire family. In truth, J. W. was upset by the move; he missed the closeness of the two-room school and good times with his teachers.

This was during World War I, and the family was doing well. Cotton prices were high. John Wootten farmed nearly a thousand acres of cotton, and he was a good cotton trader. As J. W. put it, "We were rich and living high on the hog."[51] His father thought differently. Washington, he said, had two classes of people, the rich and the poor, and they belonged to the poor. Actually, the Fannings probably were closer to upper-middle class—not rich, but comfortable.

World War I was going strong when the family moved from Tyrone, but J. W. didn't realize the country was engaged in a struggle with a foreign power. He didn't know the war affected the whole life of the community. Several local young men had gone into the Army, and some fought in Europe. J. W. remembered them coming home from the war and his father talking about the ones who died. A Canadian soldier who came to the community talked about being gassed by the enemy. One local soldier returned home with a French bride, and J. W. remembered admiring her beauty. But the woman could not adjust to the rural Georgia culture and quickly returned to France. One of J. W.'s aunts married a soldier, a Mr. Gresham, who brought home horrendous stories about the war. Actually, much of what J. W. learned about the war was from newsreels at the picture shows.

As J. W. entered the sixth grade in Washington, grades were separated into individual classrooms. His teacher was Miss Annie Fluker, a strict disciplinarian who taught all subjects. J. W. remembered how she handled an unruly situation with a classmate named Gunter: she took his hand, held it open, and whacked it solidly with her ruler.

J. W. had many friends. His adolescent years were filled with parties, barbecues, swimming, and seining—catching fish in a net—in the river. Prom parties came often and required stamina. A host would invite a group of boys and girls to his or her house for the party. Each boy was given a blank card with fifteen or so numbered lines on it. Each boy would sign a girl's name on each line for a "prom": a ten-minute walk, or promenade, along the street in the neighborhood of the host teenager. When each walk was over, the host would call the next prom number, and this would continue until the entire card was finished. J. W. had his first prom date when he was twelve or thirteen. His father hooked up the horse and buggy and took him to get the girl. All three of them went on to the party.

Barbecues were a common social activity for country folks at Quaker Springs, a place on Little River where stagecoaches used to pass. When he was about fourteen, J. W. attended a barbecue he never forgot. After the food had been served and eaten, the young man sat in a swing to pass the time. A young girl, his cousin by marriage, sat down beside him. J. W. experienced perhaps his first real attraction to a pretty girl. As he put it, "I just sat there unable to say a word, admiring her beauty, and I felt my heart take an extra flip."[52]

Her name was Lucy Lowe Hunter, and they became good friends

and visited each other's homes. They even wrote to each other when J. W. left Washington. Lucy had a sister named Nina, who was a talented and versatile musician. Young people often gathered on their porch in the evenings to listen to Nina play and to join her in singing songs. Many years later, during his final years, J. W. visited Lucy Lowe in Decatur, Georgia, to reminisce about childhood and teenage experiences.

About the easiest person to fool is yourself.

J. W.

The seventh grade under Miss Annie Neeson was a disaster. J. W.'s social life was flourishing, but his grades were flagging. "I just plain quit paying attention to my studies," he said. "I let myself go and was having fun. Those were the days."[53] At the end, J. W. was told he would have to repeat the seventh grade. J. W. was disappointed. Next time around, his teacher, again, was Miss Neeson.

This time, she did not let up. She demanded excellence in all of his subjects. J. W. met the challenge and was promoted to the eighth grade, if not with distinction. He admitted making many mistakes in his sixth- and seventh-grade years. He did not learn. He did not take advantage of opportunities.

Seeing their son repeat the seventh grade and showing little improvement in the eighth, J. W.'s parents made a decision that would change his life forever. They enrolled him at the Webb School in Bell Buckle, Tennessee, in September 1920. They had learned about the school from a cousin who had enrolled his son there.[54] Few girls attended Webb. Fewer distractions were available.

J. W.'s father rode the train with him and his cousin, Joseph Ferdinand Fanning, to Bell Buckle, and helped the boys enroll and find a place to live. The Webb School had no dormitories; students lived with local families. The two boys moved in with the Wheeler family on Peacock Street. They considered themselves lucky, because Mrs. Wheeler was an outstanding cook who served plenty of food at every meal. Her sorghum syrup and country butter on hot biscuits helped to fuel the boys' two-mile round-trip walk to the Webb School. And, few meals in his whole life matched the one Mrs. Wheeler served on Thanksgiving Day in 1920.[55]

William Robert Webb, affectionately known to thousands as "Old Sawney," founded the Webb School in 1870 at Culleoka, Maury County, Tennessee. Sawney was a versatile and forceful man who left a permanent mark on education and in other arenas. He was a Civil War veteran from North Carolina. He had learned the elements of a sound, basic, secondary education by studying in a school led by the formidable W. J. Bingham—"Old Bingham" to his students—a tough teacher and strict disciplinarian.

William Webb learned what a touch of hickory to a young man's behind would do for lesson preparation. This was the master teacher's way of communicating expectations. When a boy did not know his declensions in Latin, he got a thrashing from Old Bingham. Webb said, "That's the only school I ever saw where thirty or forty boys knew their lessons every day, and never missed." Old Sawney would apply Old Bingham's pedagogical method to instruction at his own school years later, and with similar success.

Sawney served in the U.S. Senate in 1912. His was a short but illustrious career. But his greatest contributions were in education: the establishment of the Webb School and the instruction and guidance he provided thousands of young students. He was principal of Webb from its founding until his death in 1926. Sawney's brother, John Maurice Webb, a scholar of the first rank, worked closely with him, serving as coprincipal from 1874 until 1916.

These two men made the Webb School one of America's most distinguished secondary schools. Its graduates attended prestigious universities all over the world. When Woodrow Wilson was president of Princeton University from 1902 to 1910, his faculty told him some of their best-prepared students came from Webb. Before its fiftieth birthday, about World War I, Webb counted more Rhodes scholars among its graduates than any other secondary school.

In 1886 the school was moved from Culleoka to Bell Buckle, about fifty miles southeast of Nashville. Its mission, as stated by its founder, was and is "to turn out young people who are tireless workers, and who know how to work effectively; who are accurate scholars; who know the finer points of morals and practice them in their daily living; who are always courteous." The student oath was succinct: "I pledge my word of honor as a gentleman that I will not lie, cheat, or steal." (Today the word *gentleman* is not accurate, since many enrollees are female.) Students learned the value of hard work and honesty.

Old Sawney was interested in the total person. He wanted his students to be able to function well in a complex world. He said, "Cultivate in a student self-reliance by teaching him to think and not merely to accumulate facts—the accumulation of facts being desirable only as furnishing material for thought." Sawney was described as "a walking legend, a talking museum piece, a publicity saint, a symbol of survive and prevail." In student assemblies, he would say, "You new boys, take a look at me. I'm the old cuss you've heard so much about."[56]

It was September 1920 and J. W. was fifteen years old when his father left him at the Webb School; he was initially apprehensive, even anxious. He had never lived away from home, and he missed his friends and the familiar surroundings in Washington and Wilkes County. Yet he had a sense of what was expected in this foreign environment: the school required strong self-discipline and dealt with the basics of reading, writing, and arithmetic. J. W. didn't have the self-discipline of study. But he soon learned to study. He believed that when one truly applied himself, learning was a fulfilling and rewarding experience. Strict and demanding professors soon conditioned boys' behavior; they whipped any student who did not prepare for class. Every classroom had a little anteroom where the teachers kept switches used for punishment.

J. W. never received a switching, but he knew the inspiration behind the song, "Reading and Writing and Arithmetic, Taught to the Tune of a Hickory Stick." Seeing other students switched made him a believer. He also came to dread the sting of an eighteen-inch wooden ruler across the palm of his hand.

Some school rules seemed contradictory. While faculty and students could smoke pipes and chew tobacco, a student was expelled if he smoked a cigarette. J. W. tried smoking a pipe and took a couple of chews of tobacco. Both the pipe-smoking and the chewing made him dreadfully sick, so he never tried them again at Webb. Another regulation was that no student was allowed in town when the *Dixie Flyer*, a special train of the North and South Carolina Railroad, was going through. In no way did the administrators of the school want students to be tempted to jump the train in a moment of frustration.

Leisure time, however, was not devoid of pleasure. The Tennessee countryside was appealing to students, and long walks were common on holidays. Farmers could be seen driving turkeys, cattle, and hogs to the loading platform at the train station. The boys and the few local girls who were allowed to attend Webb could talk to each other only at the movies each Saturday night and at a required devotional each Sunday afternoon.

Homesickness swept over J. W. when he was at the Webb School, despite his feeling of self-reliance from being reared on a farm. He continually wrote letters to his parents in which he pleaded to come home. They denied his pleas. John Wootten and Gertrude Fanning wanted their elder son in a tough, disciplined environment. They saw abilities in him, and they hoped he would see them in himself at Webb.

In early December 1920 J. W. once again wrote to ask if he could come home and attend school in Washington. He had learned to study, he told his parents, and he promised to apply himself. Their response: pack up and come home for Christmas. First, J. W. had to pass an algebra test, which he did, and he and his cousin, Little Joe, hurried to the train station, caught the *Dixie Flyer*, and headed south to Atlanta, where J. W.'s parents would meet them.

Spending four months away from home, especially for the first time, had seemed like an eternity for J. W. Now he had a fresh appreciation of his family. He recalled how he felt when the train arrived at the Atlanta station that day: "There my family stood, and I will never forget it. They carried me home, and I had a big Christmas."[57]

In September his father had left a boy at the Webb School, and when that boy returned to Georgia four months later, he was a developing young man. Learning was no longer a dreaded task but a passport to an exotic world around him. J. W. had conquered his Goliath; he felt the satisfaction of the shepherd boy, David, when the giant stumbled and fell. Learning would be his future.

The Christmas holidays passed, and as the time to return to Webb drew near, his parents told him of another decision. He would not return to the school in Tennessee but would attend Emory Academy at Oxford, Georgia. He was euphoric. He was thankful to remain in Georgia, only a few hours from his Washington home.

J. W. didn't want to go back to Webb, but he knew the school provided him many images. "I shall always remember," he said, "the many rules to live by, the hot biscuits and sorghum syrup served by Mrs. Wheeler, and the heating of water in the iron pot in the backyard for the once-a-week bath on Saturday night."[58] Even better, the school transformed a somewhat undisciplined farm boy into a serious student. As an adult, J. W. reflected, "The time I spent at that school was very basic in shaping my life."[59]

On January 1, 1921, J. W. became a student at Emory Academy, continuing the year in high school started at the Webb School. He would remain there until he completed the eleventh grade, the normal requirement for graduation in Georgia at that time. The academy, a preparatory high school, was housed on the campus that was previously Emory College at Oxford, which had moved to the Atlanta campus in 1919. The Oxford site continued exclusively as a high school until 1929, when it became a junior college.[60]

In the film "J. W. Fanning: A Great Georgian" that summarizes J. W.'s life, dormitory roommate Marvin O'Dillon recalled, "Each night before retiring, we would have devotional, and as a rule, he would read or I would read, and this would be followed by a prayer. That helped me wonderfully."[61] J. W. formed many close friendships at Emory, including the Shipp brothers from Florida and Ralph Fratt, also from Washington. J. W.'s ability to lead began to emerge at Emory. He was elected president of the student body during his senior year. He was editor of the student publication and a member of the debating team.

The academy curriculum was broad-based. It concentrated on English, Spanish, mathematics, and basic science courses. Military science was required of everyone. J. W. was assigned to Company A, made up of boys his age. Another company included veterans of World War I returning to complete their high school education. J. W.'s commanding officer and first sergeant were members of the armed forces who had fought in France; they made his military education much like the regular army's basic training. He liked the structure of the military work. He made corporal his senior year. Military courses were scheduled five days a week and drilling exercises for three. All military students spent two weeks at summer camp.

The military units formed their own athletic teams. J. W. played basketball. His tryout for the Company A football team, however, ended his gridiron dreams. He broke his arm on the very first play from scrimmage. A doctor in Oxford set the arm without using anesthetic.

J. W. fainted. He was told to put the arm in a sling and go to his dormitory room. He abandoned thoughts of ever playing football again.

J. W. fell in love with schoolwork at Emory Academy. It was not an entirely new feeling; he had begun to appreciate learning while at the Webb School. But at the academy the teachers were mostly college professors who preferred the familiar traditions at Oxford to the newly chartered Emory University in Atlanta. As a result, most subjects were taught at a higher level and in more depth than high school offerings at other schools. J. W. was challenged to push himself, and his undiscovered abilities soon emerged.

Classes were small and teachers got to know students personally. Even the principal proved to be "just one of us," as J. W. described Dr. J. A. Sharpe, one of the two men who directed the academy during J. W.'s time there.[62] One Saturday afternoon in May, Dr. Sharpe came by the dormitory and told the boys to go swimming in the river. The next thing they knew, their principal had jumped into the river with them.

The principal's colorful side also emerged in his habit of chewing tobacco in class. One of J. W.'s classmates, "Dance" Hodges from Bainbridge, also liked to chew. Dr. Sharpe would sit in his swivel chair in front of the class and say, "Dance, give me a chaw of tobacco." The principal would load his mouth, take a few hearty chews, swivel his chair around and spit out the window.[63]

J. W. spoke of him with respect: "Doing things out of the ordinary and seemingly out of place was his forte. His mixture of unusual intellect and a good sense of humor was an inspiration, which helped the students get a better perspective on life. He was the personification of a whole person, a complete human being who saw life as it really was rather than looking through tinted glasses. He was a great man, but at the same time, he had a way of reaching my level and pulling me up to him."[64] Sharpe left Emory Academy to become president of Young Harris College.

In his senior year J. W. and his colleagues toiled under the direction of A. W. Rees, whose demeanor was the antithesis of his predecessor's. He was strict and proper and shy on humor. Nevertheless, J. W. said he learned, from contrasting the leadership styles of the two principals, that there were more ways than one to accomplish goals and objectives.

J. W. credits Rees with scaring religion into him. He recounted the frightful tale in his characteristic, wry style: "If I became a Christian, this is when and where it happened. I will never forget it. I was called on to pray by Principal Rees in front of the entire student body of more than three hundred boys. I said, 'Lord, help me through this one.' I was challenged as never before. There I stood praying, and I will always remember this as a very high moment in my life."[65]

During the summers J. W. went home to help John Wootten on the farm. It was the early 1920s, and cotton prices had been cut drastically. Cotton yields were pitifully low because of the boll weevil. Money was thin.

J. W. knew the family was sacrificing to keep him at Emory Academy, and he welcomed any opportunity to help. He relished the chance to do farm work, his first love. When he wasn't needed on the farm, he worked at other jobs. He described the summer of his sixteenth year in a letter he wrote many years later, in 1979, to his grandson Dan Cook:

> Dear Dan,
>
> I hope this letter gets to you on Monday. I received your letter on Friday, so I am mailing this letter by Airmail-Special Delivery.
>
> Your question is what I did when I was 16 years old. That is not easy to answer but let me try to give you a few experiences I do remember.
>
> I was 16 years old on August 14, 1921.
>
> These are some things I remember about my 16th year. I hope

they prove interesting.

Grandmother and I enjoyed your stay this summer, and I am glad that you and David enjoyed the boat ride.

Best to you always.

Granddaddy F.

The following was included with the letter:

During the summer of 1921, I worked for a survey crew that was surveying a road from Washington, Georgia, to Dry Fork Creek—the boundary line between Wilkes and Oglethorpe counties. I was responsible for handling one of the two rods used by the civil engineer to sight from his compass. I remember the weather was very hot and at times we became very thirsty and would drink water from ditches beside the road—certainly the wrong thing to do. I think we were paid 25 cents per day and we worked ten hours. During the last of the summer I drove my father to Florida searching for men who owed him a lot of money which he wished to collect. We drove through Lakeland, Georgia and I remember seeing a very large sawmill receiving tremendous logs by way of a small railroad.

When September arrived I returned to school at Emory Academy at Oxford, Georgia where I was a Junior in high school. I remember the year in school was difficult but enjoyable. I stayed in a dormitory named after Bishop Few of the Methodist Church and my roommates were two boys, one named Willis Savage and one named Ralph Flynt. Willis Savage is dead but Ralph Flynt had a long and distinguished career with the Office of Education of the Federal Government and is now retired living in Alexandria, Va. Ralph Flynt was a very tall boy and was nicknamed "Longitude." He was a good student. I remember taking Plane Geometry, History, English and Chemistry. Also I took Caesar, Latin II

> under the President [principal] of the School, Dr. Joe Sharpe. The year 1921 was a very trying year for farmers and my father only made 50 bales of cotton where he usually made 500 bales. The Mexican Boll Weevil proved to be a very destructive insect. My father told me that I had to be very economical because money was short.[66]

The family's sacrifices to keep J. W. at the academy were amply rewarded. The young man excelled in practically everything he did. He earned good grades in all his subjects, and his leadership qualities were obvious. A few days before commencement, he found out he was the class valedictorian.

His parents learned of the honor when they arrived for graduation. They were proud, and J. W. made what he thought was a good valedictory speech. He recalled only one person who was astonished to hear of his accomplishments at the Emory Academy. It was Miss Annie Neeson, his seventh-grade teacher at the Washington school. His academic achievements at Emory pleased her, he said.[67]

We can take two paths to live: One, let troubles govern life; two, accept troubles and spend life overcoming them.

J. W.

J. W.'s years growing up in the Piedmont region were not typical. He often described that time as atypical for someone of his background. Outside influences affected him greatly; many people outside his close-knit family helped shape his life.

J. W. was close to his younger brother, Wootten. Wootten was born with a weak heart and curved spine and was paralyzed by the time he was fifteen. He used a wheelchair for many years. But he was a sturdy, upbeat person who never lost his self-esteem.

School buildings back then could not accommodate students with handicaps. Wootten studied at home. The Washington library was sizeable for that time, and Wootten read every book on the shelves. Blessed with a sharp mind, he educated himself. His favorite subject was science; he was gifted in putting together appliances and other complex mechanisms.

In the early 1920s Wootten built a crystal radio for the family. J. W. listened to the radio when he was at home on a break from school. The dominant station was broadcast out of Pittsburgh, Pennsylvania, but WSB Radio in Atlanta was making its debut.[68] Wootten also had a short-wave radio he used regularly to talk with people all over the world.

J. W. admired Wootten's determination, his drive, his "can-do" attitude. He also admired his father, and he learned from him: how to drive a car; how to plow with mules and horses, and how to ride them; and how to value money, farming, and a good education. His father trusted him to do the right thing, and when he did wrong, his father was quick and firm with discipline. Through example, he gave J. W. a work ethic that was to stand him well throughout life. Here was an honest, hard-working man who constantly tried to improve himself and his economic level for the betterment of his family.

Because J. W.'s sister, Emily, was seven years younger, the two of them enjoyed a different relationship. But he loved her dearly. The family bought her a piano so she could take music lessons. J. W.'s mother thought it would be good if he, too, learned to play, but after about three lessons he gave it up. His boyhood friends discovered he was studying the piano and called him a sissy. He never touched the keys again.[69]

All of the children except J. W. are buried in graves alongside those of their mother and father in Resthaven Cemetery in Washington. Mary initially was buried in the cemetery at Phillips Mill Baptist Church. But when J. W. was thirteen, the family decided to move her body to the Resthaven Cemetery. J. W.'s father told him to go to the place of her original burial and, with the help of others, to unearth her casket and take it to Washington on the back of a horse-drawn wagon.[70]

J. W.'s mother, despite her seeming rigidity, was generous with him, always available for counseling and caring. Gertrude Fanning's life was cramped by poor health, but she found time to implant deeply in her son family values and the meaning of family love. She taught him compassion and the importance of respecting others. She taught him the importance of prayer and lessons of her Baptist upbringing.

On the balance, his parents gave him freedom throughout his childhood years, but they let him know freedom carried with it responsibility for one's actions. Perhaps their most important gift, though, was recognizing J. W. had unusual talents, and doing something about it. If they had not sent him to the Webb School, J. W. might never have found himself and become the useful person he was.

J. W. learned from the people, black and white, with whom he interacted in the community. Rural folks show a special loving, caring interest for all children in their midst.

J. W.'s formative years were a continuum of daily experiences rich with successes and tainted by failures. They produced a well-rounded, highly competitive person filled with a genuine concern for others, a strong desire to be of service, and a hunger to learn. Soon he would apply these qualities to a new test: the intellectual climb up Ag Hill at the University of Georgia.

His mere presence got your attention,
and this characteristic combined with his gentleness,
smooth voice, and his intellect left you in awe.
He was the type of person whom you wanted to be around
as often as possible.

LINDSAY THOMAS,

U.S. Congressman and Leadership Georgia participant

You will never meet opportunity strolling down the street.
The greatest use of life is to invest in something
that will outlast it.

J. W.

CHAPTER TWO

University Studies, 1923–1928

J. W. Fanning would have been happy being a farmer, but his parents wanted something better for him. They knew the drudgery and the uncertainty of farming. Both wanted him to go to college, but they disagreed on what he should study. "My mother favored Emory University to prepare me for the ministry," he said, but his father was "partial toward Mercer University, wanting me to become a journalist."[1] J. W. was certain he wanted to continue his education, but not at Emory or Mercer.

He begged his parents to support his choice: the University of Georgia, to study agriculture. Several years earlier, his friend and mentor, Washington lawyer William H. Slaton, had encouraged J. W. to attend the university.

The fall of 1923 was rapidly approaching, and Georgia and the entire cotton belt were taking a cruel hit from the boll weevil, which was devouring the crop on its journey from Mexico to southern Virginia. Agriculture was in an economic panic, not only from the ravages of the insect but also from steep declines in prices farmers were receiving for cotton. Most of them were falling on hard times. No one suffered more than Georgians.[2]

Total cotton acreage in Georgia began to decline rapidly in 1921. It dropped 28 percent from its 1920 level. A report in the *New York Times* on September 20, 1921, projected losses to the boll weevil that year to exceed $400 million. The South, especially Georgia, recorded the greatest losses. Up to 90 percent of the cotton fields in Georgia were severely infested, and small farmers in particular lost interest in the crop or became disheartened.

No one could have imagined the impact of the dethroning of King Cotton. In a few years the world economy would dive into a deep and extended depression. In Georgia the depression already had begun. Because the state was predominantly rural and a high percentage of its economy linked to cotton, the demise of the crop affected practically everybody.[3]

The Fannings' cotton fortunes continued to dwindle from the devastating summer of 1921, when they harvested only fifty bales. Normally they harvested five hundred bales. The price farmers received for cotton lint that year averaged twelve cents a pound, down from forty cents a pound a year earlier. Family farms were staggered: gross income from cotton was about $3,000 in 1921. It had been $100,000 the year before.[4]

According to records John Wootten kept of his farming and business enterprises, a summary page in the early twenties contains this statement in his handwriting: "Not worth a d____."[5] (Mercifully, J. W.'s father could not foresee that 1924 would provide another disappointing harvest and that in 1925 it would not rain a drop on the farm from April to November. The family lost the entire crop that year.[6])

John Wootten Fanning was in trouble. He needed some relief. He went to the Washington Loan and Banking Company for a loan, but was refused. He flew into a rage and threw the banker through a glass window out into Toombs Street. Some of the misfortune came when J. W. was attending the private Emory Academy, but John Wootten and Gertrude never faltered in supporting his education. Their economic situation worsened when he attended the University of Georgia; fortunately, J. W. was able to pay for most of his education there.

The University of Georgia was small in the fall of 1923. Its enrollment was about 1,500 students, 275 in the freshman class.[7] Only a few female students attended then, largely because the university had become coed just five years earlier. The campus was compact, reaching from Ag Hill to Broad Street. This seemingly sleepy southern university, however, was experiencing many internal changes that were not always visible to the casual observer. Thomas G. Dyer, in *The University of Georgia: A Bicentennial History, 1785–1985*, portrayed the twenties as a time of transition for the institution.[8] David Barrow was chancellor, and he and his administration faced continual changes in student behavior, including an increase in underclass hazing, a more open social life, and a perceived rise in cheating. Dyer said "the most significant changes in student life related to the presence of women in the student body."[9] However, Chancellor Barrow believed the students were really no different than their predecessors. Some of the activities, he said, had redeeming benefits: they provided a release for pent-up emotions.[10] All the revelry would not prove to be a distraction for J. W. He had become a serious student.

In early September 1923 J. W. boarded the train in Washington for Athens and the University of Georgia to begin his freshman year. In those days upperclassmen would meet the train at the Athens depot and provide a ritual greeting of sorts for freshmen. They presented each freshman a "beanie" cap and assigned him a big brother. Every ceremonial step contained an element of humiliation. The "greener" the freshman, the more he was humiliated.[11] Following this traditional welcome, a sophomore with clippers in hand escorted the freshmen to a local barber shop, where their heads were sheared, and then to their dormitory rooms, where they received a list of rules for freshman behavior as expected by the upperclassmen.

A freshman was forbidden to walk beneath the historic Arch on Broad Street. The penalty for committing this act was a slightly less than severe paddling by his big brother. If a freshman behaved appropriately, he could traverse the Arch after the Christmas break.

Another major event was the freshman-sophomore fight held on Herty Field. It was a classic free-for-all. Weapons were not permitted, only hands and fists and feet, but scars from the fight hinted that everybody didn't follow the rule. Freshmen were introduced to the Graveyard Yell, a first cousin of the famous Rebel Yell of the Confederate Army. Freshmen also formed a shirttail parade and often ran the gauntlet at three o'clock in the morning.

Perhaps the most excruciating form of harassment, however, was to take freshmen into the Oconee Hills Cemetery, assign a tombstone for each, and order them to sit behind that stone all night. The upperclassmen scouted the place during the night to ensure all freshmen were carrying out their orders. Each student had only a candle to find the correct tombstone; if it was not located, he had to repeat the search the next night. This was perhaps J. W.'s most miserable experience at the university.

Before J. W. could register for classes, he had to pay a fifty-dollar registration fee. He didn't have the money. Luckily, John Wootten had intervened. He told the university administration that his son had been valedictorian at Emory Academy and should be entitled to free tuition the first semester. He made his point; the university provided the fifty dollars.

J. W. enrolled in the College of Agriculture that fall. His concentration was in dairy husbandry. Later he changed his major study to agricultural economics, which would give him a broader understanding of the total industry, from farm to consumer.

He had promised his parents he would earn at least part of his college expenses, and he found part-time work at the university cafeteria in Denmark Hall. J. W.'s responsibility at the "Beanery," as the students called it, was to serve three meals a day to twenty-four students, and he earned enough money to cover the cost of his own meals: sixteen dollars a month. J. W. often said it was through the kindness of John W. Jenkins, the cafeteria manager, that he was able to attend the university.

How to spend the summers was a challenge. Between his freshman and sophomore years, J. W. went home to help his father on the farm. He felt he owed it to the family. He didn't expect to be paid, but his father did provide some money to help with expenses when J. W. returned to the university in the fall of 1924. The summer between his sophomore and junior years was completely different. That was the summer he learned firsthand about people living in poverty.

J. W. spent the summer of 1925 selling Bibles in rural Covington County, Alabama, near the Florida border. He and an associate, Worley Graham, a fellow University of Georgia student, worked for the Southwestern Book Company of Nashville, Tennessee. After their training, the two were assigned the town of Andalusia in Covington County. Arriving in town, they checked into a hotel, divided the county in half—J. W. had the eastern half—and without wasting any time, they started selling Bibles.

They had been trained to get into the house, always, and to sit down with the people and make the sale: a big family Bible for $8.95. J. W. reached his first prospect outside; this farmer was killing hogs. He never got inside the house, but he made the sale in the yard. What good were some of the sales tips taught in orientation? he wondered.

At first, Worley and J. W. had to ration their few earned dollars. They lived hand-to-mouth, spending the night with customers, accepting offers of meals, and sometimes walking as much as fifteen miles a day to meet prospects. J. W.'s shoes wore out the first week, and since he was nearly broke, he used pieces of cardboard to line the soles.[12]

On weekends the two would return to Andalusia, clean up, eat meals in the hotel with the money they had collected as partial payment for the Bibles, and spend much of the time resting. The work was hard; Alabama was hot.

No matter how much work a man has done or how weary he may be at the end of the day, he will do one more thing—and then another—for a friend in need.

J. W.

Most of the families solicited lived in abject poverty. J. W. had never seen such poverty. One family made a lifelong impression on him. After they had bought their $8.95 Bible, they invited J. W. to join them for supper and spend the night. He accepted, and soon he and the family of five, which included a grandmother, were sitting quietly around a makeshift table to eat. After the father said the blessing, the mother and one of the older children started serving the food. The meal consisted of figs and water, which were consumed almost in silence and without complaint.

Before retiring for the evening, he noticed there was only one bed in the house for the entire family; pallets for sleeping were spread on the floor. The family insisted he take the bed, which he reluctantly agreed to do. First, they prayed and read the Bible together. J. W. said, "I appreciated the sincerity of the people, their great hospitality, their deep religious convictions, and their simple way of life."[13]

J. W. slept fitfully. He thought about the meager supper. He knew daylight was approaching, and he began to wonder what might be served for breakfast, if anything. The family's first meal of the day mirrored their last: figs and water.

That summer an extended revival—one that lasted many weeks—was held in Andalusia. The community built a tent for the presiding evangelist in which he held meetings every night and twice on Sunday. At the end of the revival, J. W. watched as members of the Ku Klux

Klan marched into the tent in full regalia, hoods over their heads, and handed the minister $1,500. The preacher praised them with glory as they strutted out through the flaps of the tent. J. W. said he never forgot the sickening scene.

Instinct guided J. W. through perhaps the most bizarre July Fourth of his young life; he got more than expected on Independence Day in Alabama. Hitchhiking back to Andalusia, anticipating free time for the rest of the week, J. W. saw a Model T Ford touring car as it crested the hill. The driver stopped and offered J. W. a ride. He accepted because the driver was headed to Andalusia, although he had to make a couple of stops along the way.

At the first stop J. W. overheard a conversation between the driver and another man. He learned that his driver was known as "Governor." He had already learned that Governor liked to talk and tell stories. Next, Governor stopped to buy some moonshine whiskey. He purchased a gallon and took two or three swigs. He then drove to another location, bought two or three more jugs and took several more big swallows. Intoxication began to take its toll, and finally Governor said, "Son, you had better drive this automobile, because I am not sure I can handle it." He climbed in the back seat, curled up and slept while J. W. drove.

The closer they came to Andalusia, the more J. W. thought about the situation. "Here I am," he thought, "a stranger in a foreign land with a drunk man and four gallons of moonshine whiskey in the rear seat. Suppose the local sheriff catches us. There is no doubt that I will be put under the jail house." About two miles from town, he woke the drunken man and told him he had to take another route. He got out and started walking.

The next day, an acquaintance in Andalusia asked J. W., "Why did you leave the Governor to handle his car in such a drunken stupor?" J. W. stuck to his little white lie, saying he needed to take another route into town. As it turned out, Governor had wrecked the car and found himself in jail. J. W. knew he had made the right decision.[14]

Worley and J. W. ended their summer by borrowing their parents' cars to deliver the Bibles they had sold. John Wootten sent J. W. an old Model T Roadster. Buyers paid the balances owed on the books, and the two students returned home.

J. W. deposited $400 in the Exchange Bank in Washington and drew against it for $250 to cover his college expenses. He never got the remaining $150—the bank declared bankruptcy and closed permanently.

J. W. moved into a new dormitory, Milledge Hall, when he returned to the university that fall. His roommate was Blake Pullen. His junior year was typical—filled with academic achievement and social activities. Between his junior and senior years in the summer of 1926, J. W. worked for the U.S. Department of Agriculture for fifty dollars a month. He traveled across the Southeast as part of a project involving import-export livestock products.

He and a man named Charles Null covered Alabama, Florida, South Carolina, and Georgia, finishing the summer in Savannah in late August. J. W. learned about floor products and the transportation of goods because a lot of the work was done in depots and places where records of imports and exports of commodities were kept.

To return to Athens, J. W. caught the Central Georgia train out of Savannah to Macon, where a change of trains was necessary to get to Athens. He had planned to go up to Milner, between Macon and Atlanta, and visit a girlfriend, but, short on money, he decided to return to Athens. The decision proved to be fortunate.

When he arrived, Bill Jones, his freshman-year roommate, said J. W. had a date that night in Memorial Hall, where freshmen were being entertained. A pretty freshman girl from South Georgia named Cora Lee Harvey would be his blind date, Bill said. J. W. was intrigued and went by her dormitory, Soule Hall, where he met her. He found

Cora Lee to be as beautiful as touted. She was lively and a lot of fun. Cora Lee had been reared on a farm in Tattnall County in southeast Georgia, and she knew all about farm life.

From then on, J. W. saw Cora Lee whenever he could. They did the things that many other college students did while courting. They attended athletic events—especially football games, because Cora Lee had a passion for football—went to the movies, took walks on campus, and went on picnics. They enjoyed going to concerts, often held in an amphitheater built in a ravine off Ag Drive.

Before long, J. W. knew he was going to try to "get that gal." He did: they were married five years later. It was a bond that would last sixty-one years, until her death.

J. W. relished his undergraduate experience—the friends he made, the extracurricular activities, the courses he took. His professors had outstanding reputations, but the one he admired the most was Dr. John R. Fain, professor of research in agronomy. "He, more than any other person, helped me to understand farming as a business and agriculture as a basic industry," J. W. said.[15] J. W. described Fain as a great man and a great scholar, and a practical and down-to-earth person.

Fain invited J. W. to visit him at his home in east Tennessee, in Jefferson County, where he hoped to retire. J. W. traveled there during the summer of his junior year. He recalled being taken out to the back of Fain's house, which faced the Great Smoky Mountains, and being asked to climb up on a big stump in the pasture. When he did, Fain said, "Fanning, look out across the Great Smoky Mountains and tell me how big you feel."[16]

It was a humbling experience. Fain made his point: never forget your place in the vastness of creation between these people up there who owned little farms and those in South Georgia.

During J. W.'s senior year, Fain came into possession of a 180-acre farm in Walker County, and he asked J. W. to join him in its operation. J. W. moved a family of black sharecroppers to the farm, where they grew cotton and soybeans for several years with some success. J. W.'s senior year, when he shared a dorm room in Milledge Hall with a World War I veteran, Harvey Rankins, marked the peak of his undergraduate life.

J. W. was popular with both professors and students. He was serious about his studies, and he inspired other students with his determination to excel in everything worthwhile. His curriculum in agriculture had an emphasis in agricultural economics. He took science and mathematics courses, basic English and literature, biology and botany, introductory courses in each agricultural discipline, and an aggregate of courses in his major field.

Obviously, his desire for learning stood him well throughout the entire four years, and he also kept his promise to his parents that he would earn as much of his college expenses as possible. He waited on tables at the Beanery, found summer employment, and earned two modest scholarships. His earnings covered most of the costs except for a couple of tuition payments and an initiation fee of twenty dollars to join the Gridiron Secret Society.

Faculty and students alike recognized J. W.'s leadership qualities. He met the requirements for membership in several honorary and scholastic organizations: Phi Kappa Phi, Alpha Zeta, Aghon, Junior Cabinet, Senior Round Table, Blue Key Council, Gridiron Secret Society, and the *Pandora* yearbook staff. One of his highest honors was being elected chancellor of Alpha Zeta, which essentially marked him as the most outstanding student in the College of Agriculture that year. From this position of leadership, he was asked to welcome freshmen enrolling in agriculture and occupy the podium with Dr. Soule, president of the College of Agriculture. J. W. knew he was building his leadership skills.

The editor of the *Pandora* of 1927, in summarizing his impressions of J. W., wrote: "John William Fanning, Washington, Georgia. Making every possible honor in college, J. William now leaves with enough gold to start a jewelry store and enough praise and admiration to become president of the land. He leaves us the cherished memory of an honest, persistent, intellectually distinguished student and a friend with an admirable disposition, winning personality, and a scholastic record unsurpassed by any in the history of the university." The tag line following the summary reads, "Speak only when speech is required," words that J. W. may have selected himself.[17]

On June 15, 1927, J. W. was one of 178 seniors awarded the bachelor of science degree in agriculture. He graduated with honors in agricultural economics. His parents drove from Washington to see the chancellor hand their son his diploma and recognize him for academic achievements.

The summer following graduation, J. W. went to work for the College of Agriculture conducting farm-management surveys in southeast Georgia. He was doing what he loved: driving his Model T Ford roadster from farm to farm, working with people, collecting information about management practices. All the time he was broadening his understanding of Georgia agriculture. J. W. enjoyed calling on farmers, whether in their homes or in the field. They were his kind of people. He respected their honesty, common sense, and down-home brand of humor.

J. W. told a story about a country preacher approaching a farmer hoeing in his field. "Are you prepared to die?" the preacher hollered across rows of cotton. The farmer stopped chopping weeds, looked around to see if a rattlesnake was about to strike, and then hollered back, "Why?" The preacher responded, "The Judgment Day is coming." The farmer asked, "When is it?" The preacher yelled, "It may be today, or it may be tomorrow." Said the farmer: "Well, don't tell my wife; she'll want to go both days."[18]

Following graduation in June 1927, Fain offered J. W. a chance to pursue a master's degree, something Fain believed would be required of any professional in the future. J. W. took the offer. He was to take advanced courses in economics in the College of Agriculture and write a thesis, "a scientific study of the Negro and his adjustment to American civilization."[19]

The topic was predetermined because J. W. would receive a monthly stipend from the Phelps-Stokes Fellowship, one of the few scholarships for graduate study in the Ag College. It was awarded on a competitive basis and funded African American studies. Recommended by the Phelps-Stokes Committee on the faculty, John William Fanning was appointed Fellow for the year 1927–28. The chancellor of the university, Charles M. Snelling, wrote the following as the foreword for J. W.'s thesis:

> The Phelps-Stokes Fellowship was established for the purpose stated in the following resolutions:
>
> Whereas, Miss Caroline Phelps-Stokes in establishing the Phelps-Stokes Fund was especially solicitous to assist in improving the condition of the Negro; and
>
> Whereas, It is the conviction of the Trustees that one of the best methods of forwarding this purpose is to provide means to enable southern youth of broad sympathies to make a scientific study of the Negro and of his adjustment to American civilization;
>
> Resolved, That twelve thousand five hundred dollars ($12,500) be given to the University of Georgia for the permanent endowment of a research fellowship, on the following conditions:
>
> 1. The University shall appoint annually a Fellow in Sociology, for the study of the Negro. He shall pursue advanced studies under the direction of the departments of Sociology, Economics, Education or History, as may be determined in each case by the Chan-

cellor. The Fellowship shall yield $500, and shall, after four years, be restricted to graduate students.

2. Each Fellow shall prepare a paper or thesis embodying the result of his investigations which shall be published by the University with assistance from the income of the fund, any surplus remaining being applicable to other objects incident to the main purpose of the Fellowship. A copy of these resolutions shall be incorporated in every publication issued under this foundation.

3. The right to make all necessary regulations, not inconsistent with the spirit and letter of these resolutions, is given to the Chancellor and Faculty, but no changes in the conditions of the foundation can be made without the mutual consent both of the Trustees of the University and of the Phelps-Stokes Fund. [20]

After spending the latter portion of the summer of 1927 in Wilkes County, working with his father on the farm, J. W. returned to his alma mater in September to start working toward the master of science degree in agricultural economics. He titled his thesis "Negro Migration: A Study of the Exodus of the Negroes between 1920 and 1925 from Middle Georgia Counties as That Exodus Was Influenced or Determined by Existing Economic Conditions."[21] J. W.'s charge by his graduate committee was to study why thousands of black workers left and how their leaving affected middle Georgia. Much of his data—collected by personal interview—came from Madison, Oglethorpe, Oconee, Morgan, Putnam, Jasper, Jones, and Jackson counties. He also visited Wilkes, Green, and Elbert counties, because he knew their farming well.

His research gave him a chance to visit farms and talk with people about why black people were leaving. Of course, his father was farming in Wilkes County during the period considered in the study, and a number of black people who worked with him had left. Population trends in Wilkes County told the story. In 1910 the population was 23,441, of whom 75 percent were black. In 1930 the population dropped to 15,944, with 63 percent black.[22]

For his traveling around the region, J. W. bought an old Ford Model T that had been stripped down but with enough parts to run. He paid seventy-five dollars for it. He sold it for the same price at the end of his research. J. W. enjoyed collecting information for his thesis, primarily because he got to talk with people, people he could identify with. He had lived much of the story himself. He talked with both white and black farmers throughout the area. "I worked on this study," J. W. said, "because I thought it was important. I learned a lot about people and the conditions that affect people."[23]

Both blacks and whites left; but J. W. focused on blacks' leaving, mainly for jobs in the North, where there was a seemingly insatiable demand for cheap labor. Immigration waves from Europe had slowed to a ripple because of World War I, so growing industries in the North looked to the South for new labor. Representatives of northern companies, J. W. discovered, traveled south to describe to blacks the job opportunities in Chicago, Cincinnati, Washington, New York, Detroit, and other cities.

In Middle Georgia's old Plantation Belt, black people recognized the opportunities up North. The boll weevil had stolen their income in the South. Many black workers believed their only choice was to move north. They left en masse.

Middle Georgia experienced a social and economic revolution because its income base was destroyed, and it lost much of its labor force. Cotton fields went unattended. Land, once productive, lay barren. In a few decades, it became overgrown with broomsedge and trees.

J. W. finished collecting the data, wrote and interpreted the results, and defended his work before his graduate committee. He completed it all in late spring of 1928. He concluded that blacks left Middle Georgia for two primary reasons: one, the boll weevil had taken their jobs, and two, the North offered plenty of jobs.[24]

J. W. received the master of science degree in agricultural economics from the university on August 24, 1928. Again, his parents and family—especially his father—swelled with pride. More than a decade earlier, John Wootten had recognized J. W.'s native ability, and he took charge of his son's life, for an instant, it seemed. He took him to a tough little prep school in Tennessee, gave him a well-rounded liberal and challenging education at the Emory Academy, and he changed the course of his son's life. Study at the University of Georgia was the culmination of dreams. J. W. now held two university degrees, both received with distinction. His success was real and tangible.

Money was hard to come by in the early and mid-twenties, but the Fannings bet on their son with the little extra money they could find. He had been outstanding, both as an undergraduate and postgraduate student. He not only got a good education—he left a mark on the institution. He used his winning personality, his exemplary academic achievements, his leadership to elevate the student environment at the university. Now, at twenty-three, he was prepared to move on with confidence.

But where? Jobs were scarce in 1928, but instead of being discouraged, J. W. was pleased. He went home actually hoping to stay on the farm, his real objective in life. He rolled up his sleeves and began helping his father as if his dream were about to become reality. But his mother intervened. Gertrude Harrison Fanning admonished her son to find a job, to leave farming behind. Farming had given her and her family some glory days, but it also had left painful scars. Her disdain for farming and cotton was so deeply imbedded in her psyche that she wanted to erase it from her memory. She even destroyed many family photographs to eradicate the evidence of spirits broken by poverty.

Farming was not in J. W.'s future, but agriculture was. He became an assistant county agent in Clarke County, Georgia, and began work on January 1, 1929. Years later, when his mother was dying of cancer, J. W. attended her at her bedside. She apologized for not supporting his dream. "I am sorry I kept you from being a farmer," she said. J. W. replied, "That's all right, Mama. I have made out just fine."[25]

It was my privilege to give J. W. a ride home after our Kiwanis Club luncheon one day. On the way to his house, I decided to drive through the university campus. While riding through South Campus, he talked about the great changes that had occurred at UGA through the years. One could sense that he was thrilled to have had a role in many of the changes.

W. C. MCARTHUR,

agricultural economist

In the winter of 1957 as a young assistant county agent in Carroll County I first met J. W. He was a mentor throughout my career.

TAL C. DUVALL,

University of Georgia colleague

He was a remarkable communicator and word architect.

STEVE BRANNEN,

agricultural economist

City people and rural folks have always been somewhat at odds. But that all changes when the city fellow buys a farm or when the farmer goes to town to buy a tractor.

J. W.

CHAPTER THREE

The Agriculturist, 1929–1954, 1956–1961

The days had begun to lengthen in early summer of 1928, and Gertrude Fanning had spoken. She was adamant: J. W. would not become a farmer. He began seeking employment while helping his father on the farm. But where to begin? He had vowed he would never be a teacher or a county agent, but he applied for a job with the Agricultural Extension Service in the county that was home to his alma mater: Clarke County, Athens, Georgia. He readily accepted the offer. He would be assistant to Luke Watson, county agent, and start work in the North Georgia county on New Year's Day 1929.

To go with his first job, he bought his first automobile, a 1928 Model A roadster with a rumble seat. He financed everything, both the down payment and the price of the $650 Ford, and he was anxious. "I will never forget my first night on the job," he recalled, "feeling overwhelmed with debt and an unknown future."[1]

He was, in fact, merging the two jobs he had vowed to avoid. The Agricultural Extension Service—now the Cooperative Extension Service—had been established in 1914 by the federal Smith-Lever Act; it was maintained by a combination of federal, state, and county funds. Its mission: to bridge the gap between the knowledge base in agriculture and its practice. Land-grant colleges had been established in 1862, and their initial mission was to teach agriculture and the mechanical arts. Fifteen years later, federal money for research was provided. The educational arm, added in 1914 to get information to farmers, seemed a logical way to increase agricultural production and enhance efficiency.[2]

The Extension Service also was charged with tackling home economics problems on the farm; agents would work with farming families to make their lives a little better. The Extension Service would help people move beyond the family farm to take part in worthwhile enterprises, explain work to neighbors, counsel with others on community matters, study with Extension agents about problems of the farm and home, and enlarge their vision.

A list of duties published near the time J. W. began his work in Clarke County included:

- increase the net income of the farmer through more efficient production and marketing and the better use of capital and credit
- promote better homes and a higher standard of living on the farm
- develop rural leaders
- promote the mental, social, cultural, recreational, and community life of rural people
- implant a love of rural life in the farm boys and girls
- enlarge the vision of rural people and the nation on rural matters.[3]

J. W. joined the Agricultural Extension Service when county agents served 101 Georgia counties with agricultural programs and seventy-three counties with home demonstration work. Clubs for boys operated in 106 counties and clubs for girls in seventy-seven counties.[4]

County extension work was challenging because it was as close to farming as J. W. could get. He identified with the dreams, frustrations, heartaches, and successes of those who looked to the soil for their livelihood. Being a county agent felt natural and right. He was familiar with rural poverty and low-production agriculture, but he was concerned about people of any socio-economic status and race. "I always liked diversity in life," he once reflected.[5]

Working with people was to become J. W.'s forte. After he had gained their confidence, they freely talked about themselves and their communities. Perhaps they sensed his eagerness to help—to hear the real story, not to dictate it. "If you want to know all about a town, you need to get acquainted with the people who live there," he said. "At first they will tell you its good features, especially the parts that swell their pride. But, eventually, they will come around to telling you the truth."[6]

Luke Watson was a teacher-supervisor J. W. respected and looked to for counsel. Watson taught him the basics of leadership development, something J. W. valued because of its core premise: people learning to help themselves—individually and as a community—was the best way to make a change that would stick. In an interview conducted many years later, he said, "Being a county agent allows you to see the community as a whole working and talking to themselves. My greatest enjoyment has come from working with people and being a part of what is going on."[7]

After nineteen months in Clarke County, J. W.'s former professor and mentor, John R. Fain, reentered his life. He was head of the University of Georgia Department of Agronomy. He recruited J. W. to transfer to campus, where he would work as a farm management specialist with the Agricultural Extension Service. Fain was J. W.'s supervisor, one of the attractions of the new assignment. His associates were farm management specialists Kenneth Treavor and W. A. Minor.

The new position expanded J. W.'s involvement in agriculture. His duties were to work with farmers on an individual basis. He would show them how to use farm records to make management decisions, to interpret and present research results in a practical manner so farmers could apply them, and to cooperate with other specialists on farm problems.

County agents always looked for solutions to problems. They gathered data from farmers, analyzed what they collected, and presented their findings in community meetings. J. W. liked the method. He could teach farmers what he had learned in research and help them improve their efficiency.

County agents worked with specialists to develop programs. J. W. was responsible for promoting program development at the county level. One day a plea came in a letter from George Daniel, county agent in Troup County: "Come on over into Macedonia and help me."[8] During the two-week assignment, J. W. came to know many farm families, most of whom were hurting financially but who were still good-natured.

One Saturday morning he became acquainted with a family reported to be struggling more than usual. As he arrived at their home, he found the man and his wife "prettying up" the yard with brush brooms. Both were wiry, their calloused hands reflecting the rigors of farm life. J. W. asked if they were expecting company. They exchanged a glance, laughed heartily, and said, "Our twelve sons and their families are coming for a visit." J. W. simply tipped his hat and congratulated them.[9]

J. W. enjoyed meeting farmers and their families in their own environment. He made friends across the state, learning as he traveled. He learned that families everywhere were determined to make farming work. He admired their dry wit and wisdom as they struggled to stay on the land during the aftermath of the 1929 stock market crash.

A sense of humor was one of the farmers' most important possessions; it kept them going. J. W. remembered an admonition shared by a rugged farmer one day: "A person ought never to take anything out of a bottle unless he reads what's wrote on it."[10]

The same man told J. W. about the farmer who had never ridden a train and asked the man behind the ticket window for a round-trip ticket. "To where?" asked the ticket seller. "To here, of course," replied the farmer. Another farmer told J. W., "If you don't think a feller can jump six feet high and twenty feet wide, you never have sat down on a rattlesnake."[11]

Troup County during the early 1930s was a learning laboratory for J. W. He learned about human nature. He listened to rural people's everyday problems and anxieties, their hopes and now-faint dreams.

"Listening and hearing is an art that requires patience, diligence and equanimity, and a great respect for the one from whom one solicits ideas and feelings," he said years later. "Then comes the ability of the listener and hearer to articulate the heartfelt concerns and desires of those being heard."[12]

Listening with the heart would become even more important to J. W. as farmers in Georgia and the rural South suffered further economic setbacks. Houston County, in middle Georgia, had essentially an agricultural economy: a large portion of the land, 147,500 acres, was farmland. The average farm comprised about 175 acres. Across rural Georgia, family income was slipping fast. In Houston County the gross value of crops in 1930 was $101 million. A year later it had declined to $78 million.[13]

A message from County Agent F. C. Chandler, whom J. W. later would replace, explained: "The decrease occurred despite a substantial increase in production. Except for peaches, the outlook for cash crops that are grown in this county does not present a very promising picture. However, it is part of the farm business that we must go ahead to the best of our ability. The home garden is the most valuable plot of ground on the entire farm and should be kept going to full capacity."[14]

On August 20, 1931, eleven farmers from Houston County and nearby Peach County appealed for help in a telegram sent to the Georgia General Assembly. It read: "Fifteen cars of watermelons on track offering for $10.00 per carload, unable to sell. Our backs are to the wall of accumulated debts. We are flanked on our right by the $20,000,000 state highway holy fund; on our left there looms on the horizon five-cent cotton. Nothing left but straight ahead into the land of financial despair. Deliver us out of the hands of W and A railroad loan sharks and further taxation."[15]

The cost of growing cotton in 1931 was fourteen cents a pound for the average farmer. Problem was, the farmer expected to get only nine cents a pound at harvest time. The South faced its darkest time since just before the Civil War.[16]

J. W.'s reputation, in the meantime, extended beyond the state. The University of Arkansas invited him to teach a course on program development to its county agents and others across the South.

The work was serious, but on his own time, J. W. was having fun. He focused on Gainesville, in North Georgia, where he would marry the gal he vowed he'd get, Cora Lee Harvey, the captivating blind date of his undergraduate days. Cora Lee had graduated from the University of Georgia and now was a home economics teacher at Chicopee Village, a mill community near Gainesville. J. W. and Cora Lee set their wedding for December 22, 1931.

A man must have a certain amount
of intelligent ignorance to get anywhere.

J. W.

J. W. asked Kenneth Treavor, his colleague and friend, to be his best man. The two of them picked up The Rev. Dr. D. B. Nicholson and some flowers before leaving Athens to travel to Gainesville. They were barely under way when the car became mired in deep red mud. J. W. and Treavor jumped out of the car, leaving the minister inside, clean and dry. After much pushing, foot sliding, and tire spinning, the car was going again. On the way, the groom and best man stopped at a barber shop to clean off the mud and grime.

Cora Lee was living in a house in Chicopee Village, where the wedding ceremony was performed. Treavor remembered, "It was a beautiful wedding, and everything went along all right. After it was over, we put Fanning and Cora Lee on the road, and that was that."[17] The newlyweds spent their wedding night at the Henry Grady Hotel in Atlanta. Their honeymoon traced a circular route: they traveled to the central Georgia town of Macon for the second night, and south to Tattnall County for the third night, at the home of Cora Lee's parents. Before the honeymoon ended, they had visited the coastal city of Savannah; northeast, land-bound Augusta; and had spent one night with J. W.'s family in Wilkes County. "This was a honeymoon for seventy-five dollars in the Depression of 1931," J. W. said.[18]

While J. W. and Cora Lee were enjoying marital bliss, the Great Depression was sinking deeper. Twenty-five percent of the U.S. work force needed jobs. The stock market crash and other economic weaknesses had devastated the cotton belt of Georgia.

The boll weevil had allies. J. W.'s family and neighbors were taking more hard hits: the price of cotton fell to five cents a pound; families couldn't pay their debts; some lost their farms to bank foreclosures.[19] J. W. told the story of a judge in Washington, Georgia, who had presided over many foreclosures. Finally a group of angry residents tied him to a pole, tarred him and ran him out of town.

In major cities across the country, lines of people without jobs stretched around blocks leading into soup kitchens. The farmers at least had food in their fields and gardens. J. W. felt fortunate that he and his wife were employed, even though they would have to live apart until other arrangements could be made.

Before Cora Lee returned to Chicopee Village, however, J. W.

checked by his office at the University of Georgia and found a note on his desk from the director of the Extension Service, Phil Campbell. The Extension Service faced serious budget problems, the note said. J .W.'s job as farm management specialist would end. J. W. couldn't believe it. Then he read on: he was to be transferred to Macon, where he would continue in the Extension Service as a special agent for the sale of Georgia products. "The opportunity for another position was truly a relief," he remembered.[20]

The transfer to Macon was completed on January 1, 1932, and Cora Lee went back to her job at Chicopee Village. Staying apart was not easy for the newlyweds, and after six more months at Chicopee, Cora Lee resigned and joined J. W. in Macon. A few months later, Franklin Delano Roosevelt was elected president of the United States. He was sworn into office in January 1933.

J. W.'s new assignment was to promote the sale of all Georgia agricultural products, something needed for the slow economy. He became acquainted with the people who made things happen, primarily the people who handled and bought farm products. Curb markets were common—places where farmers sold their goods from trucks and where people talked about prices and demand for Georgia products. Such information was sent regularly to C. G. Garner, marketing specialist in Athens. J. W. persuaded a dealer to buy a truckload of fresh cabbage from the North Georgia mountains. The vegetable had never been sold on the Macon market.

J. W. also processed farmers' applications for what was termed the "Seed Loan" program—emergency loans administered by the U.S. Department of Agriculture. He traveled to Jones and Wilkinson counties, where he took farmers' applications for special loans, practically the only source of farm money because banks had stopped lending to most farmers. J. W. presented the applications to county committees to approve or reject. President Roosevelt ordered all banks closed for a short time when the Emergency Farm Loan Department was processing applications. "Instead of panic," J. W. said, "I was surprised how calm the people were. They were hurting financially but saw a glimmer of hope in the president's drastic edict."[21]

In February 1933, J. W. transferred south to Perry, in Houston County, to serve as interim county agent for six months. He was standing in for F. C. Chandler, the regular county agent, who was on leave to serve as the officer of a Civilian Conservation Corps (CCC) camp. In 1933 Congress had approved the CCC primarily to provide jobs for young men.

People were searching for hope, and J. W. learned the importance of dispensing it. "We each seek the brighter side," he said, "and we ask our leaders to find that side." Focusing on the possible fueled hope, J. W. believed. He frequently used this quote by a minister: "Men sing at midnight not because of the darkness, but because morning will come."[22]

J. W. got to know the leadership in the county, and one of the first persons he met was Colonel Sam Nunn Sr., who found in J. W. a quick and eager student. The two men would drive around the county discussing the agricultural issues of the day and the people affected by them.

On one trip, he and the colonel found themselves studying a whiskey still operating on some bottomland. Nunn told J. W., in his distinctive, gentle drawl, that this was one way some people made their living in Houston County. The colonel also worked with J. W. on a national program that paid farmers to plow up acreage to reduce the quantity of cotton on the market. The project was successful, and a deep and lasting relationship grew between the two.

When the six-month assignment in Houston County ended November 1, 1933, J. W. was transferred to South Georgia to serve as a farm management specialist in Tifton.

During his first month on the job, he visited families around the state who had sons enrolled in the local Abraham Baldwin Agricultural College. He learned from them about farm operations across the state. But his stay in the county would be brief. And Houston County was calling again. The county he had left only weeks earlier sent a delegation of county commissioners to Tifton to lure him back when the former county agent J. W. had replaced chose not to return after his stint with the CCC. The recruiting party offered to raise his pay twenty-five dollars a month, and upon the recommendation of Extension Director Harry Brown, J. W. accepted. He and Cora Lee returned to Perry on December 1, 1933. The interim position had become permanent. The Fannings had made many friends during their first tour of duty, and they were happy to return.

Government programs to help cotton farmers were in full swing in the early 1930s, and J. W. became involved immediately in a sign-up campaign for people who wished to "rent" cotton land to the federal government—agreeing not to grow the crop on a parcel of land—at a payment based on past yields per acre. Confusion reigned among farmers who hoped to be paid a fair price by the government, which would determine so-called "acreage allotments."

J. W., as the county agent, was responsible for explaining the program, receiving applications, and appointing a committee to approve them. His days were hectic. Farmers sought fair and equitable treatment, but sometimes they themselves were not fair. They overestimated prospective yields per acre, trying to get more money from the government. J. W. learned several lessons in human nature by observing the bargaining process of the committee and the farmer.

Nobody knows the troubles I have seen,
but we keep trying to tell them.

J. W.

Humor was the salvation of the day—the common denominator in stores, feed mills, and other gathering places. Farmers were signing up to be paid for reducing their cotton production, and some of the federal regulations they had to follow amused them. One story making the rounds had its roots in the government programs: a hog farmer was going to be paid money by the government not to produce hogs. His toughest problem: which type of hog he should select not to produce.

J. W.'s leadership ability was tested, but his knowledge and common sense helped him to get through. He said he learned at least two things from the Great Depression: "One is never to take good fortune for granted, and the other is to never underestimate the ability of people to overcome adversity."[23]

The Farm Credit Administration, established by executive order in 1933, supervised the Farm Credit System, which provided loans to struggling farmers. Farmers now had a new, sorely needed source of credit; local banks had lent about all they could. J. W.'s office helped make the programs work.

Electric power was another relief program. In 1935 only 12 percent of U.S. farms had electricity. Money from the Rural Electrification Administration turned on lights in farmhouses, churches, schools, and other buildings once lighted only by oil lamps.

Money was scarce, but at least families could grow their own food supply. Most farms had fresh vegetables and fruits during the growing season, and canning and food preservation extended their usefulness throughout the year. Before electricity, a lot of food spoiled, and winters often lasted longer than the food supply. But J. W. brought to the people electrical equipment for pressure canning. The mobile unit allowed neighbors to come together to process their fruits and vegetables. Meat from slaughtered animals was canned as well. Canning sessions became social celebrations.

Although J. W. was in Houston County for only a short time, his community involvement was considerable. Aurelia Evans, a resident of Perry born in 1902, remembered him as a wonderful man who made friends across the county.[24] But J. W. still wanted to become a plain old "dirt farmer," and now he had a wife who supported his dream.

A farm near Perry, offered at a low price, tempted the Fannings, but they decided to consider a more attractive option: a 250-acre farm in Bulloch County being sold by the Federal Land Bank for $2,500.[25] They took off for Bulloch County in the early spring of 1934 to visit the farm. On the way, Cora Lee became ill and they stopped for a day. Time ran out, and they returned to Perry without even seeing the farm. His dream of becoming a farmer once again was put on hold.

Cora Lee's "illness" was not unexpected. When the couple had returned to Houston County after their month in Tifton, she was pregnant with their first child. A doctor was found in nearby Macon to advise Cora Lee during her pregnancy, and when delivery was near, she was admitted to the Macon Central Hospital. Sibyle Frances Fanning was born at 5:30 p.m. June 30, 1934.

The fee for the doctor who attended Cora Lee during her pregnancy and at the birth was ninety dollars, which J. W. had paid in advance at the rate of ten dollars a month. Mother and daughter were healthy, but the doctor still required a ten-day stay in the hospital following the birth and, for Cora Lee, another three weeks in bed at home. The couple lived in Perry in a rented house, the Gilbert House, next to the First Baptist Church. A local woman stayed with Cora Lee and Sibyle during the recovery time at home.

A month later, another chapter of J. W.'s life was about to begin. It was late July 1934, when Extension Director Harry Brown sent a message for J. W. to call him. J. W. learned the truth of the adage "Never say never," because he was being asked to do the second of two jobs he vowed he would never do: teach. The chancellor of the University System of Georgia in 1934, Philip Weltner, believed a role reversal was in order: county agents would serve as classroom teachers in the College of Agriculture, and teachers would serve as county agents. At that time the Department of Agricultural Economics had a vacancy.

Partly because J. W.'s two degrees were in agricultural economics, he was offered the job and advised by the director of Extension to take it. The role reversal, a bold experiment, was to be a success.

The family was moving again, this time packing up and heading to Athens in August 1934. J. W. became an assistant professor in the Department of Agricultural Economics, under the direction of his department head, Professor J. William Firor.

In truth, he had always been a teacher. His classroom had simply changed location, from barn to school, and his students no longer were farmers and 4-H children, but college students. J. W. was responsible for three classes: a basic course in agricultural economics, an advanced course in farm credit, and a basic course in farm management. He discovered that criteria for becoming a good teacher and a good leader were remarkably similar. One thing was clear: teaching, regardless of the setting, is "sharing of oneself."[26]

J. W. now was a lecturer. Preparation was demanding. He spent hours in the library coming up with fresh, stimulating information for the classroom each day. On the other hand, campus life had one great reward not available in county work: time to be with his wife and baby daughter, Sibyle. He and Cora Lee one day would label those years the "highlights."[27]

Dozens of the hundreds of young men who passed through his classrooms became loyal friends for life. Some became presidents of banks, others prominent in the political arena. Some became educational leaders, and still others were successful in farming and business. They found that J. W.'s wisdom and philosophy served them well throughout their careers.

Edgar L. Rhodes, a farmer from Bremen, Georgia, who would become a member of the Board of Regents of the University System of Georgia, was one of those students. More than fifty years later, in March 2000, Rhodes remembered J. W. as one of his best professors. "He was what I called a true professor in the College of Agriculture," Rhodes said, "always placing the student first. He cared about students."[28] Earl Cheek of Perry, an agricultural education major, remembered that his professor was practical—a benefit of his years as a county agent.[29]

J. W. never failed any students. Most students knew that. Instead, when he discovered a student in trouble, he tutored him or her through the difficulties. Said Edgar Rhodes: "There is no doubt that his legacy will encompass many areas in which he served, but I remember him most of all as being an outstanding professor."[30]

J. W. , however, could provide constructive criticism when it was needed. Joseph Marshall, who would be a participant in the first leadership program of which J. W. was godfather, wryly recalled, "I remember him telling me one time that I was too conservative, not in politics but in the leadership area."[31] Marshall actually grew up with J. W., in a sense. They met, Marshall said, "when I was a 4-H Club member in Columbia County in the late '40s, [and] Mr. Fanning visited our farm with our county agent. Later I knew him when I was an undergraduate and he was chairman of the Ag Economics Department. He encouraged me to go to graduate school and wrote one of my recommendations."[32]

J. W. also worked with students outside the classroom. He became chairman of the College Placement Committee, which helped graduates get jobs when jobs were scarce. He was devoted to the classroom—in his two short years he became one of the university's best-regarded professors—but he still missed working in the field with the people of Georgia. He would not be content professionally unless he could return to the Georgia soil, and the farmers and agents. So in August of 1936, he rejoined the Agricultural Extension Service on campus as a farm management specialist, welcomed back by Kenneth Treavor, his friend, best man, and former colleague. J. W. would remain in this position for eighteen years.

J. W. was truly in his element. He came to know and help leaders in farming, business, and just about every other arena in the state. His leadership responsibilities grew, and he worked at motivating himself and others to do more than they thought they could. He knew that motivation required knowledge, confidence, inspiration, and warmth. "Thomas Jefferson defined a leader as one with a knowing head and a loving heart," J. W. said. Another comment revealed his inborn affection for others: "Loving people is a requirement in effective leadership."[33]

J. W.'s diverse talents and experiences enlivened his years on the job. Shortly after he became farm management specialist, the Extension staff moved into a new building on Lumpkin Street named for Senator Hoke Smith. Smith was coauthor of federal legislation establishing the Cooperative Agricultural Extension Service. In February 1938, from his new office, J. W. supervised a somewhat unusual assignment: planting crops at Reidsville Prison, a state-owned institution in Tattnall County.

Because the Extension Service was the applied arm of the university's agriculture college, it managed all farmlands at state-owned institutions. J. W. was sent to Reidsville to get the planting under way; planting season comes early in South Georgia. His lifelong desire to farm was close to being realized—certainly not in the manner he expected, certainly not with prison labor. For two grueling months, J. W. would do enough farming to satisfy his appetite for a long time.

At the prison, J. W. found fifty mules and one old tractor to "break" and prepare the seed bed for planting two thousand acres of land. The superintendent of the prison did not welcome J. W.'s help and authority. In fact, the situation was so tense that J. W. was unable at first to get the keys to the fertilizer sheds. He not only got the keys, he got fifty more mules from the state prison at Milledgeville. Two teams were assembled, one to break and prepare the land for planting corn and the other to distribute the fertilizer and plant the seed. Other teams were to prepare the land and plant vegetables such as tomatoes, peas, and squash.

This mammoth task did not proceed without problems; working prison laborers had its limitations. Two managers, one in charge of hogs, the other of cattle, were selling animals on the side. When it was discovered that the swine manager had allowed several hundred male pigs to become shoats—uncastrated animals—a day was set aside for the castration. That evening, prisoners enjoyed the by-product, "Mountain Oysters."

When J. W. left the farm in April, planting of all but 165 acres was completed. A replacement superintendent was named, and the farm prospered under good management. J. W. considered his Reidsville journey a valuable experience, but he had no desire to supervise another prison farm.[34]

Within the next two years, four important events—destruction, construction, birth, and death—occurred in J. W.'s family. Destruction came in the early evening of May 7, 1939, when a tornado ripped through Wilkes County, causing great damage to the family farm. The home was severely damaged; the roof and top floor were blown away. Large trees were uprooted, and a tenant house occupied by eight people was blown from its foundation. No one was injured, and friends and neighbors pitched in to help clean up.

In early 1939 J. W. and Cora Lee contracted for the building of their first home—on Parkway Drive in Athens. It was completed six months later, and the family moved in on June 12. A twenty-five-year mortgage was arranged at 4 percent interest. The monthly payment was forty-one dollars. This was to be the home that lasted through their entire married life. The first winter, a storm dumped fifteen inches of snow onto the area, and temperatures plunged to minus eighteen degrees. Still, the family was comfortable. "This presented no problem with a furnace-heated house," he said.[35]

On June 20, 1939, their second child, John William Fanning Jr., was born at St. Mary's Hospital on North Milledge Avenue. Dr. Marion Hubert was the attending physician. Cora Lee's nephew, Alfred "Carlyle" Harrison, lived with the family for the first two years in their new home and helped with household chores.

Harrison found his uncle's love of the university was contagious. "I remember going to one of the farms with him to treat some hogs," he said. "This was my first experience close up with this procedure, and this set the stage for me to decide to go to the University of Georgia."[36]

Sorrow darkened the household shortly after John William Jr.'s birth. J. W.'s father, John Wootten, who had continued to suffer shock and disappointment after the tornado's devastation, died in May 1940. The man who was the model of ambition and drive for J. W. would miss many of his son's later successes.

In the coming years, J. W. worked closely with the Georgia Farm Bureau Federation. He helped in planning programs, explaining national farm policy, and providing information on agricultural outlook. He knew agricultural leaders from across Georgia, and he earned respect within the organization. When he was courted by one of its presidents to succeed him, J. W. declined.

The Farm Bureau, however, provided J. W. with fulfilling experiences. He led discussions of problems facing groups of farm people. He listened to their comments, summarized each discussion, and frequently led the people to recognize their problems and to do something about them.

You never meet opportunity strolling down Easy Street.

J. W.

Whether working with a group or with an individual, J. W. followed the principle of self-determination: helping oneself. That principle was never illustrated better than in the family of J. P. and Montene Morris, who lived in Appling County, in southeastern Georgia. The Morrises had met the Fannings in the late 1930s, a few years after J. W. became a farm management specialist with the Extension Service. J. P. and J. W. held each other in high esteem, and throughout their lives they looked to each other for advice.

In 1941 the Morris family was growing tomatoes to be sold as green tomatoes at a nearby State Farmers Market, a newly developed project of the state and the University of Georgia. Without warning, the market for green tomatoes bottomed out. J. P. and Montene were caught with twenty-five acres of beautiful tomatoes that were turning red quickly.

Visiting relatives in a nearby county, J. W. and Cora Lee stopped by to see the Morrises. J. P. told J. W. what had happened: the twenty-five acres of tomatoes would be a total loss. J. W. contacted Frankie Parker, home demonstration agent in Appling County. She, in turn, reached a former classmate working in the university dining hall. After a little persuading, the manager of the dining hall decided to buy a soup mixture with Morris tomatoes as a basic ingredient—along with corn and okra, canned in quart jars. The soup was to be served to students during the winter months.

That's not the end of the story. The university at the time was promoting county-operated-and-owned canning plants. So the Morrises contacted the plant in Appling County to see if they might use the plant to can the soup. The county management agreed, the Morris Canning Company was created, the first Georgia Quality soup mixture was canned, and the canned soup was delivered to the University of Georgia in August 1941.[37]

Eventually, the Morrises built their own canning plant, and the home demonstration agent taught the soup formula for more than forty years. (The formula: combine and cook ten 10-quart water buckets of ground tomatoes mixed with five 10-quart water buckets of one-half-inch-cut okra, along with one 10-quart water bucket of whole corn kernels.)[38] This start-up business grew and annually used more than five hundred acres of tomatoes grown locally, hundreds of acres of okra grown in another part of Georgia, and hundreds of acres of sweet corn grown by local farmers.

Morris Canning Company grew from five employees to nearly two hundred. Most of them lived in the same county; their wages were spent locally, boosting the economy of Appling County. Georgia Quality & Montene Morris Vegetable Mixture became the brand name of the soup. J. W. helped the Morris family to help themselves, and they, together with countless other farm families and Georgia agriculture as a whole, profited.[39]

J. W. had an uncanny knack for seeing the big picture in agriculture and what might happen. He analyzed a situation by getting facts, and he sought out people who knew how to make the right things happen. He committed himself to situations that dealt with the growing, marketing, and processing of agricultural commodities. His frequent comment underscored his life's commitment: "There is a great future in farming."[40] J. W. was totally engaged in agriculture.

From about 1940 through 1945, farmers had a tough time finding workers. About twelve million men and women were serving in the U.S. Armed Forces, and many others were working in factories producing materials and machines needed in the World War II effort. The shortage was worse during the harvest seasons. Soon came the Emergency Farm Labor Administration program, administered in Georgia by the Extension Service.

The director of Extension, Walter S. Brown, called on J. W. to take charge of the program as farm labor supervisor for the state. He would oversee the work of all county agents and home demonstration agents. Using federal emergency money, they recruited volunteers to help harvest crops. The program was successful because most Americans in the South were dedicated to the war effort and to farm production as well.

Labor was sought from all sources. Even Italian and German prisoners of war (POWs) were used. In one instance, five hundred Bahamians were recruited to harvest peaches.[41] The presence of POWs on American soil required an adjustment on the home front. For years propaganda reminded Americans that the Italians and Germans were their enemies. Many local people—particularly those whose sons and daughters were overseas—were skittish about the presence of POWs in the community.

The first POW camp in Georgia was in Americus, Sumter County. Its first occupants were five hundred German prisoners who fought in the North African campaign. Before the war was over, more than nine thousand German prisoners were located in Georgia—at large military camps such as Fort Gordon, Fort Benning, and a few other sites. County agents made arrangements for the work, and the POWs received compensation, a portion of which each placed in safekeeping to be received after the war.[42]

Despite the awkward beginning, the POW labor effort was without incident. In fact, J. W. rememebered, several POWs said they wanted to return and become American citizens. "The German POWs," he said, "made a significant contribution to the harvesting of Georgia crops, especially peanuts."[43]

J. W.'s job was encouraging the POWs to work hard in the fields. So he offered them a deal, one that was creative and, to those who knew him well, uncharacteristic of the man. He told them that if and when they completed all the work scheduled for that day, he would serve them free beer. Their response was enthusiastic. Production increased accordingly.

Just before the end of World War II, Cason Callaway of Blue Spring Farms, Hamilton, Georgia, offered another challenge. Callaway was a retired textile magnate, a member of the Board of Regents of the University System of Georgia, and a director of many large corporations in America. He styled himself as a successful farmer and in the 1940s created the Georgia 100 Better Farms Program. A new wrinkle in Georgia agriculture, the program was an outstanding innovation in the state.

The idea was presented at a luncheon in Atlanta in August 1944 before a group of business and civic leaders. Callaway was persuasive as he told them of his dream: "Form one hundred corporations, covering as much of the area of the state as possible. Each corporation will have seven stockholders, each of whom will put up one thousand dollars. . . . Each corporation will employ a farmer and buy one hundred acres of land costing about three thousand with the remainder of the money being used to build up the soil. After the soil has been built up, each corporation will borrow not more than three thousand from the bank."[44] The plan was to operate the program for three years, and each farm would have federal and state agencies at its disposal for advice and suggestions. Farms would be graded and prizes awarded for accomplishments. Corporate signers came forward enthusiastically. The program was launched.

Callaway had proposed that the Agricultural Extension Service serve as a key collaborator. He asked Director Walter S. Brown to make J. W. a member of a committee of three to provide technical services to the 100 Better Farms. Permission was granted, and J. W. began a four-year working relationship with Callaway. J. W. knew Callaway was a leader who saw a revolution in the making, and he wanted Georgia to be ready. "Mr. Callaway's contribution born of his sharp insight and caring was to help Georgia leaders to see the future with new eyes and great courage," J. W. said.[45]

J. W.'s committee visited each farm. He and other committee members told farmers how to build up their soil, how to select their enterprises and how to use their capital. Budgets were prepared for each of the farm owners, and Callaway invited farmers to his own Blue Springs Farm to sit down and discuss opportunities in agriculture. A few years later, about 150 farmers and interested colleagues traveled to Maryland, Pennsylvania, Illinois, and Iowa to see what was doing well. Callaway's goal of the tour: to help Georgians to raise their level of thinking about what was possible in farming practices and management. Almost every farm in the program paid its own way through the three years and was liquidated at a profit.

J. W. and two of his university colleagues, W. T. Fullilove of the Georgia Experiment Station and L. M. Awtrey of the Georgia Coastal Plain Experiment Station, wrote a book that served as a classroom text and a resource for farmers. The book, *The Business of Farming*, was based on statistical material accumulated at Blue Springs and by the 100 Better Farms. The book focused on problems and exercises in determining profits, planning operations, and keeping records on farms.

Callaway wrote the preface, which began: "The training of farm youth in the business of farming is one of our greatest responsibilities and opportunities. . . . A new system of agriculture, which should be more profitable but will require larger and longer term credit, is developing in Georgia and the South. To take advantage of this opportunity and merit the needed credit, all farmers, large and small, should possess knowledge of how to plan and put into effect simple budgetary controls."[46] The book became popular among high school ag teachers and college professors teaching farm economics.

J. W. learned much from Callaway by participating in the program. He saw how Callaway's charisma attracted people and how his vision moved them to act. Callaway was a motivator who sought diligently to influence the business leaders and farmers of Georgia to do more than they thought they could. He was slow to anger. His mind and spirit brimmed with aspirations, ardent wishes, strong feelings, and an iron self-discipline. He could express pleasure and happiness freely, but he contained his displeasure, disappointment, and unhappiness. "To work for him was an inspiration to me," J. W. said later, "and I was helped greatly in my own career to emphasize the qualities of foresightedness and motivation."[47]

J. W. was to build his own reputation for knowledge, efficiency, and leadership. He had learned to communicate well with a diverse public. He was adept at face-to-face exchanges, and he also was an accomplished writer. Following the Georgia Better Farm Program, J. W. began a seven-year relationship with *The Progressive Farmer Magazine*. He wrote an article each month—more than sixty on topics dealing with successful farm management. His articles were read across the Southeast and reached thousands of farmers. The writing, he said, helped him discipline himself and develop clear-cut thinking and speaking.

He would hold three positions at the university while writing for *The Progressive Farmer Magazine:* veteran farm management specialist until 1954, founding director of a new community education center from 1954 to 1956, and department head and division chairman. J. W.'s knowledge, love of education, and disciplined thinking merged in his articles, which ranged from an economic treatise on farming efficiency to the simple story of Earnest Blakey.

J. W. liked to write success stories about small farm families, and the Earnest Blakeys of Barrow County, Georgia, fit the mold perfectly. He titled his story about them, "Six Steps to Farming"; and it appeared in the July 29, 1958 issue of *The Progressive Farmer Magazine.*[48] He was dedicated to the proposition that farmers in Georgia had much room for improvement, and his writings were often admonitions to do a better job of farming. In the November 1, 1953, issue of *The Progressive Farmer Magazine,* he discussed "Six Ways to Judge Efficient Farming."[49]

1. Receipts must be greater than expenses.
2. All resources must be fully used.
3. Yields must be above average.
4. Volume turnout per man must be large.
5. A high return must be made on the investment.
6. Capital investment must be pprotected.

(The complete text of these two stories appear in Appendix H.)

Other titles of J. W.'s articles included: "Livestock Farming with a Future," "Milk from Forage Costs Less to Produce," "In Farming, You've Got to Do the Best with What You Have," "It's Time to Watch Those Hogs," "Things Ought to Be Better in 1955," "Stay with Those Hens," "Storage Pays Off in Grain," "How Much More Dairying," "You Can Still Bank on Beef," and "How Much Credit Is Enough?"[50]

In 1961, *The Progressive Farmer Magazine* named J. W. "Man of the Year" in service to Georgia agriculture. The following citation accompanied the honor:

> Everybody likes to hear Georgia's J. W. Fanning talk economics—he makes it "come alive." And after they hear him talk on the subject, they go out and quote him. Mr. Fanning speaks and writes on agricultural economics. And he puts it to work by serving groups who are making Georgia farming a more profitable business and a more satisfying way of life. . . .
>
> Since 1956, he has been head of the department and chairman of the Division of Agricultural Economics at the University of Georgia College of Agriculture. That's a heavy title. But Mr. Fan-

> ning can bring economics to everyday language. . . . As Extension Service economist for more than twenty years, he has done more than any other person to guide county agents and their cooperating farmers in providing program planning.[51]

Another challenging request came from the chairman of the Board of Trustees of Berry College, John Sibley, in the late 1940s and early '50s. Sibley was one of Georgia's giants in banking and was passionate about the wise use of our natural resources. In the 1940s J. W. was asked to join Clarence Walker from the college to help develop budgets for all the farm enterprises.

Berry College, founded in 1902 by Martha Berry, was a school for enterprising rural boys at a time when few public schools existed in Georgia. Work experience continues to be offered as a part of every student's development; from 85 to 90 percent of the students work on campus. The natural environment, conducive for learning, comprises 28,000 acres of land—fields, forests, lakes, and mountains.[52]

At Berry, farming its land is a long-standing practice that not only produces food for the college and for income, but also provides work opportunities for the students. J. W. loved being involved with a large-scale farm operation, because challenges were presented that he never encountered on family farms.

Later in the 1950s J. W. served as a visiting consultant to Berry. He advised the college on the overall operation of the farms and the proper use of its physical resources. Working with him were Charles N. Shepardson of the Federal Reserve System and Dr. D. R. Dodd of Berry College. The three men submitted their report, titled "An Appraisal of the Berry Schools Program with Particular Reference to the Agricultural Activities," to the president of the college, Dr. John R. Bertrand, in August of 1958.[53] The detailed report covered training and employment activities to be undertaken, financial aspects of training activities, student labor, and agricultural enterprises and operations.

The report confirmed the notion that Berry College was managing a large-scale, integrated farming operation. General farming consisted of 800 acres of crops, 40 of gardening, and 35 of orchards; 600 head of beef cattle, 125 head of milk cows, and 70 head of brood sows; an 8,000-capacity broiler house, 3,000-capacity laying house, 12 smaller laying houses, a central feed mill, and 25,000 acres of forest land. J. W.'s work with Berry College in the 1950s opened the door for a relationship that was to continue long beyond his retirement.[54]

His eighteen-plus years as a farm management specialist with the Agricultural Extension Service in Athens was one of the greatest chapters in J. W.'s professional life—probably because it came closer to "dirt farming" than anything else he ever did. He did not till the soil or plant and raise cotton and other crops to maturity, but he advised countless farmers and families who were exacting a livelihood from the soil. He knew the real estate of Georgia and its tenants, from Rising Fawn to Tybee Island to Donalsonville. He was at home working with a small farmer or the corporate owner of a plantation. He lent himself, his knowledge, and his expertise to make farming a profitable pursuit for people across the state and Southeast.

*More than anyone else I've ever known,
J. W. had a vision of how rural communities could improve
the quality of life of their citizens and how to turn this vision
into practical results. He was always eager to do everything
possible himself but had an uncanny knack of extracting
as much as possible from the people like me
who admired and trusted him.*

JIMMY CARTER,

*former president of the United States
and Governor of Georgia*

*Commandment number one
of any truly civilized society is this:
Let the people in a community be different.*

J. W.

CHAPTER FOUR

Community Development, 1954–1956, 1961–1965

In March 1954, J. W. resigned from the Extension Service to become associate director for community services of a new, intriguing entity known as the Georgia Center for Continuing Education. The university had submitted a grant proposal to the W. K. Kellogg Foundation in Battle Creek, Michigan, to build a center to house its planned continuing education program. The grant was awarded in November 1953.[1] J. W.'s focus would remain research and teaching, but the new position would provide a segue into community development—an area that would become his passion.

Discussion about community and area development was beginning to emerge at the state level in the mid-1950s. The major players were the Area Planning and Development Commissioners' Association, the Georgia Municipal Association, the Association of County Commissioners of Georgia, the Georgia Power Company, the Industrial Development Division at the Georgia Institute of Technology, the Electric Membership Cooperatives, and the State of Georgia Department of Planning. It was a pioneering endeavor, and J. W.'s counsel and experience were valuable in forming the area planning and development commissions. He was the University of Georgia's official representative. As such, he was instrumental in carrying the process statewide. His writing began to show a flavor of community development, rural-urban balance, and regional planning. Former President Jimmy Carter remembered:

> After I returned home from the U.S. Navy in 1953, I became deeply involved in almost everything going on around the Plains community. I had been away from home for twelve years, so I also had to learn about farming and our warehouse business. I utilized every opportunity to learn from J. W. and was soon attending sessions at the community development center in Athens, most of which were orchestrated by him. I was involved in the earliest stages of regional planning commissions, organized what was first named Middle Flint Planning Commission, and became the first statewide president of the Georgia Planning Commission. All of this was done under the tutorship of J. W. Fanning. He was always diplomatic, and able to coordinate the potentially diverse efforts of private citizens, Georgia Power Company, Georgia Electric Membership Corporation, and officials in the state government.[2]

President Carter's hunger to know his community was an instinct in which J. W. strongly believed. In one of his submissions to *The Progressive Farmer Magazine,* J. W. wrote:

> Are there things happening in your community? . . . Town folks moving to the country? Farm folks moving to the town? New industries going up? Idle farm land on the increase? Lines between rural and urban fast disappearing? How many of the changes in your community in the past fifteen to twenty years were planned, —given direction,—or controlled? How many do you wish you didn't have? How many were you against that turned out alright [*sic*]? How many were you for that turned out bad?
>
> Is your rural community stronger or weaker now than fifteen years ago? How about your urban community? How close are your rural and urban leaders working together for total community improvement?[3]

Knowing your community meant learning the answers to those questions, and J. W.'s memory served him well. He met thousands of Georgians during his lifetime and astonished most by remembering their names. Hill R. Healan, who served as the executive director of the Association of County Commissioners of Georgia for twenty-six years, marveled: "I worked very closely with him on legislative matters. He was a great civic club speaker and was in that capacity for many years. He knew everybody!"[4]

Yet J. W. detoured from community development for five years. After he had worked two years with the Georgia Center for Continuing Education, the dean of the university's College of Agriculture asked him to serve as head of the Department of Agricultural Economics and chairman of the Division of Agricultural Economics. J. W.'s love for agriculture resurfaced, and he assumed the dual positions on July 1, 1956. He was responsible primarily for teaching and research, both strongly tied to the extension programs. Being chairman of the entire Division of Agricultural Economics was a herculean task requiring strong leadership.

J. W.'s interest in community development, however, didn't diminish. He continued to attend regional meetings throughout Georgia. He enjoyed the five years he spent in research and teaching—especially the basic course in agricultural economics.

His talent for teaching had been recognized for years, and students with varied interests and goals registered for his classes. He valued his connection to the classroom: "A teaching relationship is a great one and profound in nature," he said.[5] He continued to provide students with individual attention. He was their mentor when they needed advice; he was their advocate when they needed a job.

Not everyone who benefited from his guidance, however, was one of his students. That was the case with Gaylord Coan, who arrived on campus hoping to concentrate on agribusiness. The trouble was, the course catalog did not list this major. So Coan sought out J. W., who essentially created a curriculum and suggested a number of appropriate courses. After graduation, Coan received an interview at Gold Kist, Incorporated. J. W. had arranged the interview. Coan went on to become CEO of Gold Kist. His most poignant memory of J. W., however, was when he and Cora Lee called on the Coan family, encouraging them to visit their church.[6]

During his time as department head and division chairman, J. W. was an invited lecturer at the School of Banking of the South, a two-week summer program at Louisiana State University in Baton Rouge. He spoke on the economics of agriculture. After a few years he was asked to serve as director of the banking school's agricultural economics section, organizing the teaching program and recruiting the faculty. He was among some of the best agricultural economists in the nation invited to lecture. The program put him in contact with five hundred to six hundred leading bankers from across the South. In a few years he assumed responsibility for lectures on farm credit. By this time, he was staying in Baton Rouge for two weeks each summer.

J. W. was an active faculty member of the School of Banking for twenty-five years. The school's reputation for high-quality instruction was well-known. Each group of students attended the school for three consecutive summers, covering management of bank funds, credit, basic banking and economic problems, and banking law in the first year; agricultural credit, agricultural economics, investments, bank management, and real estate financing in the second; and profit planning, senior management case, foreign trade and international finance, bank marketing, trust department, and computer utilization in the third and final year.

Students in the program were eager to improve themselves. They absorbed everything in the classroom. J. W. challenged himself to meet their expectations. But he looked upon his position as leadership development—helping these young banking leaders find the courage to think and act, and to keep abreast of the developments in agriculture.

J. W. revered life. He valued every assignment. Walt Denero, who would work at an institute named after J. W. years later, described him: "Standing straight and tall, he towers above those who seek to be served, rather than to serve. His gentle touch and influence have helped bring healing to those who dwell in dark rooms of ignorance and joy to those who once despaired. Ever optimistic, for Dr. Fanning, no challenge is too big and no concern too small to escape his notice and attention."[7]

By this point, leaders across the state—people in Atlanta boardrooms and the offices of the Georgia Chamber of Commerce—knew of J. W.'s ability to lead. Industrial development had always been among the top priorities of the chamber, and agriculture was the state's largest industry. The chamber established a committee to promote agriculture through extended processing of raw products from farms, such as canning of fruits and vegetables, processing of livestock and poultry, and other agricultural production requiring further treatment before it reached the consumer.

J. W. was selected to chair the Agri-Industry Committee, and he and other members emphasized the importance of processing agricultural and forestry products in Georgia to keep and create jobs inside the state. He continued to earn the confidence and respect of Georgians. When effective leadership was required—particularly to make the seemingly impossible happen—he was one of the people most likely to be recruited. The man had a well-developed sense of humor, and he used levity skillfully to make his points. Much of his humor reflected his experiences in dealing with rural citizens, because he loved their way of life and the way they approached challenges.

He was committed to service, wherever and whenever needed. "His challenge to me was to strive to become the best in promoting and providing for those who need assistance in any way possible," said Clifford Hardwick III, who would work with J. W. as a colleague at the university.[8] An intriguing opportunity arose during the late 1950s, when the Georgia Department of Health called for a regional program in community health. Instead of centralizing activities at the Milledgeville Mental Health Administration, more control would be given to local entities.

In Clarke County, professionals wanted to organize a Northeast Georgia mental health association, which would serve Clarke County and the nine counties surrounding it. Margaret Broun, then-president of the Athens-Clarke Mental Health Association, asked J. W. to help. He accepted the challenge because he supported the idea. He knew the process would require the patience and perseverance of supporters if it was to succeed. He also believed in conducting a thorough exchange of ideas; everyone's opinion was important to him. J. W. was skilled in keeping people focused and involved. After several years, the Northeast Georgia Mental Health Center was organized and located in Athens General Hospital.

What he accomplished with the organization of the Mental Health Center was repeated throughout his career. It was uncanny how J. W., working with all types of people, could enable each member to express his or her own ideas and still build a consensus. He worked in nearly everyone's suggestion. The Clarke County program was so well accepted that an optional sales tax to fund the erection of a new medical facility passed in a local referendum.

The health center's multiple-county setup was in step with the times. By the latter part of the decade, area planning and development regions were beginning to emerge in the rural reaches of the state. More than a decade earlier, metropolitan counties had banded together to create the Atlanta Regional Commission, and the concept was being considered for undefined regions outside the city.

In 1957 the Georgia General Assembly passed legislation creating the Georgia General Planning Enabling Act, which stated: "Any two counties are authorized to create a joint planning commission. Any one or more counties and any one or more municipalities in any one or more counties are authorized to create a joint planning commission."[9] To receive local, state, and federal money, the new association must have legal status. When endorsed by law, an association of counties could pool its resources across governmental jurisdictions.[10]

In Rome, Georgia, in the middle of the Coosa River Valley, the forward-looking editor of the *Rome News Tribune*, Colin Fawcett, was asking about regionalism—about getting thirteen counties in the area to work together to meet challenges. So the Rome/Floyd County Planning Commission hired Sidney F. Thomas Jr. to be the director of a new association. Thomas, Fawcett, Harley Harper, chairman of the Rome/Floyd County Planning Commission, and Fred Starr, a regional representative of the Georgia Power Company, collaborated in writing a plan to create a county association. These four men gave impetus to the idea of regionalism in northwest Georgia.

Outside experts were brought into the picture, including J. W. Fanning, representing the University of Georgia Department of Agricultural Economics, Noah Langdale of Georgia State University, Frank Hood of the Georgia Power Company, Kenneth Wagner from the Industrial Development Division of Georgia Tech, and a representative of the U.S. Army Corps of Engineers. Senator Richard B. Russell also became interested. These people lent their skills and experience and gave legitimacy to county regionalism.[11]

The idea of pooling resources across regions had inherent appeal, but the road to cooperation among governments was tortuous. J. W. and others had learned what was needed in helping to form the Coosa Valley Area Planning and Development Commission. They just took that knowledge to the rest of Georgia, reshaping experiences from time to time to suit the needs of the various proposed regions.

Joining J. W. in this often daunting effort was a faithful corps of regional organizers: Frank Hood of the Georgia Power Company; Joe Tanner of the Rural Electric Membership Corporation; Elmer George, executive director of the Georgia Municipal Association; and Hill Healan of the Association of County Commissioners of Georgia.

Tanner remembered J. W.'s effectiveness in presiding over the meetings: "The tone of his voice and his Southern accent almost immediately commanded respect. I have told people that if you were ever in a room with J. W., it would not take you more than two seconds to realize you were in a room with somebody who was different and special."[12] J. W. demurred. He said he just took the common-sense approach. He defined common sense "as that stuff on the end of a coon dog's nose that told the dog which tree contained the coon."[13]

Hood of Georgia Power would work with J. W. for more than thirty-five years. He remembered, years later: "He was without a doubt the finest developer of a program I have ever known. He was able to pull people together and to get them to talk and to discuss their problems. He was able to get them to really want to take action to correct deficiencies in the towns and cities in which we worked. It is my belief that he is one of the greatest moderators of a community discussion that the state has ever produced."[14]

J. W.'s curriculum vitae began to lengthen as he continued working in regionalism, community planning, and leadership. Elmer George, then directing the Georgia Municipal Association, later remembered a meeting he had with J. W. and Hood at which they discussed population change, economic development, and problems and challenges facing Georgia. The result was a series of joint city-county district meetings held in early 1958 that focused on pooling resources for the good of the extended community. Panelists in addition to J. W. were a faculty member or two from the Georgia Institute of Technology, representatives from the Georgia Power Company, professionals from planning associations, real estate developers, and representatives of federal agencies.

The ten meetings attracted local city and county officials, state legislators, regional and local educators, media, business and agricultural leaders, and members of the public. George said the meetings brought together city and county officials in a collaborative program. The South was entering an era of progress and prosperity unprecedented in its history. Presenters urged participants to pool leadership resources and work together for the benefit of all Georgians.

J. W.'s enthusiasm for community collaboration and planning was apparent in an article entitled "Community Planning," which he published in the July 1958 issue of the *Georgia Local Government Journal*. His challenges were clear:

> Past and prospective developments have great implications in community development. New community patterns are developing. The number of strictly farm and non-farm communities is declining. The line between the rural and the urban is fast disappearing. The urban area is backing out into the rural—bringing with it both desirable and undesirable developments—and brand-new communities.
>
> Greater community interdependencies are coming. Education is now a community-wide activity. Water, sewage disposal, roads, recreation, industrial development are problems of the total rural-urban community. . . .
>
> What kind of community is wanted? . . . What kind of community do you want? You can have whatever you want—if town and country together draw the blueprint—and cooperate in the building.[15]

Town and country, business and industry, constituent and politician were represented at Berry College near Rome at the first regional conference, held May 7, 1959. Leaders of northwest Georgia came together to discuss mutual problems. J. W. spoke of the potential benefits that might accrue if counties shared services. "A new Georgia is in the making," he predicted.[16] As a result of the discussions, twelve northwest Georgia counties formally established the Coosa Valley Area Planning and Development Association. Later, an additional county joined, for a total of thirteen.[17]

The first annual meeting of the association was held July 21, 1960. It resulted in the adoption of a plan to establish the association as an official planning commission. The Coosa Valley Area Planning and Development Commission was the first of its kind in Georgia and one of the first in the country. Financial support for the program came from local governments of the participating counties and Governor S. Ernest Vandiver, who provided matching money to establish a regional office of the Georgia Tech Industrial Development Division in Rome.[18]

J. W., in the meantime, continued his teaching and research at the College of Agriculture. The dean, C. C. Murray, asked J. W. in 1960 to accompany him on a trip to Cambodia and South Vietnam as a consultant. The dean was considering sending agriculture faculty for two years to help establish colleges of agriculture in Cambodia. A similar college already existed in South Vietnam.

J. W. had never before traveled abroad and was moved by the despair—and warmth—he encountered:

> We spent three days in Cambodia and three weeks in South Vietnam. The year was 1960, which was just prior to the start of the war in Vietnam. Tension was in the air and ghastly stories about the Viet Cong abounded. But life as we saw it was fairly stable. Cambodia was very peaceful, but South Vietnam was experiencing a lot of misery. Faculty were sent to Cambodia for two years, and some for one year in South Vietnam before the war.
>
> On the trip, we had the opportunity to enjoy short visits in Hawaii, Bangkok, Tokyo, and Hong Kong. We met many officials of the two countries as well as staff members of the Office of Foreign Aid. The war that came afterwards devastated all efforts

> to make improvements in agricultural education, and we were saddened deeply by the civil war in Cambodia which was very cruel to a people whom we found to be peaceful and hopeful.
>
> This was my first trip abroad. I learned much about foreign affairs and the environment in which people of different races lived. The agelessness made a profound impression on me. I learned that a smile and a friendly handclasp are universal among beautiful people of all races.
>
> I came to understand more than ever the role of the leader in the custody of values. I saw how values differ from one culture to another. Also, how those values as reflected in the lives of people are not always respected by some in authority. I returned home with a profound respect for the way the values we have established in our form of government hold fast and the great responsibility resting on our leaders to serve as custodians of those values.[19]

J. W.'s appreciation of leadership's complexity—as "custodians of values," motivators, visionaries, communicators, and individuals of persistence and self-discipline—grew with his travels. His own ability to communicate, clearly and persuasively, drew widespread recognition.

Most people spend more energy going around problems than trying to solve them.

J. W.

The university, perhaps stirred by the regionalism movement, now was moving toward collaborative problem-solving. President O. C. Aderhold talked about having the university's expertise help with societal changes. The president was concerned about the university's commitment to a broad service: helping to solve pressing urban problems and generating more jobs in Georgia.

During one lively discussion, Aderhold asked J. W. what he considered to be the university's opportunity. J. W. responded, "More focus is needed on community and regional opportunities for development."[20] To the amazement of nearly everyone assembled, Aderhold agreed without argument. The Institute of Community and Area Development was created.

Aderhold wasted no time in asking J. W. to be director. He would leave behind his duties of head of the Department and chairman of the Division of Agricultural Economics. He had begun work in the field in 1930 as a farm management specialist. As much as he loved agricultural economics and working with people on improving farm practices, directing this new institute presented a challenge like none in agriculture. It was a chance to be of greater service.

The University of Georgia Annual Report, 1960–1961, carries an item from the minutes of the June meeting of the Board of Regents in 1961: "Institute of Community and Area Development: Approved for operation July 1, 1961. This Institute will bring all of the resources of the university to bear upon helping areas and communities in the state plan for future development in land utilization, recreation, industrial and commercial development, cultural improvements, and so on. Mr. J. W. Fanning has been named Director of the Institute which will perform research and service functions."[21]

His appointment to director became effective August 1, 1961, and so began "the most active and involved years of my life—and very enjoyable ones," J. W. said.[22] J. W. began choosing staff members of the institute, a talented and experienced group that initially included Howard V. Schretter, chief planner for Clarke County Planning Commission; James A. Burgess from the North Carolina League of Municipalities; and Robert J. Hill from the field of landscape architecture. Joining them were Ernest E. Melvin from the Planning Department of the city of Chicago and Gene A. Bramlett of the university's Department of Agricultural Economics.

In an article for the *Georgia Municipal Journal*, published in November 1961, J. W. described the university's newest academic service to Georgians, its challenges and how it would address them.

> *The Institute of Community and Area Development*
>
> A vast array of problems descended upon the communities of Georgia during the past ten years. Some arose from outside forces. Others came about from internal adjustments. All have been disturbing. They come in many fields including population, government, industry, agriculture, forestry, business, education, recreation, land use planning, housing, health, water, and just about every other segment of community life.
>
> No community or area has been able to sidestep one or more of these problems, nor the accompanying change and adjustment. Never, therefore, have the people of this state been more concerned nor more busily engaged in community and area development programs.
>
> Georgia is driving hard to solve these problems and to mold the new communities which appear certain to come. From the looks of things now, these communities will differ markedly from those of past years. They will be products of mid-twentieth century developments which have shortened the distance between people and expanded their demands for things that contribute to rising levels of living. All indications point to there being communities encouraging functional consolidation of city and county governments for greater efficiency in providing services.
>
> *Problems Are Interlocked*
>
> These new communities will be confronted with many interlocking relationships. For example, efforts to improve one segment of life will affect others. The addition of industry will cre-

ate problems in land use, government, education, recreation and agriculture. It will be necessary for all communities and areas to draw upon a broad base of resources and assistance for full and well-rounded development.

The state has made much progress on its approach to community development. Planning commissions are found in many municipalities and counties. Area Planning and Development Associations are becoming more numerous. Voluntary planning groups are meeting regularly in many localities. City and county governments are making adjustments in their operations to meet the complex situations they face. Other examples could be cited, but they denote the determination of Georgia's communities and areas to move forward.

University Has Responsibility

The University of Georgia has responsibility to all communities and areas in the state, and it is deeply concerned with the difficult adjustments which they confront in building anew. The university seeks to make available the knowledge and skills of its faculty and staff to every community and area on the many perplexing problems which they face in this period of transition. To more adequately discharge the service obligation, the university has recently established the Institute of Community and Area Development.

Purpose of Institute

The purposes of the Institute are to strengthen and expand the services of the university to communities and areas. The many colleges and schools of the university are vast reservoirs of knowledge and skills in such fields as government, education, business, agriculture, forestry, land use, water and mineral resources, landscape improvement, recreation, community organization, population, creative arts, and others.

Some Examples

The program of expanded services of the Institute of Community and Area Development will embrace a wide variety of activities. The following are examples:

1. More research on community and area development.
2. Widespread distribution of facts to local groups on a wide variety of subjects, such as: assistance available to communities, landscape improvement of streets, and financial administration in local government.
3. Studies within communities and areas on problems of local concern including tax assessment, tourism and recreation potentials, and business expansion.
4. Consultation and technical services on a wide range of problems such as government purchasing, financial administration, business projection, and implementing the comprehensive plans which many communities have contracted for.
5. Assistance in conducting and organizing leadership seminars and conferences on a wide range of subjects such as community planning, economic development, population shifts, labor resources, vocational training, recreation, and others.
6. Assistance in forum and panel discussions to provide for a better understanding of growth and development problems within the community and area relating, for example, to such fields as schools, roads, industrial development, intergovernmental cooperation, et cetera.

The Institute's Director will be responsible for administering this expanded service program in Colleges and Schools. All technical staff of the Institute will be on the staff of the departments of their respective interests and specialities.[23]

The establishment in 1961 of ICAD—the Institute of Community and Area Development—brightened the future of area planning and development commissions. J. W. believed regionalism was a way for small towns and sparsely populated rural counties to improve their quality of life. Many of them were losing population, a carryover of the demise of the cotton crop. Fewer farm workers were needed because of mechanization; workers were fleeing to job opportunities in larger urban centers.

In fact, the 1960 census revealed that more than one hundred Georgia counties lost population in the previous decade.[24] And from 1940 to 1960, the number of tractors on Georgia farms increased from nine thousand to more than one hundred thousand.[25] J. W. knew rural Georgia would have a hard time surviving. Services demanded by local residents could not be provided, given limited tax bases, so the common-sense solution seemed to be to pool resources across governmental jurisdictions. One by one, J. W. convinced counties and cities that regional commissions could do more for them than they could do alone.

ICAD rapidly became an effective research and service program in the state. For the first time in the history of public service at the University of Georgia, academic resources could be tapped across an array of disciplines found in the colleges and schools, institutes and centers, to enable ICAD to speak to practically any human concern.

J. W.'s love of loyalty to the University of Georgia was a thread that ran through his work and his excitement about how regionalism could strengthen small governments and communities. "In 1962, J. W. interviewed me in Atlanta about the Northeast Georgia Area Planning and Development Commission director's job, which I took in March 1963," Burt Sparer recalled:

> I got to know him mostly as a mentor, guiding the APDC planning program in the 1960s. . . .
>
> My most memorable single experience with him was when he gently scolded me for even thinking those population and eco-

> nomic studies should be done by Georgia Tech when UGA was in our very front yard! Also, many times he urged us—me—to "show the big picture" about Northeast Georgia's future—in part through a set of population and economic studies done by APDC.[26]

The Augusta regional development director, Tim Maund, who met J. W. in late 1962, confided in J. W. his "innermost thoughts about APDCs and how I felt about the profession and the direction that was being taken. I always felt that he would come on a moment's notice if I needed him and once here would be able to help solve whatever crisis had brought him. He was like a father to me."[27]

Maund did not forget a lesson he learned about professionalism when J. W. spoke to his Augusta board of directors. "We met on the third floor (the attic) of the Town Tavern," Maund recalled. "Somehow, we got caught up in a budget 'confusion' and it was 11 P.M. before we called on J. W. He gave his thirteen-minute speech and then asked for questions as if it were only 8:30. That taught me patience. That taught me that no matter what happens in a meeting, nor how long it lasts, you can always make your point. You can always be gracious."[28]

J. W. was known for helping people help themselves. His combination of talent and leadership resulted in innovative programming at the local and regional levels. To a great extent, ICAD represented change and challenge for higher education public service and outreach.

During his earliest days as director of ICAD, J. W. became heavily involved in developing leadership because he believed nothing happened in a community unless strong local leaders took people from where they were to where they needed to go. "I remember his ability to see and articulate the Big Picture of so many issues, especially as they related to leadership development," said colleague Tal C. DuVall, a close friend of J. W.'s.[29]

In 1961 the city of Savannah was interested in establishing a leadership program for its future civic leaders, and with help from a political science professor, J. W. directed the effort, based on an idea first tried at the University of Pennsylvania in the 1950s.

An account of the program's beginnings appeared in the June 21, 1961, edition of the *Savannah Morning News*. The story, "Businessmen Plan Leadership Course," reported:

> Plans for a seminar designed to train Savannah's future civic leaders were announced yesterday by a special committee at the Desoto Hotel. Some 40 young business and professional men, selected as the first candidates to attend the seminar, were at the dinner meeting. It was named the "Savannah Community Leadership Seminar." The steering committee for the project is composed of Reuben Clark, Joseph H. Harrison, James R. Lientz, George S. Patterson, John Riley, Sam Adler, Jr. and H. Hansell Hillyer. Hillyer and Adler were elected co-chairmen of the seminar.
>
> The steering committee, in setting up the seminar schedule, will work with the University of Georgia. Attending the meeting yesterday and giving their views on the project were Dr. J. W. Fanning, director of the new Institute of Community and Area Development at the university, and Dr. Morris W. H. Collins, political science professor at the university. . . . Fanning said the Savannah seminar is a pilot project for the state.
>
> "This is the first contact our new institute has had with a seminar of this type," he said. . . . Hillyer and Adler said that the purpose is to assist the community in preparing "promising young executives" for the volunteer responsibilities with non-profit business, civic and citizen organizations.
>
> The seminar will be divided into eight sessions during the coming year. After this class has finished the course, another class will

> begin. . . . Fanning and Collins will work with the group in selecting community problems to be studied at each session and will assist in lining up experts in each field to lecture and lead discussions. . . . "The ultimate objective," Hillyer said, "is to help government operate effectively to the end that Savannah may enjoy sound development."[30]

For eight years J. W. served as advisor for the Community Leadership Program in Savannah. The format of the meetings called for university experts to write background papers on selected topics: Savannah's growth, economic health, welfare services, cultural facilities, government, and city planning. Copies of the prepared papers were given to participants long before the sessions began. Participants gathered in the late afternoon once a month for a speech, dinner, and lengthy discussion.

Leadership Savannah has been conducted annually ever since the initial effort in 1961. Only men were selected for the first several classes, but women soon became regular participants. The project served as a model for similar programs across the state.

J. W.'s ability to read a situation and formulate an agenda to fit expressed needs was on target when he dealt with leadership development. He could see the big picture. He could define a problem accurately, assemble diverse and competing groups to analyze a complex situation, gather support for a cooperative solution, and motivate the people to act. He was firm without being dictatorial.

ICAD's early programs succeeded because of J. W.'s leadership, many have said. His enthusiasm for community development work was contagious; his staff could not help but get excited. He likened a community to a living organism comprising and affecting the people who live there.

J. W. usually would begin his comments with some quip to get the audience's attention. He would say, "Ladies and gentlemen, we are delighted that you thought enough of this meeting to come out. Believe me, it will not last late into the evening. As Henry VIII would always say to a new wife, 'Don't worry, I will not keep you long.'"[31] He would make people feel comfortable. Each participant would express his or her personal views, and, before it was over everyone usually agreed on the issues. J. W. was a consensus builder. He would conclude the meeting by saying, "Ladies and gentlemen, you have just heard a community talking to itself. When communities start talking to themselves, accomplishments begin to happen."[32]

J. W. would never give advice at a community meeting, but he would provide information and push participants to make decisions themselves.

It is good policy for the leaders of a community to keep the citizens well-informed. Otherwise, they will begin to speculate that all manner of evil is going on down in City Hall. Facts tend to curb a lot of speculation.

J. W.

ICAD staff members traversed the state during the 1960s. They held many meetings, convincing leaders in almost every county that they should belong to a regional commission. The meetings bore positive results. These collaborative development centers remain forces for change today.

Rallying the residents of several counties to accept regionalism was not without challenges—and even hazards. To many local leaders, regional commissions threatened the status quo. One afternoon, advocates and educators in one area in South Georgia were meeting in a motel, planning the agenda for a meeting later in the evening. Suddenly they were interrupted by a rap on the door. Standing in the doorway was the local sheriff, who advised them to get out of town because the folks did not appreciate outsiders telling them what to do. They listened to the sheriff and drove away unscathed—only to return another day for a successful gathering of local leaders and prominent residents.[33]

Such extreme opposition, however, was nearly nonexistent. ICAD's philosophy was to respond to what members of the community said they needed, not to strike out looking for something to do. Requests for assistance in forming development districts came from all over Georgia, and by the middle of 1963, a majority of cities and counties had joined together to create planning and development commissions. ICAD's role was to prepare a document describing the characteristic of the region under consideration and provide a forum for local residents to meet and hammer out their differences.

Howard Schretter, who had training and experience in economic geography, usually prepared the documents given to participants. A year earlier, in May 1962, he had produced "Central Savannah River Area Economic Conditions and Trends," which was intended "to promote a better understanding of economic problems facing the area, and by doing, point up the need for unified local action to combat these conditions."[34] Detailed sections of the publication were devoted to population and urban changes, labor force issues, income, and housing.

Another document compiled by Schretter underscored the ambitious tasks facing these nascent, collaborative commissions. Issued October 18, 1963, and titled "The Area Planning and Development Commission: Its Relationship with Local Planning Programs," the volume included a foreword by J. W. He wrote: "Area Planning and Development Commissions offer to Georgia's communities an opportunity to join together for the solving of common problems and the developing of areas' potentials. . . . Since the development of a program and the selection of a director still lies ahead for most of the state's area planning and development commissions, basic questions that will shape their future are yet to be made. . . . The concern [of this report] is with the formulation of an area commission's program, the relationship of this program to local planning activities and the nature of a commission's director and staff."[35]

ICAD staff members drove thousands of miles and spent countless days and nights helping groups of counties establish area planning and development commissions. They usually rode from Athens in J. W.'s easy-riding Chrysler with its spare tire mold on the outside of the trunk lid.

J. W. rarely spent a night on the road; he had spent enough time away from his family as an agricultural extension economist. Sometimes he had to drive all the way home from cities as far away as Waycross, arriving in Athens as late as three or four in the morning. The travelers often were close to exhaustion, but the next day they would be at their university desks by eight. J. W. usually got there first. He also worked a half day on Saturdays and expected his staff to be there, too.

ICAD colleague Gene Bramlett remembered: "J. W. had boundless energy but he never appeared rushed. Once, the two of us worked hard on a project all day, which included an early morning, out-of-town trip. I was weary by 6:30 that evening and departed for home, leaving J. W. to catch up on a few more things not related to our project. Listening to the car radio on the way home, it was announced that J. W. Fanning was to be the featured speaker that night at some organization in a nearby town. . . . I remember thinking that if I had to speak that night, both the audience and I would probably go to sleep. I do not know what time J. W. left the office or when he got home that night, but I do know he made the speech."[36]

As a result of the work of ICAD and leaders and residents across the state, eighteen area planning and development commissions were created. They included almost every county and city outside the Atlanta region. J. W. often was referred to as the father of the APDC movement. While he did not launch the idea, no one gave more time to the movement than he did.

Perhaps the angels who fear to tread where fools rush in used to be the fools who rushed in.

J. W.

Schretter, one of ICAD's first staff members, described J. W.'s legacy: "J. W. was in the forefront statewide in guiding Georgia communities and their leaders into difficult transition from rural to urban, from opposition to cooperation, from provincialism to regionalism, from economic and social exclusiveness to inclusiveness, and from traditional, top-down to bottom-up decision-making. I believe more than any other single individual, J. W. charted the path. We are still following in his footsteps."[37]

ICAD had other work to do in cities and communities. In early 1963 leaders in the city of Royston asked the ICAD staff to help prepare a program for local development. Bob Hill and Howard Schretter prepared a booklet, *Royston Georgia—Guidelines for an Over-All Development Program.* It was the kind of publication produced for most of the communities ICAD assisted. The contents, written for local residents, listed some of their goals and gave comprehensive guidelines for community development.[38]

Community projects were divided into two categories: major planning and resource analysis. Major planning concerned the physical development of the community; resource analysis was aimed at taking advantage of the community's development potential. The staff included a call for local action to make things happen and urged all residents to provide support. The entire community must not only stand behind the development efforts, but also be willing to act. Communities responded with enthusiasm.

Elmer George of the Georgia Municipal Association recalled J. W.'s contributions: "When J. W. Fanning was named director of ICAD . . . a new era of service to community and area development resulted. . . . J. W. was a visionary, pragmatically appreciating the past, understanding the need for change, quietly working with others. In this environment of change and opportunity, J. W. influenced literally thousands, involving them, and giving them credit—he is a man to be appreciated, loved, and remembered."[39]

His colleagues in ICAD respected him; their praise might appear excessive to people unfamiliar with J. W. Fanning. He was their mentor, and they admired his ability to articulate a vision, his speaking passionately about the "new Georgia" he foresaw. J. W. knew that if the educational capacity of the University of Georgia was tapped, its wealth of resources could help communities and regions to solve their problems.

Search for the good and praise it.

J. W.

Hazel Glenn, who was J. W.'s personal secretary for more than ten years, remembered:

> Mr. Fanning was a great supervisor. He was always very thoughtful and courteous, making you feel good about yourself and proud to be working for him. You could sense his greatness by the manner in which he dealt with everybody and how he approached his administrative duties.
>
> Only once did he ever register any displeasure with my work. A gentleman, who was one of the speakers for the Leadership Sa-

vannah Program, called the office one day wanting to speak to Mr. Fanning, who was attending a meeting in another part of the state at the time. I was very reluctant in giving the telephone number where he could be reached. The caller became very demanding in his request, and finally, I gave him the number. The next day, when Mr. Fanning came in, he walked in front of my desk and stood there for a minute and finally inquired, "Did a certain gentleman call here yesterday?" I admitted giving him the telephone number. Mr. Fanning stood rather erect and stoic and simply said, "That man reached me and called me out of a meeting and talked for forty-five minutes." With that Mr. Fanning went into his office and did not say anything else.[40]

J. W. avoided unpleasant exchanges. His silence often communicated more than words. At one meeting on the road, J. W. concluded his remarks about the importance of planning and development, and the question-and-answer part of the meeting began. Bramlett, assistant director of ICAD at the time, remembered that a crude fellow stood up and berated J. W. and others on the entire concept. Among other things, he said, planning was communistic—an attempt to take control away from the people. Someone jumped in immediately, asking a question much kinder than the first. J. W. answered it, choosing to ignore the first speaker. Bramlett felt the rude fellow should not have escaped so easily, and he knew J. W. could have handled him with even-tempered skill.

As the ICAD staff was driving back to Athens, Bramlett asked J. W. why he didn't respond to the ridiculous question. J. W.'s answer: "I did not have to say anything. That fellow cut his own throat without me saying a word. He lost any position of leadership he might have had in his own community. . . . Incidents like this often work themselves out without you having to do anything." Bramlett followed J. W.'s example many times during his career: An audience usually knows when a speaker or questioner is talking nonsense, and the best tact is to be polite and move on.[41]

Young Donnie Morris, the son of J. W.'s old friends, J. P. and Montene, rode with the ICAD staff members for two weeks as they spread the seeds of regionalism. He remembered, years later, hearing J. W. say he detested negativism. When negative ideas were presented in a meeting, J. W. would usually excuse himself if he thought the attitudes could not be turned around. He would say, simply, "Ladies and gentlemen, I have done about all I can do. Thank you." And he would leave.[42]

"My daddy thought the world of J. W. Fanning," Morris said, years later. So he wasn't surprised when his father announced, "Donnie, I'm going to give you the best experience and education a father can give his son." Donnie was twenty-two years old, with a new bride, but his father asked him to ride the state with J. W. as he presented the area planning and development concept to Georgians. "I didn't do much but carry their bags and listen," Morris said. "I probably learned more during those two weeks than any other time in my life. And ever since, my Daddy's statement—'this would be an experience to remember'—continues to ring in my ears." Morris learned many lessons observing J. W. He remembered J. W.'s saying, "Towns and cities, like persons, need identity. With identity comes pride, dignity, and inspiration—and a determination that motivates residents to establish a living community." Donnie later marveled, "Little did I know at the age of twenty-two years old I was witnessing the shaping of Georgia's history."[43]

In summarizing his vision for the new Georgia, J. W. once said: "For Georgia, imagine if you will, a time in the future when the state's landscape is dotted with communities that include a blend of renewed small cities, new towns and growing rural villages—each in a cluster with its own jobs and industries, its own schools, its own medical center, its own cultural entertainment and recreational center, and with an agriculture fully sharing in the prosperity."[44]

Compelling others to support his vision, J. W. planted seed after seed. With each talk he moved people to take positive action and to empower themselves. "Perhaps the most remarkable trait of J. W. was his ability to persuade," Bramlett said. "He could have been a great preacher, a great lawyer, banker, counselor. . . . He not only perceived what was true or right, he could persuade others to take the higher road. He had valid visions of what communities and individuals could become and was able to express them convincingly to those affected."[45]

The wisdom of life is to endure what we must
and change what we can.

J. W.

J. W. had believed in the principle of self-empowerment all of his life. And while most people didn't know it, his brother, Wootten, was the inspiration behind that belief.

As a boy, he saw Wootten's determination to be like other boys; he saw the power of individual to overcome negative predictions about his abilities. Wootten had struggled to navigate life in a wheelchair during his teen years, but, finally, the adult Wootten had had enough. He telephoned his older brother in Athens and said, "Bring me a pack of Camel cigarettes. I am going to get out of this chair."[46] From that day forward, he never again used the wheelchair. J. W. would come to admire Wootten for far more than his will power; he would come to idolize his brother quietly.

In 1935 Wootten had moved with his parents to a farm about two and a half miles east of Washington, on U.S. Highway 78. About five years later, he began running the farm, left to him after his father died in 1940. A few years earlier his younger sister, Emily Greene, had a son, John, known as Buck to the family. After a divorce, Emily and young John came back home to live. She worked for the U.S. Department of Agriculture in Washington for a time. In 1945, Emily died of an unidentified infection at the age of thirty-three; John was only seven. J. W. and Wootten discussed what to do about rearing young John. At Wootten's insistence, John remained on the farm, and Wootten exhibited the loving care of a devoted parent, rearing him into manhood.

They made money from laying hens, rabbits and other farm enterprises. They kept records of their activities separately. On their seventy-five acres of land, they grew oats, wheat, corn, sweet and Irish potatoes along with a neatly kept garden full of all kinds of vegetables. In addition, they always had twelve to fifteen head of cattle, and they produced a few hogs for their own consumption, plus some to sell.

The relationship went much further than the fields. Wootten took John to church two times a week, on Sunday and Wednesday nights, and he made certain that John had a balanced social life as well as an opportunity to participate in high school sports. Every Saturday they went to the local theater to see the featured matinee special. John was active in the Boy Scouts; he received the Eagle Scout award.

The relationship between J. W. and Wootten grew even stronger as the years passed. J. W., working for the University of Georgia, would leave Athens on the weekend to travel to Washington and help Wootten and John on the farm. Sometimes he would drive his car, but often he took the bus on Saturday mornings, arriving at about eleven o'clock. He would change into his work clothes, hitch up the mules, and work the land. About five in the afternoon, he would catch the bus back to Athens.

J. W. spoke of his younger brother with devotion and, at times, awe. He once spent the best part of a morning reflecting about his brother's many talents and sharp intellect. "If Wootten could have had all the things I had, physically," he said, "Wootten would have been a millionaire two or three times over. He had a great mind, but his health was against him." Wootten was a "perpetual inspiration," J. W. said. "His ability to do things with his hands was uncanny. When I think of the crystal-set radios he used to build, I realize that he brought the family into the radio era."[47] Wootten actually learned his skills by reading books. He made telegraphs, and he often acquired automobile parts, put them together, and sold the cars. It was his brother's ability to do what others believed he couldn't that sparked J. W.'s respect.

The last time J. W. saw Wootten alive was when he stopped to visit his younger brother on the way to Savannah. The two men enjoyed a long talk about a number of things, but mostly about the family and Wootten's welfare. When J. W. checked into his hotel in Savannah, he was given a message that Wootten had died. The physical trauma of a fall he had experienced that day was more than his heart could stand.

It was 1964—a significant year in J. W.'s life, both for the painful closing of a chapter in his personal life and for a chapter in his professional life that was about to open.

J. W. saw that I got out into the state to meet residents
and to develop an understanding of its economy,
and the two of us traveled all over Georgia.
I soon realized that his understanding about service
and outreach was well developed and sound,
the kind of program that was serving the people, communities,
governments, and industry in an effective
and almost unbelievable fashion.
[He] saw the service program as central to the mission of the
institution, as a part of the total teaching program.
Service faculty were teachers in a nontraditional classroom setting,
delivering educational programs at their finest.
I was perfectly willing to leave the service program
completely in J. W.'s hands. To a great extent,
he was a constant mentor, not necessarily verbally and instructive,
but by his very presence and demeanor. . . .
He established the most comprehensive program
of university outreach in this country—I expect in the world—
and powerful programs of citizen leadership development.

FRED C. DAVISON,
University of Georgia colleague

People respond positively to praise and negatively to criticism.
So, if you have to reprimand an associate, first find
something good about which to commend him.
Then deal with his faults in terms of opportunities
for him to become even better.

J.W.

CHAPTER FIVE

Vice President for Services, 1965–1971

President O. C. Aderhold had not yet exhausted his mental list of what J. W. Fanning could accomplish at the University of Georgia. Aderhold embraced the three missions—instruction, service, and research—prescribed for all land-grant institutions of higher education. To balance the three, he envisioned a structure in which vice presidents for each of the functions would report directly to his office as equals. During the academic year of 1964–65, he filled two of the vice presidents' positions, one for instruction, the other for service. He named George Parthemos as vice president for instruction and appointed J. W. Fanning as the vice president for services, effective January 1, 1965. The following year, Robert C. Anderson became the vice president for research.[1]

In his career at the university, J. W. had climbed from assistant county agent to the second tier of university administration as a member of the president's cabinet. Many congratulated him. The late Lamar Dodd, distinguished professor of art, sent the following message on January 8, 1965: "I cannot tell you how pleased we are over your appointment as vice president. I can think of no better choice for the job. Over the years you have given this university and this state your very very best. No challenge has been too small or too great. We are fortunate in having a man of your caliber, and the university can take pride in its having you as its newly-appointed vice president."[2]

J. W.'s now-adult children, Sibyle and Bill, told their father how proud they were in letters of congratulations. From his daughter Sibyle: "We were so thrilled when we received the clipping from Mother. I don't think there is another man who deserves such a position and honor as you do. It is a wonderful thing to know that a truly honest man can climb to the top in his profession. Please ease out of the job you are doing now so you can be in a managerial position and cut down on the travel. We want you around for a long time."[3]

Bill wrote: "Dad, Sandra [Bill's wife] and I are very proud of you. . . . I must say that my chest swells with pride when someone asks me if this Mr. Fanning is my father. . . . I sure hope your travel will be reduced with this new assignment."[4]

An article on the front page of the January 1965 issue of *University of Georgia Fortnight*, the biweekly newsletter for faculty and staff, quoted J. W.'s vision for his new assignment:

> Grand opportunity to help Georgia. . . . As I see it, the University is being challenged as never before to extend, to make stronger, to make more effective the services it is rendering to the people of Georgia. Problems people face today can't be solved individually but as they relate to other problems. Solutions are becoming complex in character and diverse in approach.
>
> Our opportunity is in working as a total unit—a team—to combine the magnificent jobs the individual schools and departments have been doing in the area of service. I look forward to serving by the side of the deans, department heads, the faculty, and all the other many different units.
>
> We've always felt a close kinship with the people of Georgia and have always been desirous of extending our services—knowledge, technical competence, and consultative ability—to them.[5]

President Aderhold charged Fanning with directing and coordinating public service functions of all schools and colleges, continuing education, bureaus, institutes, and centers. He was now responsible not only for the work of his former units, the Cooperative Extension Service, the Institute of Community and Area Development, and the Georgia Center for Continuing Education, but also the Institute of Government, plus the service activities of thirteen colleges and schools and all of their institutes and centers.

Aderhold's establishing a cabinet position for public service at a major university was a forward-looking step. The president himself had played an integral role in the university's long history of reaching out to its sponsoring public. From his first day in office, Aderhold emphasized reaching all segments of society—not isolating resources in the proverbial academic ivory tower.

When the Board of Regents approved the position of vice president for services, there were scarcely more than three major land-grant universities in the United States that mirrored Georgia's emphasis on the public service function.[6] The decision thrust the public service commitment of the University of Georgia into the national limelight, and J. W.'s ability to articulate its significance was critical.

Few positions in higher education are equal in influence and impact. J. W. had at his fingertips the total resources of the university to improve the quality of life in Georgia. He knew how to match the university's know-how to people's needs, and how to get faculty and students engaged in worthwhile projects.

He was uniquely suited to the position. He had traveled the state as a farm management specialist, learning its geography, its people, and their temperament. He repeatedly proved he could recognize problems and identify solutions; he believed people could solve their own problems if they believed in themselves. J. W.'s enthusiasm had spread across the state. Now it would spread across the campus.

A vice president for services is a consummate educator, one of the most visible representatives of the university. Students were particularly drawn to the work of public service. J. W. often shared the mission and work of public service with students in seminars and occasional lectures in a variety of courses.

Lord, grant that I always desire more than I accomplish.

J. W.

J. W. demonstrated his humility when he chose as his office Old College on North Campus. It was the same office he had when he directed the Institute of Community and Area Development. Colleagues admired his innate talents, yet were moved by his ethics and principles. "His broad, holistic vision was backed up by an incomparable set of values," recalled Jack Burke, former university associate vice president.[7]

To guarantee a smooth transition, J. W. remained director of ICAD for about a year. Later, Ernie Melvin became the director. J. W. said he saw his new position as "a very delightful assignment and privilege—one of the finest responsibilities that has come my way."[8]

Under J. W.'s leadership, academic public service at the university grew rapidly. He could identify needs across the state that could be solved with university expertise. "J. W. knew administrative responsibilities, and he knew the duties of a director," remembered university colleague Cameron Fincher. "He was always totally supportive of directors and other decision makers. He never pelted those under him with lengthy memoranda or unsought advice. His hand was gentle, but when firmness was demanded, he could make the tough decisions, almost always correctly. I never reported to a wiser or better person whom I respected more."[9] His employees in Old College appreciated his administrative abilities. Bob Rowan, J. W.'s assistant for his entire tenure as vice president, marveled at the smooth manner in which staff meetings were conducted.

What J. W. did for public service, perhaps more than any other accomplishment, was to raise the level of awareness among faculty of the critically important contribution of public service to the university's overall profile and mission. J. W. was a working vice president because that's what he wanted—to be among Georgians and their communities—and because that was the nature of the job. To be effective, he had to have daily contact with the people to understand their concerns. He placed a high priority on matching the resources of the university with the concerns of the people. He continued to speak to civic clubs, travel with his colleagues to community meetings, moderate sessions on a wide variety of issues, and answer countless inquiries. He created new programs to fill voids; existing activities were expanded and reshaped to meet educational needs. Two additional major public service units were established: the Rural Development Center at Tifton and the Marine Extension Service.

In the late 1960s a number of task forces were formed under the leadership of J. W. and L. W. Eberhardt Jr., director of the Cooperative Extension Service, to develop the structure and concept of the Rural Development Center. This agency of the University System of Georgia was to focus resources on programs to benefit Georgians living and working in rural and small-town areas of the state, especially the Coastal Plain.

Many of the state's leaders were convinced agriculture in the area needed to accelerate its pace of growth. So J. W. needed to ensure that the University System would build and maintain a close working relationship with leaders and residents of towns throughout the region while continuing to be supported by larger towns. He knew that in order to adjust agriculture production, programs must move beyond the farm and enfold the surrounding community.

Task forces created a concept for a collaborative program involving primarily the University of Georgia College of Agriculture and Abraham Baldwin Agricultural College at Tifton. A director, to be an associate dean of the University's College of Agriculture, would be located in Tifton with three assistant directors: director of the Coastal Plain Experiment Station; director of the Agricultural, Forestry, and Home Economics Division at Abraham Baldwin Agricultural College; and an assistant director of the Cooperative Extension Service.

The defined mission of the Rural Development Center was to use the resources of the University of Georgia, Abraham Baldwin Agricultural College, and appropriate state and federal agencies to improve the quality of life for rural Georgians. Four "thrust coordinators" and a program director would keep the center focused on agricultural and forestry production, marketing and utilization of forestry and agricultural products, community development, and personnel training. The center officially began its work on July 1, 1969.

For a number of years, the RDC's broad, vigorous program consisted of conducting short courses, conferences, and seminars on topics related to rural development; holding expositions oriented toward farm commodities such as beef cattle, swine, and forestry; conducting applied research, and establishing and enriching agricultural enterprises.

Among its accomplishments were two of significant proportions: creation of a new crop and a major agricultural show. A blueberry industry, established in Bacon County and the surrounding area, would become a multimillion-dollar crop in Georgia.[10] The Sunbelt Agricultural Exposition at Moultrie had an equally large impact on the economy of the area.[11] Many of the programs originally conceived by the RDC have been dispersed among various factions of the Cooperative Extension Service, but the physical facilities at Tifton remain a major conference site for rural South Georgia, and the offices serve a number of extension specialists.

Another significant service program of the University, conceived and established in 1970 during J. W.'s tenure as vice president, was the

Marine Extension Service. Its development resulted from two major forces: the driving interest of legislators and state residents to enhance the economy of Georgia's coast and J. W.'s vision of providing educational programs for the fishing industry. Skidaway Island, off the coast of Savannah, was identified as the logical site because Chatham County residents—believing research would bring a new prosperity to the fishing industry—had persuaded the Georgia legislature to fund a marine research center on the island. They approved a bond issue to build a bridge connecting Skidaway to the mainland to ensure access to the island facility.[12]

J. W.'s concept for marine extension was compatible with local residents' vision for economic enhancement in coastal Georgia. Once endorsed by the research group, J. W.'s proposal moved forward. Dr. Ed Chin, who had been recruited from Texas A&M University's Marine Laboratory at Galveston to coordinate the University System of Georgia's marine programs, was given the responsibility of launching the extension program. Chin's meeting with J. W. took place during an automobile trip to the research institute on Skidaway Island.

Chin remembered being impressed by J. W.'s dedication to the university, his sensitivity to the needs of the people, his quiet dignity. He listened as J. W. proposed giving him the additional responsibility of developing a marine extension service. J. W.'s gentle persuasiveness convinced Chin to take the job. J. W.'s guidelines were simple: Do what you can to help the seafood industry, improve the quality of life for folks who live on the coast, and in general, "do good." J. W.'s postscript was delivered with a smile: "Whatever the problems you find, you solve them."[13]

With a little seed money from J. W., Chin spent the next few months getting a grasp on the local area's economic problems. The federal government provided money to build the Skidaway Marine Extension Education Center; subsequently, Chin obtained more federal money to fulfill J. W.'s plan to build a marine extension service facility at Brunswick, where the seafood industry also needed help.

Some state leaders suggested that Marine Extension should operate as an arm of the Cooperative Extension Service. But J. W.'s idea for it to stand alone won support. He was convinced the Marine Extension Service would lose its identity in an organization as large as the Cooperative Extension Service. As a result of his persuasiveness, the University of Georgia became the only major university in the country to have separate marine and agricultural extension programs. Operated at two locations, Skidaway Island and Brunswick, the Marine Extension Service would quickly develop a national reputation for its direct service to the seafood industry, providing training and education, information dissemination, and basic research.

J. W. also served as an advisor to the two university presidents, O. C. Aderhold and his successor, Fred C. Davison, on critical issues facing the institution. People in top leadership roles in state and local governments and industry sought his advice and counsel.

J. W. had known Davison before he became president. Davison asked him to deliver the invocation for his presidential inaugural dinner in 1967. He said of J. W.'s effort: "It was a constant reminder of what our priorities should be."[14]

Invocation for Inaugural Dinner for President Fred C. Davison
Thank you, Father, for this occasion and those assembled here.
We are grateful for this institution
For its sturdiness
For its involvement in the life of this state and nation
For its determination that boys and girls and men and women shall possess the knowledge and understanding and wisdom and character to embrace those values which are eternal in building

civilizations that endure through the strains and stresses and joys common to the family of man.

May this great university, Father, continue to teach and inquire into the nature of things, for in so doing, it shall not go where the path may lead but go where there is no path and leave a trail.

For this young man and his wife who will lead this university to heights yet unattained, we are so thankful.

May they continue to grow in wisdom and in favor with God and man.

May they succeed in their determination that all young men and women shall learn that "Happiness comes with struggle and change and making hard decisions."

May they bring to the faculty the understanding that "not failure but low aim is a crime."

And may they inspire all Georgians to reach ever for the attainment of their God-given potentials.

We pray thy special blessings upon Fred and Dianne in the days and years ahead.

Give them, we pray, the strength to stay alive as long as they live.

For this food, we wish to express our deepest appreciation.

Amen.

Davison so treasured the invocation that a framed copy hung on the breakfast room wall of his home for the nineteen years he served as the president.[15]

J. W. received many honors during his university vice presidency, but perhaps the most significant came from Mercer University on August 15, 1969, just one day after his sixty-fourth birthday. He received an honorary doctor of laws degree, presented at summer commencement at Mercer, for which he was the invited speaker. The *Athens Daily News/Athens Banner-Herald* carried a story about this significant recognition on August 3, 1969:

> Few men, if any, have contributed more to the growth and development of education in Georgia in recent decades than Mr. Fanning. . . . He has been a member of the faculty at the University of Georgia since 1929 and is currently serving as vice president of services. . . .
>
> [Fred Davison] had this to say about him, "Mr. Fanning's concept of the service function of higher education is unmatched. He is dedicated to making Georgia communities better places in which to live. . . . His many associates in education and elsewhere have long recognized him as a leader, mediator, and friend, as well as an outstanding educator."[16]

Yesterday is experience. Tomorrow is hope.
Today is getting from one to the other the best we can.

J. W.

Much of J. W.'s address at Mercer focused on the difficult issues of the times. He urged graduates to remember that Americans had encountered many periods of anxiety. At times, he said, the American Dream appeared to be slipping away. Yet it would not: the determination to eradicate poverty, hunger, disease, and ignorance would persist. J. W. warned that cynics would attempt to destroy institutions created to solve problems. He quoted Abraham Lincoln: "Property is the fruit of labor; property is desirable; it is a positive good in the world. That some should be rich shows that others may become rich, and hence, is just encouragement to industry and enterprise. Let not him who is houseless pull down the house of another, but let him work diligently and build one for himself, thus by example assuring that his own shall be safe from violence when built."

J. W. concluded: "No, the American Dream has not been lost. It remains strong and inviting and challenging and eternal in character. It is yours to have and to nurture and to hand to your children and grandchildren. Thus we can make the great Dream come true. . . . The American Dream lies deep in the hearts of disciplined, responsible, concerned, dedicated, and persevering individuals. May the American Dream become your dream and may you persevere all of your days after the truth of a life more abundant."[17]

Two years later, on the last day of the year—December 31, 1971—J. W. Fanning retired from the University of Georgia. His distinguished and distinctive university career spanned forty-three years, the last seven as the vice president for services. His accomplishments were legendary; his positive influence on and off campus was impossible to measure. To learn how the university could best serve the public, he traveled to every county more than once. He became well-acquainted with the people and their communities and concerns. One of J. W.'s favorite sayings was, "You know where you have been by the lights you have lit."[18] He had lit many lights in many corners of the state; they would glow for generations to come.

J. W. had a passionate affection for the state. In his several positions with the university, he had come to observe and to know the varied faces of the state: its poverty and despair, wealth and comfort, weaknesses and strengths, and diverse leaders and followers of all races and ethnic backgrounds. He understood the people's desire to remove the shackles from the oppressed, utilize and protect their natural resources, and improve the quality of life for all Georgians. J. W. found great satisfaction in applying resources of the University of Georgia to the challenges of the state's communities. He not only made things happen; he made the right things happen.

Athens newspapers carried a number of stories documenting J. W.'s contributions to the University and the state. On December 31, 1971, his last official day at the University, the *Athens Daily News/Athens Banner-Herald* highlighted a "Service Career to End," underscoring a few of J. W.'s accomplishments during his university tenure:

> Through Fanning's efforts, university programming reaches virtually every community in Georgia . . . the University of Georgia has one of the broadest areas of public service of any institution in America and is as responsive to the needs of the people as any state institution.
>
> Fanning is retiring from a job that takes him more than 20,000 miles across the state each year in terms of what he calls a program of outreach. . . . But the miles traveled have not affected his concern with bringing university services to Georgians. "I love this work trying to give people something that will be valuable to them. It's been a lot of fun."[19]

An editorial complementing the story said: "Few persons, if any, have contributed more to the growth and development of education in Georgia in recent decades than Dr. J. W. Fanning. . . . Numerous Georgia communities are better communities and numerous Georgians enjoy a better life because of Dr. Fanning's efforts to share the university's resources and knowledge with the people of the state. . . . His concept of the service function of higher education is unmatched."[20]

Fragrance stays with the hand that gave the rose.

J. W.

A few months after his retirement, on April 6, 1972, more than 450 friends and well-wishers from across the state attended a dinner for J. W. at the Georgia Center for Continuing Education. Leaders from higher education and the private sector gave glowing testimonies to J. W.'s work. University of Georgia President Fred C. Davison, a long-time friend under whom Fanning had worked since 1967, said, "In his own way, J. W. has directed the lives of more people and more institutions than any man of whom I am aware. . . . I'd have to characterize him as the greatest citizen and the finest man I've ever known, and the best friend I've ever had."[21]

Fanning sat quietly through the long string of tributes, laughing at jokes and listening to reminiscences. Called to the lectern to make his own remarks, he smiled and quipped, "My grandfather always told me that living is like licking honey off a thorn, and I'm beginning to understand what he meant." He closed with two of his favorite prayers: "Oh Lord, keep me alive as long as I live," and "Oh Lord, teach me when to let go."[22]

Davison would later reflect, "I will never know all the ways he provided me with invaluable assistance. The interesting thing is that J. W. understood very well that he was helping me in a special way—not wanting any credit, only wanting the university and me to be successful." Davison was particularly struck by the affection J. W. had for the people in the state—and the degree to which it was returned. "As we traveled over the state, it was obvious that J. W. knew every back road in Georgia," Davison recalled. "We never went the same route twice, and he could tell me who lived in many of the houses we passed, even in the remote areas. Oftentimes, he would repeat the names of the children, even their cousins and other kinfolks. There is no question in my mind about J. W. being the most widely accepted and loved person in Georgia during the twentieth century. If everyone in Georgia were to pick their own heroes listing the top four or five, certainly, J. W. would be one of them."[23]

Friends noted that J. W. had traveled across the state for forty-three years, and it was time, they said at the retirement celebration, that he and Cora Lee became acquainted with the rest of the world. They were urged to use a portion of their monetary gifts for overseas travel. They gladly complied, exploring Italy, Switzerland, Germany, and enjoying other Western European countries, especially those of Scandinavia and western Russia.

Consequences do flow from our decisions,
and the time for choosing does, finally, run out.

J. W.

After enjoying some time for reflection, J. W. was asked in an interview if he ever experienced any serious disappointments or frustrations during his professional career. He revealed, somewhat wistfully, that his love of farming had endured throughout his tenure. In fact, at one juncture he thought he was prepared for a broader management position, but the position was given to another person. He wanted the job, he admitted, and was severely disappointed when it eluded him. Yet J. W. said he prayed he would not become bitter. And he was successful.

J. W. often paraphrased an Old Testament verse: Jeremiah told the Israelites, "Keep your mouth shut and go to work."[24]

In retirement, J. W. would correspond with county agents he had known. A year before he died, in a letter August 9, 1996, to Ralph Griffin in Haralson County, J. W. wrote:

Dear Ralph:

Thank you for your letter of August 5. Your written words are close to your oral words. I do believe you are the same Ralph Griffin that I knew as a County Agent in Haralson County 50 years ago. . . . May I wish that you will be alive as long as you live. . . . D.W. Brooks, you and I are about the only ones left of those whose names you listed in your letter. On August 14, I will be 91 and I can hear St. Peter shaking the Pearly Gates for my entrance. At least I hope he will let me in. . . .

As to those two small farmers who wanted me to tell them what to do, I tried to lay before them the world of change they would face. They were smart enough to know the answer but the answer was a hard one to take, so they no longer are present being overwhelmed by circumstances over which they had no control. As a friend of mine says, "Things are not what they used to be and never wuz." About the only successful farmer left is a part-time farmer with a job in town.

The going has been tough and will get rougher. . . . Since leaving Extension in 1954, my career has taken many turns and twists—most of which have been in my favor—but most of which I did not contemplate any better than the small farmer contemplated his. Now comes a future that will be Exciting, Demanding, Dangerous, Challenging. The road ahead will be tough for those not prepared to go with the bumps. I would like to take on the next 25 years. . . .

Thanks for your letter. It caused me to open my memory box and let the memories flow—some good—some not so bad. As Winston Churchill said, "This life is good to live once." . . .

Best to you,

J. W.[25]

Because J. W. lived that life so fully, focused as he was on the betterment of Georgians, his impact was widespread. His colleague Asa Boynton said, “He was possessed with a burning desire to help his native state rise above the ‘doormat of the national image’ that came out of the Great Depression. He loved his family and the University of Georgia, but he was passionate about making Georgia a better place to live for future generations, and in my judgment it surely is.”[26]

One of the things J. W. taught me is that people come and go all the time, but they are put here for a purpose—to make a difference to their fellow human beings. There are many individuals who do deeds for themselves, but J. W. showed me that he would do things for unselfish reasons, so why could not I do the same thing?

ASA T. BOYNTON,
University of Georgia colleague

I think his legacy is his gentle counseling to whoever was willing and interested in talking to him, his enduring love of life and all that was in it, and his unselfish disposition to work behind the scenes but let others take the credit. When you think of J. W. Fanning you have to think in terms of a very special style of leadership.

HELEN MILLS,
University of Georgia colleague

We need to be not more than we are;
neither do we need to be less than we can be.

J. W.

CHAPTER SIX

The Personal J. W.

Everyone who knew him knew that J. W. Fanning was a man of principle. He was slow to anger. He did not gossip. He found a way to compliment others, and he never criticized anyone's personality. He had a presence about him, but he never walked into a room as if he owned it. He wasn't one to work a crowd. He was reserved in approaching people, but once a conversation started, he gave the other person his undivided attention. He did not make people feel uncomfortable; he never put them down. On the contrary, he put people at ease. His smile came easily and his words softly. He had a knack for remembering your name, and once he asked about your children, he likely would remember their names, too.

J. W.'s handshake was warm and strong, so strong, in fact, that some women would brace themselves as he approached to greet them, especially if they were wearing rings on their right hands.

He was not an imposing figure physically. He was about six feet tall with white hair that was quite thin. His shoulders were broad and rounded, and his dress was always neat. But he was not a "clothes horse." He never paid top price for what he wore. He wanted people to call him simply J. W., but some participants in Leadership Georgia insisted on calling him Dr. Fanning. His demeanor seemed to be on an even keel at all times, but his closest friends knew he sometimes churned inside. He developed ulcers and other internal problems that were symptomatic of his occasional unrest.

If J. W.'s life had any shortcomings, his friends said, it was that he was not at home with his family as much as a father wants to be, especially in the 1940s and '50s. He was constantly taking care of responsiblities at the University of Georgia or traveling and speaking so often that surely he was needed at home part of that time. J. W. took care of the urgent first, and the urgent often was his work.

Overall, though, J. W.'s life was one of constants. He had a serene demeanor and adherence to spiritual principles. The consistency in his spiritual life was one reason behind the consistency in his everyday life.

"Anyone who knew J. W. reasonably well knows that his Christian faith was genuine, alive, and continuous," remembered his longtime friend and colleague Gene Bramlett, former assistant director of the newly established Institute of Community and Area Development.

> Religion was a favorite subject of ours when we were on a trip together. I learned he was tolerant of most other religious denominations. His theology was not narrow or rigid. . . .
>
> I would suggest, however, that J. W.'s overall attitude and moral behavior did not rest entirely on the fact he was a Christian, in the sense that he was struggling to conform to its moral principles. Rather, to a great extent, his own views and behavior happened to correspond closely with the moral principles of Christianity. I think he would have been a person of high moral standards even if he had not been a religious person.[1]

J. W.'s daughter, Sibyle, echoed those sentiments. "He showed me the true meaning of kindness and being considerate of other people," Sibyle said. "He never judged his fellow human beings, and he believed that everyone has value and worth, and something to contribute. Being kind to others was a lesson seen in him every day—even though the persons he encountered might have done something earlier against him."[2]

A life built around fear is terrible.
To fear is to live backwards. To have faith is to live forward.
A life built around faith is a magnificent thing.

J. W.

His acceptance of people extended to people of every race. Bill Fanning recalled that his father passed along the lesson he'd learned from his own father: that people of all colors and stations in life should be respected. "One thing my father told me was the great relationship that existed between his family and black people," Bill said. "Growing up among a heavily black population made my dad extremely concerned about all people, regardless of race or status in life. There was no doubt that the Fanning family never showed any serious animosity toward blacks."[3]

Those standards were evident in J. W.'s activities outside the circle of his career. His life reflected the seamlessness of his philosophical integrity. In his personal life J. W. applied the same energy, humility, respect for others, optimism, and leadership he brought to his teaching and administration.

"Dad knew the Bible," Bill said, "but he did not impose it on other people because he believed that religion was a very private matter."[4] But J. W. enjoyed weaving together and sometimes challenging his and other people's understanding of spirituality. He would become one of the most active members of the First Baptist Church of Athens.

Although his activities are not well chronicled for the first ten years, much of his participation was recorded and remembered. J. W. assumed leadership roles on the board of deacons. He was chairman of the deacons, a member of the finance committee, and a Sunday school teacher for decades.

He began teaching the men's Bible class in Sunday school in 1955 after he was approached by fellow church members. The class had begun about thirty-five years earlier. "I accepted the responsibility with fear and trembling," J. W. said. "I did not feel worthy of following two great teachers . . . . But, for approximately forty-one years, I enjoyed the fellowship of the class and their active participation in the discussions of Christian concepts and principles."[5]

The written preparation for the first lesson on record was for Sunday, August 26, 1955. J. W. emphasized "The Art of Human Living." A quote from the lesson plan gives a list of eight desirable qualities important to living a life of fulfillment:

1. Quit looking for a knock in your motor.
2. Learn to like your work.
3. Have a hobby.
4. Learn to like people.
5. Learn to be satisfied when the situation is such that you can't change it.
6. Learn to accept adversity.
7. Learn to say the cheerful human things.
8. Learn to meet your problems with decision.[6]

A member of J. W.'s class, Dr. Edward E. Best Jr., an associate professor emeritus of classics at the University of Georgia, presented a tribute to J. W. at his funeral service more than forty years later: "Possessed of such character, plus his knowledge of the Bible, he made a model Sunday school teacher. . . . After reading scripture aloud and then applying it to the current world situation, he would go around the class asking each member for his response. . . . This procedure, on occasion, evoked vigorous, sometimes heated discussion. Individuals might even disagree with J. W.'s interpretation, but he never seemed to mind. How generous, how respectful of our views, and how patient he was with us. By this method he led us to growth and understanding and betterment."[7]

Growth also came from J. W.'s ability to create a safe learning environment in which people could voice their opinions and thoughts. A member of his Sunday school class recalled a session about profanity, and J. W. was using his trademark procedure of asking questions of the group. Said Julian Cave, "He asked one of the members, 'John, why do you think we use profanity?' The fellow paused for a moment and then answered, 'I'll be damned if I know, J. W.' This was an indication of his openness to the group process and the class being free to interact with him."[8]

In the early 1980s the First Baptist Church was without a minister, and Upshaw Bentley led a pulpit committee looking for a new pastor. Three members of the committee would visit other churches to evaluate ministers. The entire committee marveled at J. W.'s ability as an evaluator; it seemed he was consistently on target. (Hoping they wouldn't be recognized in the process, members found anonymity was impossible when they visited a church inside the state and J. W. was among the group.)

Prospects on the "short list" were invited to Athens for interviews. Bentley and J. W. met with candidate Jon Appleton at a local restaurant, and after completing the interview, J. W. told Bentley, "I do not know about you, but I have found my preacher."[9] The congregation accepted Appleton, and he ministered to the church for more than two decades.

Appleton remembered meeting J. W. and telling his wife, "I have met a man like no other I have ever known."[10] J. W. would have a major influence on the church, Appleton recalled: "I was his minister for twenty-one years, and he was my mentor, counselor, encourager during the entire time. My most memorable experience was when our congregation voted [on whether] . . .women could be elected to the Diaconate. When the congregation was in conference, J. W. spoke, saying, 'If Paul were alive today, he would say, O, you foolish Athenians, how can you refuse women a role in church that they are already practicing?' Once J. W.'s voice was heard, the vote was called for. The ensuing vote was overwhelmingly that women be accepted on the deacon ballot."[11]

Conscience is what tells you the difference between right and what you want to do.

J. W.

J. W.'s ability to encourage all people to voice their ideas, synthesize what he heard, and find a consensus amid dissention was also apparent in the community development work J. W. now tackled in his own community—Athens and Clarke County. In the 1960s some local leaders were interested in consolidating the city and county governments, and for the first time, they gained enough support to discuss the proposal openly among residents and leaders. Twice over the next twenty years, however, the issue was placed on the ballot, only to be defeated by voters. In the late 1980s a group of twelve residents once again promoted the cause, initiating a course of action to put the issue before the public again. This group was informally called "Randolph Holder's Roundtable," named for its meeting place at a round table in radio veteran Holder's business office.

J. W., a member of the group, contributed his long experience in working with cities and counties that pooled resources. The university's Institute of Community and Area Development and Institute of Government also furnished expertise. After much debate, elected officials in the city and county agreed to put the issue to the voters for a third time. Pat Allen, a banker and chairman of the Athens–Clarke County

Unification Commission, thought of only one person when he needed someone to chair the group and educate the public about consolidation. It was J. W. Fanning.

On the Tuesday of the vote, in August 1990, Allen, attending his Kiwanis Club meeting, asked people at his table if they had voted or if they had questions about unification. J. W. had been president of the club in 1961 and had continued to be active. One man said firmly, "I don't know anything about that charter. But I do know this: If J. W. is for it, then so am I."[12] The third attempt to unify the governments was successful. E. H. Culpepper, Athens resident, and one of the most energetic proponents, said, "If J. W. Fanning had not become involved, consolidation of the two governments would not have happened."[13]

Gene Bramlett remembered J. W.'s ability to bring people together on the issues: "He had a wonderful ability of making complex issues seem simple, and of proposing solutions to them that seemed genuinely plausible. . . . J. W. made things sound good and reasonable by the way he said them. That, in my view, is one of the secrets of his leadership."[14] Said his minister, Jon Appleton, "J. W. had the gift of discernment, the art of bringing consensus reality from divergence to acceptance."[15]

The skill of his oratory was well known, and J. W. was asked on occasion to speak at public gatherings. He participated in numerous ceremonies at the Athens Regional Medical Center, where he was a member of the hospital authority for many years. John Drew, president and CEO of the medical center, spoke of J. W.'s greatest contribution to the center in terms of his genuine and heart-felt concern for people. His impact was substantial, and in the late 1980s the Athens Regional Medical Center Foundation established the annual J. W. Fanning Humanitarian Award, presented to the person who made significant contributions not only to the hospital but also to community service that improved the health, welfare, and quality of life for residents.

When Margaret Beasley Broun, a dedicated contributor to the hospital, died in early 1981, J. W. communicated at her memorial service the essence of her generosity. In doing so, he unwittingly described himself as many others did: "Margaret felt that things did not have to be as they often are—that ugliness need not be—that human suffering could be relieved—that the mind of a person could be restored to noble service."[16]

One of his most heartfelt speeches was given to the Northeast Georgia Council of the Boy Scouts of America—another group to which J. W. was committed. He was on the board of directors of the Cherokee District, and his speech was not unusual—it revealed his passion for helping others to find the best of themselves. "The great concern which each of us, as parents and grandparents, possess is the bundle of experience which our boys and grandsons are putting together," J. W. said. "Does that bundle contain experiences with those moral and spiritual values upon which we established this society? Does that bundle contain experiences that teach respect for law, compassion for our fellow man, love for our enemies, the dignity of work, and the pursuit of knowledge and understanding? . . . It is not the oath of the Scout organization that makes the boy; it is the boy who makes the oath."[17]

J. W. also stood in the pulpit at First Baptist Church, asked to preside at morning worship services and other church gatherings. Once, speaking on wisdom, he asked the congregation to honor traditional and enduring values:

> The world cries out today for wisdom and understanding as it struggles with momentous decisions on how to live a good life amid conflicting values. What is truth? What is right? What is eternal?

> The answer is that we must turn to those who have gained wisdom and understanding through many years of successful living. Even though we have seen great change in how we live, the basic values of life have not changed. There is nothing new in love or faith or hope.[18]

God gave us a memory
so we could have roses in December.

J. W.

J. W. possessed a deft, poetic touch and unusual capacity for leading others in prayer. He composed most of the prayers himself. When Sibyle lost her first husband, childhood sweetheart Rodney Cook, in a tragic accident in 1985, J. W. sent the following prayer to provide her solace:

> Surely, in the beginning, you willed that spring would come after winter—a spring that would speak to us of the eternal love and offer of redemption. A spring that offers reservations after long nights of despair and suffering. A spring that says, as did Jesus, "I bring you life, and I bring it more abundantly."
>
> Father, help us to fall in love with life all over again this spring, and find in you a peace that passes all understanding. And a faith so strong and enduring that we can endure to the end as obedient children of Thee. Help us in the dark moments of fear to light our candles of hope.[19]

Sibyle, now married to Bob Jenks, lives in northern Virginia.

In honor of the many contributions of J. W. and Cora Lee to the First Baptist Church, the congregation voted to name a new addition to the church the Fanning Building. It was dedicated on August 28, 1994. A newspaper story about the dedication in the *Athens Daily New/Athens Banner-Herald* quoted J. W.: "There is just one condition.

Cora Lee's name must come before mine. She's the reason why I am here."[20]

He spoke the truth. J. W.'s parents and siblings primarily attended Methodist churches, but Cora Lee had a strong Baptist upbringing in South Georgia and was determined to remain in the Baptist fold. J. W. and Sibyle were baptized the same day in 1945 at the Athens house of worship selected by Cora Lee, First Baptist Church. "He and I were sitting together in the sanctuary," Sibyle remembered, "and I decided to walk down the aisle to profess my faith. In the process, I just grabbed his hand and said, 'Let's go!' He arose and walked with me, and we were later baptized at the same time."[21]

J. W. taught Sunday school until the week before his death. He actually prepared a lesson he was never to teach. His notes for his 10 a.m. Sunday school class for July 27, 1997, were in his possession. The subject of that day's lesson was temptation. J. W.'s notes indicate he would introduce the topic to the class using the admonition of the Lord's Prayer, "Lead us not into temptation." This was to be followed by the question, "Does God ever lead us into temptation?" J. W. would conclude God never leads one to sin.[22]

Bramlett was struck by his humility and desire to help others achieve their goals: "Many great men have big egos which beg to be fed regularly through recognition and praise. Not J. W. He took pleasure primarily in the development of others and seeing improvements beyond himself come into being. He rarely took credit for anything, and whenever possible he gave credit to others. As far as I know, he had no hobbies or diversions beyond his church work, and working on his [Booger Hill] farm, which occurred mainly after he retired. His hobby was people—and he spent as much time with people as he could."[23]

J. W. spent a great deal of time away from Athens in his work, but he carved out space in his busy life to contribute to his community. He tried to assume the helm of organizations and causes when he was asked. When he did accept a position or task, his unwavering attention to it usually ensured success. Simply stated, he didn't say no. Cora Lee once observed, wryly, "If you do not want him to do the job, then you had better not offer it to him."[24]

Upshaw Bentley, a former mayor of Athens and a longtime friend, had worked with J. W. on many projects and had seen, firsthand, his unflagging spirit and service to community:

> J. W. had a vision for everything he did, and the 'servanthood' aspect of his life surrounded all of us. The total well-being of the Athens-Clarke County community is much healthier today because he passed this way. He was a role model for all of us . . . .
>
> His advice was always sound, and he had an unusual way of planting ideas and concepts in my mind that I somehow thought I had conceived on my own. He never looked for credit. J. W. helped me as he helped hundreds of persons in our community.[25]

Before and after retirement, J. W. welcomed the many people he encountered to be a part of the Fanning family. The couple enjoyed having people visit at the farm. Cora Lee had known J. W.'s dream to be a dirt farmer had never died; she also had a rich and memorable rural childhood on a sizeable farm in Tattnall County in South Georgia. In the early 1960s they began to search for the right property, and found it in Madison County: seventy-three acres along Booger Hill Road, just off Georgia Highway 106, about twenty miles north of Athens.

The rolling property was bisected by an energetic stream, Hodge Creek, named after one of the early settlers in Madison County, William Hodge. The creek spilled over a small dam; the dam and surrounding terrain would become sites for a cabin and picnic shelter. Much of the land was home to stately oak trees, which formed a canopy for hundreds of dogwoods. Along the banks of the stream, lush mountain laurels flourished. There also was sufficient open land with soil suitable for gardening, a vineyard, and a pasture for grazing animals.

The couple bought Booger Hill Farm, as it came to be called, in 1965; Cora Lee would buy it when J. W. was ill, a rare occurrence. Sibyle was thirty-one at the time, and Bill twenty-six. Sibyle remembered, with a chuckle, that she and her husband and children were living in Florida when her two-year-old daughter, Carolyn, became ill with the mumps, chicken pox, and strep throat, simultaneously. Cora Lee had visited during that time, and two weeks after returning to Athens, she contracted the mumps. At the time, people who lived in the same household were urged to get a vaccination to lessen the severity of the illness, in the event they caught it. J. W. reluctantly visited a local pediatrician. "Dad was 60 years old at the time," Sibyle recalled, "and he found it rather amusing to be sitting in a pediatrician's office with a group of young mothers and children." J. W. contracted the mumps, however, and was put to bed. "This is when mother purchased the farm," Sibyle said. "We children have always embellished the story by saying mother went out and bought the farm when my father was confined to the bed with the mumps."[26]

His close friends might be surprised that J. W. would pay the cost of a seemingly nonessential vaccination. They knew how frugal he was. Bill's first memories of his father were accompanying J. W.—then a farm management specialist—to meetings in Washington, Georgia, and elsewhere in the state. "I was just a little tot then," he said, "but I can remember Dad in these settings so very well. We would drive to the meetings in his car, which I recall with some agony as not having a radio or a heater, because those two items would have added significantly to its cost. It was the kind of car that had automatic windshield wipers, but you had to hold a lighted candle under the windshield inside during the winter to prevent the water spray from freezing. If you wanted to keep warm inside the car on cold days and nights, you would have to wrap yourself in a quilt."[27]

Bill believed his father's frugality was a carryover from the tough times of the boll weevil epidemic and the Great Depression. "As children growing up, Sibyle and I had to make our way financially mostly on our own," Bill said. "From the time we were old enough to work, jobs were held to earn extra money."[28] Bill and J. W. worked together on a 4-H project to raise laying hens; Bill delivered the eggs to regular neighborhood customers. When the hens became too old to produce enough eggs to cover production costs, they were eaten, usually in soup.

The project continued for two to three years, but a neighbor or two apparently didn't approve. At the time the Fannings lived in Athens, at their home on Parkway Drive, and they kept a light on in the chicken house at night. Sometimes the chickens got a little noisy. Early one morning, a neighbor opened her kitchen window, placed her radio on the sill, and turned the volume to full blast. Her message: she was sick and tired of being disturbed by chickens at night. "We immediately got out of the chicken business," Bill said.[29]

Sibyle, too, recalled how carefully her parents watched their pennies. Cora Lee, out of necessity, made all of Sibyle's clothes, and mother and daughter sometimes searched for bargains at Miss Sallie's Hat Place in Athens. "My family struggled and worked really hard to make every penny count," Sibyle said. "One year, I got a new coat for Christmas, and when I went down to see my uncle and cousin in Washington to carry them presents, I backed up against the wood stove and burned a hole in the brand new coat. I had to wear it repaired. Mother worked hard to pinch pennies to give us nice clothes, even if she had to make them."[30]

In fact, the Fannings' money was downright tight at times; the low salaries paid by the university were barely enough to cover the costs of running their household, partly because J. W. was supporting his family in Washington. To get extra income, J. W. and Cora Lee modified their home to accommodate live-in students and often their wives after World War II, when veterans flooded the campus as new students.

Sibyle recalled: "During the war, we had people living all over the house. There was a couple in my bedroom in the back, on the first floor. Upstairs in rearranged areas, there were two couples. Mother and Dad had a bedroom and bath downstairs, and my brother and I slept on bunk beds in the kitchen. Mother went over to the Navy Supply School and picked up the bunk beds, and, in addition, she painted a lot of furniture. We all had places to sleep, even if they were in inconvenient locations, but the rent paid by the couples really kept the family solvent."[31]

Money to buy the Booger Hill Farm came when Cora Lee sold to her sister the land inherited from her parents. She then had the money to begin to look for the farm they both hoped to find in the Athens area.

Life is a gamble whether you are picking out a wife or a cantaloupe.

J. W.

Friends remember that despite their differences—Cora Lee's quicksilver chatter and straightforwardness stood in sharp contrast to J. W.'s understated, thoughtful approach. The two were a strong suit. "J. W. and Cora Lee were a great team," Fred Davison said. "On the surface, she was more outgoing, expressing her thoughts and opinions more freely, but underneath all this was a person who had the same values and philosophies as he did."[32] Family friend Donnie Morris remembered watching the couple together. Cora Lee was "a mover and shaker"—and "totally in love with J. W."[33]

But Cora Lee proved she could keep a secret. Macon minister Howard Giddens, a close friend, recalled that when Mercer granted J. W. the honorary doctor of laws degree, Cora Lee "knew that it was going to be granted, but she said nothing to him about it. He was surprised that she could keep a secret."[34]

Bill remembered observing his parents relate to each other: "We, the family, would go to Camp Wausega where the Cooperative Extension Service faculty would take their families with them during training programs, which were great opportunities for recreation. It was at that camp that I first saw my mother and dad square dance. That was really interesting, because they were laughing and having such a good time."[35]

J. W. and Cora Lee worked as a team in the kitchen, but just so far. "They worked together in the kitchen with foods—not cooking, mind you, because Dad did not know how to cook," Sibyle said. "They both killed chickens, cleaned them and cut them up. We actually had a minifarm in the back yard, and from Dad's garden they canned a lot of food. They had tremendous respect for each other, but Mother was a very independent person with a strong will."[36]

"Cora Lee and J. W. were opposites on a continuum," Bill said. His father could be so pensive and quiet that he wouldn't speak for hours on a car trip, but his mother talked continually. "When mother was in the car," he said,

> she would sit in the front seat and do all the talking. She was the dominant talker, and he was the quiet one. He never did talk much around the table, being very quiet and reflective.
>
> Perhaps it was because he had talked so much on the road during the week that he preferred tranquility around the house; he did a lot of reading. He would come home late on Friday nights, completely exhausted.

The children did their best to soothe their father. "Many times Sibyle and I would scratch his head. He thought that was the greatest thing in the world."[37]

Bill also recalls one of many dogs the family welcomed into the house. His name was Joby, a favorite of J. W.'s. "My dad took a liking to that dog," Bill said.

> He would come home from work, and Joby would start running around the house, and Dad would be waiting for him to make a complete circle. Joby would come running and jump on him, and then run around the house again. He did that about ten times before he would literally collapse. Dad thought this was the funniest thing he had ever seen.
>
> One night, we were in our parents' bedroom upstairs having Bible reading and prayers—a very religious moment. Dad and mother were sitting on the edge of the bed in their pajamas. My sister and I were sitting close by, and so was Joby, with a devilish look in his eye. Dad started to pray, and Joby bit hard on dad's big toe. Dad's prayer proceeded this way: "Dear Lord—let go of my toe!" This was a funny sight, and we fell, sprawling, with laughter, on the floor.[38]

Childhood friends found her father equally entertaining, Sibyle said: "He was a wonderful reader with young people. He could read stories, and you would be absolutely enthralled with them." One story, she said, was about a family of skunks, a favorite with Sibyle and her friends. "We would fall over laughing when he read it," she said. She and her father were close; in fact, they shared a special connection that she did not have with her mother. "I don't remember having any real conflicts with my dad, probably because of his quiet and sincere method of dealing with me, which was different," she said. "He was always supportive of all I did and always very proud of what I did. We had

[the] rapport of being able to talk to each other. I don't guess I was a rebel."[39]

Bill recalled that Sibyle "was very close to my dad. She was well-suited to academia, and I was dyslexic coming through school [and] not knowing what the condition was. This made learning difficult for me. . . . Sibyle was just exactly the opposite, and Dad was naturally inclined toward her, being an academician himself."[40]

The close father-daughter bond was first forged when Sibyle was a child, traveling with her father before her baby brother was old enough to make the trip to Washington to visit J. W.'s parents. "Dad and I would just go," she remembered. "The forty-two miles in each direction seemed such a long way when I was a child."[41] Father and daughter, travel companions, came to know each other in the intimacy of the automobile, making its way to and from family members.

For Bill and J. W., it was hunting trips together. When Bill was old enough, J. W. took him to Wootten's farm in Washington. "I formed an early impression of my dad that he was a very quiet and learned person who would never speak much about himself," Bill said. "He never spoke about his feelings—never about his yearnings and desires."[42]

J. W. seldom mentioned his disappointment over not being selected for another position of leadership, but, characteristically, the disappointment became a catalyst. "[It] was a serious disappointment for him, but it was also a motivational factor," Bill said. "He simply worked harder, it seemed. Oh, there were his frustrations, which he kept to himself, and he had a very nervous stomach, which was probably because he would not vent his emotions."[43]

He used his disappointments for two lessons he passed on to his son. "I have had a terrible experience," he told Bill when he was passed over for the position. "I lost, but I want to tell you something. I've taken and will continue to take any job anybody gives me. I will do the absolute best I can, no matter what comes—if it is sweeping down the halls, writing policy, or traveling—whatever it takes, because eventually, it pays off."[44]

Sibyle also learned the importance of applying oneself totally to a task, even if it was not anticipated or initially welcomed. "One very meaningful attribute that I learned from my dad is that hard work pays off," Sibyle said.

> He was a person who kept totally focused on his profession, and he gave each assignment his utmost attention, never leaving a job undone.
>
> Of course, the values I learned from both of [my parents], growing up, have served me very well throughout my life. At the top of the list are honesty, love, and self-respect. I was taught a lot about self-esteem and to value honesty in myself and in others, and to always try to understand people's actions. Another admonition was to try not to judge people and do not set yourself above others. Mom and Dad were both in total agreement on those important values.[45]

Not only did J. W. encourage his children to understand other people, he urged them to move further to discover and appreciate their best qualities. "If you always look for the good in other people and if you always have something complimentary to say about them, you will, in the long run, be rewarded by developing loyal friends," J. W. told his son.[46]

But as much as he explored and learned about people—and how to treat them with respect—J. W.'s unstudied affection was for the land. "One thing of paramount importance to him," Bill said, "was that he always wanted to be a farmer."

> If he really wanted to be anything else, I never detected it. I think the thing that impressed me the most about my father's involvement in Georgia was his enthusiasm for the farming industry. He

> wanted to see Georgia become a state that could compete in agriculture throughout the United States. His interest in agriculture was deep and dynamic, and when you combine this with his enthusiasm, many folks caught the same spirit.[47]

With farming in their blood, Cora Lee and J. W. had no choice but to return to their roots. When they bought the farm at Booger Hill, J. W. had six years to figure out how he would take advantage of farm ownership in retirement. Cora Lee, however, with a considerable amount of time on her hands, jumped into developing the farm. While J. W. was completing his university career, Cora Lee made plans for developing the seventy-three acres, her new obsession—and had plenty of work for J. W. to tackle on the weekends.

Cora Lee's take-charge nature took over when the bulldozer arrived to grade a road to the site where a cabin would be built. She strode in front of the bulldozer as it cleared its way. When the job was completed, Cora Lee learned she had escorted the operator onto adjoining property. J. W. studied the situation and talked to the neighbor, who was unflappable, saying he didn't mind the new road. However, J. W. reminded him, while *we* may not mind, our children might, in the future. He suggested they settle the matter on the spot, and made an offer to become owner of the parcel. "This was the most expensive piece of land I ever purchased," J. W. said, good-naturedly.[48] Twenty-five years later, Lynwood Hall, a Georgia Artist of the Year, captured Cora Lee's walk in the woods in an oil painting titled "The Road Less Traveled."

Booger Hill would become a special place for J. W. and Cora Lee; they spent most of their time there after J. W. retired, coming into Athens mostly on weekends. Cora Lee had planned well. The focal point for the construction of the cabin—built according to plans drawn by Cora Lee—was a two-and-a-half-acre lake that lay at the base of a slope, its gradient running toward the creek. The site provided beautiful vistas from the cabin, located on a knoll overlooking the lake and Hodge Creek, which ran along one side. The structure of the cabin had several distinctive features, one of which was a fireplace built wide and deep to Cora Lee's specifications.

Another feature was lodge poles to support the roof over the family room and screened porch. Cora Lee wanted them to have a clear, natural, rustic finish because they were going to be exposed. When the Langdale Company of Valdosta delivered them to the contractor on site, however, they had been marred with creosote. This was unacceptable to Cora Lee, but she found the problem could be corrected by scraping the poles with a knife.

She was determined to remove the creosote stain. If visitors came calling during the process, Cora Lee handed each of them a knife and put them to work. University President Fred Davison and his wife, Dianne, drove out to Booger Hill one Sunday afternoon to see how the cabin construction was progressing; they had barely arrived when Cora Lee handed them knives for scraping.[49] Whatever was required to complete the structure, Cora Lee tackled. The entire family, including children and grandchildren, was able to celebrate Christmas at the cabin shortly after its construction.

The road Cora Lee laid out for the bulldozer operator wound its way to the cabin and provided a stunning view across a meadow leading to the lake. J. W. thought the meadow would be just the right site for pine seedlings, which were sure to grow to a marketable size in record time. He consulted with a forestry expert who supervised the planting.

In a few days, Cora Lee noticed the little trees, and it did not take long for her to realize the pines would block the view to the lake and beyond. Pine trees in the meadow were not a part of her plan, and she would have none of it: she promptly pulled up all the seedlings by hand. Today, the meadow remains filled with lush grass and is void of trees, just as she intended.

Cora Lee was a gardening enthusiast. She planted more than a thousand nursery-grown azaleas around the lake and replanted native azaleas in clear view of the cabin and picnic shelter. She made certain the existing dogwood trees had every chance to brighten the woods in the spring. The mountain laurel was special—it normally was not found in the region. She tended it extra carefully to ensure it would reach its greatest beauty on Mother's Day each May. From the middle of March to the middle of May, the "garden" was filled with blooms, and there was green vigor all summer followed by spectacular fall foliage. Booger Hill was in harmony with nature.

Cora Lee possessed a strong imagination for tasteful landscaping and a passion for working with her hands. She donned her old overalls and hat on many pleasant afternoons to indulge both urges. One day an old friend stopped by and, not recognizing her in her work uniform, asked, "Where do the Fannings live?" She said, "Sam," and he replied, "Cora Lee!?" It was Sam Dunlap from Leadership Georgia—a man she had known for years.[50]

Taking care of the farm and all the plants was no small task, and Cora Lee often looked for part-time help, often from the young sons of acquaintances. She expected much from the young men and gave her work orders in firm terms which the workers wanted to fulfill. A story has it that one son came home from a long Saturday at Booger Hill with scorched holes in his shoe soles. In response to one of her requests, the young man had stepped on hot coals near a burning brush pile in attempting to heap fresh-cut limbs on the fire. Another source of labor was out-of-work men in downtown Athens. J. W. was not enthusiastic about her bringing jobless men to the farm by herself. One time when she and J. W. were riding in her car, J. W. told her he was concerned about her safety. Without hesitation, she reached under the driver's seat and brought out a two-foot machete. "With this protection," she said, "you do not need to worry about me, J. William."[51]

J. W. liked everything his wife had done and joined her with his own special interests. He planted muscadine grapes—both black and white varieties—and blueberry plants. He also tended a garden of about two acres with his good friend Whitey Bryant. The garden yielded sizeable quantities of beans and tomatoes and other vegetables, which he enjoyed harvesting and canning. Often, he could provide a case to each child and grandchild. (One great-grandson, Andrew, would eat only Gramp's canned beans.)

The grape and blueberry plants also produced good yields every year. When the berries were in season, so it seemed were visitors. J. W. and Cora Lee bought a Shetland pony named Smoky for the grandchildren and their friends to ride and to pull a two-wheeled cart.

One way to save face is to keep the lower half closed.

J.W.

To make good use of the pasture land, J. W. bought ten beef heifers in Tattnall County and brought them to Booger Hill, where their calves provided much enjoyment, and headaches, for years. The cattle were special to Cora Lee, primarily because their bloodline could be traced to animals her father had owned. As the years went by and J. W.'s time was consumed with other pursuits, he grew tired of the cow business, decided to clear them out, and negotiated with a local buyer to take the entire herd.

He rejoiced. He told Cora Lee to look out for the "cow trader" the next morning, because he would be coming to get the cows. Cora Lee reminded J. W. there was a special relationship between her and the cows—one that could be traced to her father's farm—and she had no intention of severing that link. J. W. insisted the deal was closed, and he did not think it best to break his word.

But after a lengthy discussion with Cora Lee, he made a midnight telephone call to tell the man to forget about the cows. They remained in J. W.'s care for a few more months, until he succeeded in getting them loaded on the buyer's truck, a move that required the mental dexterity of a magician.[52]

Cora Lee and J. W. delighted in welcoming visitors to Booger Hill for the twenty-plus years they managed it. Their visitors' book contained more than a thousand names of people who had shared the solace and beauty of the land with the Fannings. Frequent visitors on Sundays were the Davisons, Fred and Dianne, and their small children, Bill and Anne.

Like many others, they would find themselves enjoying Cora Lee's cooking at the picnic shelter near the creek. The university president often would walk the length of the stream as it traversed the farm. "A visit to the farm was very therapeutic to me," Davison said. "Oftentimes I would be tired, not really wanting to expend the energy to make the trips, but once there, they were some of my most pleasant memories."[53]

In 1986, J. W. celebrated his eighty-first birthday; and in reaching this milestone, he made the decision to relinquish his role as advisor to Leadership Georgia, a position he had held since the organization was founded in 1972.

With the move, J. W. began a period as senior statesman in community and church activities, and kept in closer touch with his many friends. The telephone rang frequently with calls from former colleagues, Leadership Georgia graduates, and other well-wishers. Many of them sought J. W.'s advice on numerous issues, and he patiently counseled them. Visitors dropped by as they always had done, greeted by his warm, firm handshake.

Life is a journey in growing old—not in becoming old.

J. W.

As a couple, he and Cora Lee found this stage in their lives to be richly rewarding. It was also a time they enjoyed the sunset years with their children, grandchildren, and great-grandchildren. The Fannings and their visitors reaped the rewards of the years spent making the little Booger Hill farm a place of striking beauty. "Mother and Dad really enjoyed the farm for many, many reasons," Sibyle said, "and entertaining friends from church and the university was a high priority for them, especially [for] my mother. She was more social than Dad. They also had big Christmas parties at the home on Parkway Drive, a tradition that I have long remembered."[54]

They enjoyed their time in the Athens residence, reminiscing about the past and looking to the future. They savored past experiences. Yet, J. W. often would say, "It is all right to go back to the past—just don't stay there."[55]

In May 1992 Cora Lee celebrated her eighty-seventh birthday, and J. W. wrote a gently teasing piece for her:

> An angel appeared at the S.A. Harvey residence to talk to a baby girl on May 29, 1905. Here is the message of the angel to the baby named Cora Lee:
> "I like you.
> You have a destiny to fulfill.
> You need not imitate anybody."
> And the angel also said:
> "You need not be more than you are, neither do you need to be less than you can be."
> Now, eighty-seven years later, the baby Cora Lee, now a mature lady, is known
> to say:
> "I rise in the morning, dust off my wits,
> Pick up the paper and read the obits.
> If my name isn't there, I know that I am not dead,
> So, I eat a good breakfast and go back to bed.
> When I was young, my slippers were red.

I could kick my heels right over my head.
As I got older, my slippers were blue,
But I could still dance the whole night through.
Now that I'm old, my shoes are black.
I walk to the store and pant my way back.
The moral of this tale, as it's been told,
Is that you and I are getting old."[56]

After sixty-one years of marriage to the day—on December 22, 1992—Cora Lee died after suffering a heart attack. One of her last activities was baking a cake for an upcoming Christmas party. "She loved doing for people," Sibyle said, "and so did my father." J. W. would write, shortly after Cora Lee's death: "She was a great person—a wonderful wife and an understanding mother and grandmother and great-grandmother. We had a good life together."[57]

What is the beauty of old age?
The beauty that steals inward as one grows old—
wisdom, understanding, patience, long-suffering, compassion,
forgiving, faith, hope, abiding love.

J. W.

J. W. would live four years and seven months after Cora Lee's death. He sorely missed her but continued to live an active and productive life, attending church and Kiwanis Club on a regular basis. The telephone at home kept ringing, and he remained interested in the world around him. He read books and magazines voraciously. It was a normal habit of his to read two books at once, keeping them in separate rooms. Visitors from all walks of life continued to see him; he showed a compassionate interest in their concerns, as he had all his adult life. It was as if he continued to ripen with wisdom, and was willing to share it.

Bill remembered his father's nature of giving back to others: "He was generous and kind to his fellow human beings, an encourager of good deeds, loved to see people excel—he was there to praise and to thank them. He never focused on himself."[58]

Many of the experiences of his childhood continually ran through his mind. He wanted to return to the Isle of Palms, and in the summer of 1993, he persuaded his nephew John Greene and his wife, Sue, to drive him there. A lifetime earlier for most folks—seventy-six years, in fact—J. W.'s father had given him and two other twelve-year-old boys permission to drive the family Buick from Washington to Augusta. It was summer 1917, and the boys were nearly giddy with the sense of adventure. They took the train from Augusta to the Isle of Palms Beach on the coast of South Carolina near Charleston. The place afforded many opportunities for exploration and spirited, boyish fun. The trip with his nephew allowed J. W. to relive the adventure. They stopped along the way and spent a couple of nights on the coast. They walked briskly each day, at least one mile, up and down the boardwalk. J. W. recounted in detail what he and his friends had done so long ago. When J. W. learned the Ferris wheel was no longer there, he was disappointed. "Shucks!" he said.[59]

Mary Dowdy, J. W.'s nurse and housekeeper from 1994 to 1997, came to his home four hours a day, six days a week. Her duties were minimal, mostly cooking and being of help here and there. For the most part, J. W. took care of himself. Dowdy said of all the people she cared for, he was her favorite because of the positive effect he had on people. She remembered that hundreds of people came to visit, made innumerable telephone calls, and wrote to seek his advice, or to wish him well. She reflected,

> He found touching the lives of others to be his most rewarding experiences. He was a giant of a man—but, yet, he was a simple

> man. The approach he used in dealing with people was to study them personally before forming judgments about them or making decisions that might affect them. He analyzed everybody, figured them out—their strengths, their weaknesses, and their desires.
>
> Always, always, he looked for the goodness in all people. To him, everyone had unusual talent and potential, and he searched to discover what they were. It was remarkable how he could encourage people to do more than they thought they could do. Never did I hear him dwell on the dark side of people, and he found no pleasure in talking about himself. He wanted to know you. He knew himself.[60]

William Greer Jr. was one of the people J. W. encouraged. When he faced challenges, he thought of his mentor. Greer, a Leadership Georgia alumnus from Norfolk, Virginia, remembered: "He was a man of brains, integrity, and vision. He taught me by example that growing old could and should be a very exciting time in one's life. Hardly a day goes by that I do not ask myself, 'How would J. W. Fanning respond in this situation?'"[61]

Joseph C. Hammock, who met J. W. when he was vice president at the university and would be his colleague and close friend, said simply, "Knowing him and being involved with J. W. have led me to view him as one of the three most significant influences in my life."[62]

Recalling their exchanges and her observations of her employer during the last years of his life, Dowdy said:

> I never met anybody with such good qualities, and I never heard any comments to indicate that he disliked anything or anybody—his church, neighbors, colleagues, all people. The man nurtured good in society.
>
> My favorite moments with him were when he would talk about

> his family and his farm, and he would convey the image that he never wanted to be a "big man." I concluded that his feelings for other people were developed and nurtured to a larger degree during the summer he was selling Bibles in South Alabama, when he encountered people living in poverty, yet proud of what meager things they had. It was the pride these poor people exhibited in sharing what they had with him unashamedly.
>
> He related to the simple life. His friends and family meant more to him than gaining money or fame. You could relax with Dr. Fanning, and you could talk with him, being totally at ease. He never complained, even when he went to the doctor with much pain from angina, showing no emotion toward being sick. Once, he tried to drive his car to the mailbox, and the car became hung on the curb, which required outside help to free it. He said he would not attempt such a thing again if I would not tell Sibyle—which I never did.[63]

Joel Giddens, J. W.'s next-door neighbor and a University of Georgia scientist, often spent quiet time with J. W., who enjoyed hearing Giddens's scientific perspectives on the issues of the day. Giddens recalled, "I had the opportunity of carrying his paper, mail, and other things to his house and driving him in some instances to places he needed to go. It was during these times that I was most impressed by his personality, kindness, integrity, sympathy, and religious convictions."[64]

A man is not old until his regrets
take the place of his dreams.

J. W.

As J. W. neared his tenth decade of life, few contemporaries remained with whom he could share memories. But he learned about a year after Cora Lee's death that a cousin by marriage, whom he knew as a teenager, was living in a retirement home in Decatur. It was Lucy Lowe Hunter, the beautiful girl who sat beside the adolescent J. W. in a swing at a social gathering. J. W. contacted her, and made several trips to Decatur to visit. Dowdy remembered how much J. W. enjoyed talking to Miss Lucy about memories of the old days. They had much in common.

She wrote a letter to Dowdy two weeks after J. W. died. Here is an excerpt: "I cannot realize he is gone. I have been thinking about the times when we were young and he would visit my brother and me, and we would go down to Washington whenever we could. . . . He just always seemed like another brother to me. . . . I feel sorry for Sibyle and Bill and all the grandchildren and great-grandchildren. . . . I know we will never get over the shock of William's death."[65]

Late in life, J. W. realized a long-term dream: to own an Oldsmobile Ninety-Eight. He had become too incapacitated to drive, but he made several trips with a driver to visit Miss Lucy. One Saturday evening he made his final visit to Decatur for a special occasion: the celebration of Miss Lucy's ninety-third birthday. It was a happy event; several of her friends were present. J. W. presided over an informal program. With his usual sophistication and natural style, he read a poem he'd written for the occasion:

Age is a quality of mind.
If you have left your dreams behind
If hope is lost, and you no longer look ahead
If for you, ambition's fires are dead
Then you are old.
But if from life you take the best
And if in life you keep the best
If love you hold, no matter how the years go by
No matter how the birthdays fly

You are not old.
Lucy, you are not old
You are just over ninety.
Happy Birthday.[66]

On their way back to Athens, J. W. said to the driver, "If you do not mind, I wish to keep my thoughts to myself tonight, and reflect on the good time I have just had. We can talk later." The two were silent all the way to J. W.'s home.[67] The next morning, next-door neighbor Giddens made his usual Sunday morning call to offer J. W. a ride to First Baptist Church. The rear door of the house was locked. Normally it would have been open by that time of day. His calls unanswered, Giddens returned with a key J. W. had given him for emergencies. He discovered J. W. in his bedroom. He had died during the early morning hours.[68]

J. W. had a private wish that he expressed to his longtime friend Fred Birchmore on their way home from the last Kiwanis Club meeting J. W. attended. J. W. said that when he died, he wanted it to be in his own bed at home.[69] The wish was granted.

The date of his passing was July 27, 1997. He was just three weeks short of his ninety-second birthday. J. W. had honored the wish he had for others. He had "stayed alive as long as he lived."

I think that each of us must come to terms with death and the future before we can live today.

J. W.

In an interview in July by the scholar Sherry LaBoon just fifteen days before his death, J. W. answered two questions: How would you sum up your life? For what would you like to be remembered most? J. W. responded:

Well, it has been a good life, [a] challenging but full life. I have a few regrets, but not many, and throughout there have been some of life's challenges that have kept me on my feet and kept me moving. The challenges gave me something to do [in order to] stay active. It was all fun through life, and it is not over yet . . . .

I would like most of all to be remembered by the fact that I liked people and worked with people. My wife said that when I get to heaven, if St. Peter has a committee for work to be done, he would make me the chairman. What she was saying was, that in her opinion, I had some ability to work with committees and to lead discussions. I love that; I love that. I love being honest and square with all people, and I love them getting together.

If I have any skill at all, it is getting people together and seeking a consensus. If I can be chairman of the group, we are going to talk long enough to where we get all the views on the table and in the open, and we will come to some agreement about the way we should proceed. I enjoyed that.

This is how I would like to be remembered—that I loved people and found a way to work with them that was harmonious.[70]

Welcome Fanning, great-great-grandfather of J. W.

Source: Agrarian Arcadia, 1996, p. 78.

William Parks Fanning at 12 years old, grandfather of J. W.

Source: Fanning Family collection.

William Parks Fanning as a soldier in the Civil War, J. W.'s grandfather.

Source: Fanning Family collection.

Laura Wootten Fanning at 64 years old, grandmother of J. W.

Source: Fanning Family collection.

(Above left) John Wootten Fanning and Gertrude Harrison Fanning, J. W.'s father and mother at Hot Springs, Arkansas.

Source: Fanning Family collection.

(Above right) Gertrude Harrison Fanning and her daughter, Mary Laura Fanning, approximately four months old.

Source: Fanning Family collection.

(Bottom left) John Wootten Fanning and Gertrude Harrison Fanning with sons, Wootten, three years old and J. W., six years old.

Source: Fanning Family collection.

J. W. at approximately four years old in Surrey with his father.

Source: Fanning Family collection.

Headstones for graves of Mary E. Fanning, J. W.'s step great-great-grandmother, and Welcome Fanning, J. W.'s great-great-grandfather. Located in the Colley Family Cemetery north of Washington, Georgia.

Source: Gene Younts.

(Top) Headstones for the graves of W. P. Fanning and Mrs. W. P. (Laura Wootten) Fanning, J. W.'s grandfather and grandmother. Located in the Independence Methodist Church Cemetery, Tignall, Georgia.

Source: Gene Younts.

(Middle) Headstone for the grave of Gertrude Harrison Fanning, J. W.'s mother. Located in the Resthaven Cemetery, Washington, Georgia.

Source: Gene Younts.

(Bottom) Headstone for the grave of John Wootten Fanning, J. W.'s father. Located in the Resthaven Cemetery, Washington, Georgia.

Source: Gene Younts.

(Top) Headstone for the grave of Mary Laura Fanning, J. W.'s older sister. Located in the Resthaven Cemetery, Washington, Georgia.

Source: Gene Younts.

(Middle) Headstone for the grave of Wootten Fanning, J. W.'s brother. Located in the Resthaven Cemetery, Washington, Georgia.

Source: Gene Younts.

(Bottom) Headstone for the grave of Emily Fanning Greene, J. W.'s younger sister. Located in the Resthaven Cemetery, Washington, Georgia.

Source: Gene Younts.

Phillips Mill Baptist Church founded in 1785 in the Tyrone Community where J. W. and family worshiped in his early years.

Source: Gene Younts.

"Dinner on the Grounds," by artist Jack C. DeLoney, Ozark, Alabama.

Source: courtesy of the artist.

Griffin Store in the heart of the Tyrone Community, replaced an earlier structure managed by J. W.'s father.

Source: Gene Younts.

The Griffin Home, Tyrone Community. J. W.'s first grade school teacher, Miss Addie Sue Griffin, is thought to have lived in this home.

Source: Gene Younts.

Tyrone Community School where J. W. attended grades one through five.
Source: Lamar Cofer, Griffin Store, Tyrone Community.

J. W.'s family home at 506 Spring Street, Washington, Georgia, beginning in 1916; as it appears today.
Source: Gene Younts.

The United Methodist Church, Washington, Georgia,
where J. W.'s family worshiped after moving from Tyrone.
Source: Gene Younts.

Old high school in Washington, Georgia,
attended by J. W. in the 6th, 7th, and 8th grades.
Source: Robert E. Willingham Jr.

The last home owned by John Wootten Fanning, J. W.'s father.
Located on Old US Highway 78 west of the city of Washington, Georgia.
Source: John Greene.

John Wootten Fanning's home on Old Highway 78, severely damaged by a tornado in 1939, as it appears today. The upper story of the home was not replaced.
Source: Gene Younts.

Sarah Josephine Slater Harvey at 18 years old, mother of Cora Lee Fanning.

Source: Fanning Family collection.

Cora Lee Harvey Fanning at five years old (in the middle) with her two sisters.

Source: Fanning Family collection.

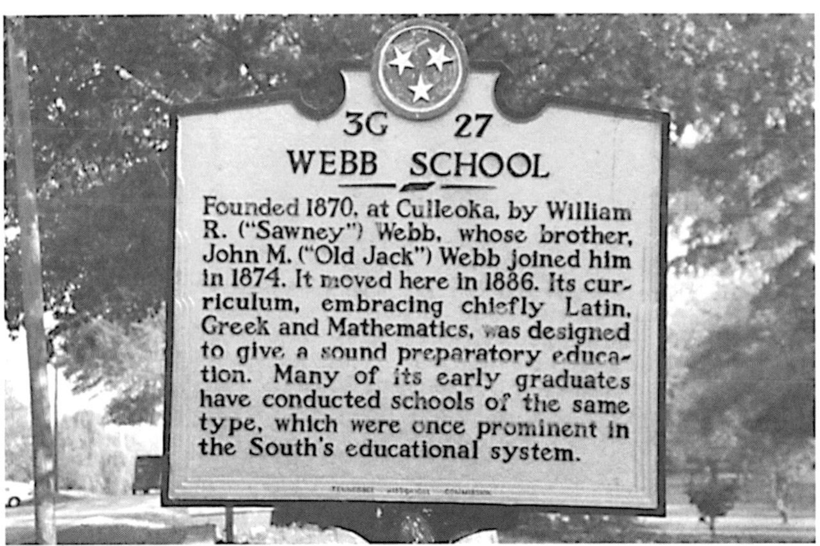

Historical marker of Webb School in Bell Buckle, Tennessee. J. W. enrolled there in the fall of 1920.

Source: Gene Younts.

The Wheeler Home on Peacock Street, Bell Buckle, Tennessee, where J. W. and cousin Joe Fanning roomed and boarded while students at the Webb School.

Source: Gene Younts.

The Registration Building on the Webb Campus, one of the few structures of J. W.'s time that remains today.

Source: Gene Younts.

The Junior Room on the Webb School campus, a museum today. In 1920 each class had its own building.

Source: Gene Younts.

Male students in the required dress code on the Webb School campus.

Source: Gene Younts.

Raymond Wells who worked for the Webb School in the 1940s. One of his duties was to gather willow switches from nearby ditch banks. The switches were used by the teachers to maintain strict discipline in the classroom.

Source: Gene Younts.

Old Library, Webb School. J. W. spent many hours studying here.

Source: Gene Younts.

Main downtown section of Bell Buckle, Tennessee, as it appeared in 2000.
Source: Gene Younts.

The folks in Bell Buckle, Tennessee, live a quiet and peaceful life. Even the dogs rest easy.
Source: Gene Younts.

First Methodist Church, Bell Buckle, Tennessee, constructed in 1807. J. W. attended here while a student at the Webb School.
Source: Gene Younts.

Former train station in Bell Buckle, Tennessee, remembered by students as the principal mode of transportation in and out of town. Photo of picture hanging in the Junior Room Museum.

Source: Gene Younts.

Train tracks leading out of Bell Buckle looking south toward Georgia, J. W.'s route home for Christmas, 1920.

Source: Gene Younts.

Seney Hall on the Emory at Oxford College campus, 2001, appearing today as it was when J. W. was a student.

Source: Gene Younts.

J. W. 18 years old, his senior year at the Emory Academy.

Source: Fanning Family collection.

Cora Lee standing between two friends visiting Ruby Falls.

Source: Fanning Family collection.

J. W. and Cora Lee Harvey during student days at the University of Georgia, 1928. Just courtin' on the grounds of the old amphitheater.

Source: Fanning Family collection.

House in the Chicopee Mill Village, Gainesville, similar to the one where Cora Lee and J. W. were married.

Source: Gene Younts.

Home of J. W. and Cora Lee on Meeting Street, Perry, Georgia. He served as a county agent in Houston County in the early 1930s.

Source: Gene Younts.

Fanning home on Parkway Drive, Athens, Georgia.
Source: Gene Younts.

J. W. with children, Bill and Sibyle, and the family dog.
Source: Fanning Family collection.

(Above left) Cora Lee Fanning at 26 years old.

Source: Fanning Family collection.

(Above right) Cora Lee Fanning and the two children, Sibyle and Bill.

Source: Fanning Family collection.

(Left) J. W. with children, Sibyle and Bill, at the home on Parkway Drive.

Source: Fanning Family collection.

Wootten Fanning at the home on Old US Highway 78 west of Washington, Georgia.

Source: Fanning Family collection.

Earl Cheek and Louie Newberry. Mr. Cheek was a student of J. W. at the University of Georgia in the 1930s. Mr. Newberry was a member of the Middle Georgia Area Planning and Development Commission Board, 1960s.

Source: Gene Younts.

J. W. as a farm management specialist addressing an agricultural assembly in the 1950s.

Source: Fanning Family collection.

J. W. as vice president for services at the University of Georgia in 1966.
Source: Fanning Family collection.

The Progressive Farmer Magazine *editor, A. B. Copeland, presenting the "Man of the Year in Georgia Agriculture" award to J. W. in 1961.*

Source: Fanning Family collection.

J. W. ready to receive his honorary degree from Mercer University. With him are Dr. P. Harris Anderson and Dr. Paul E. Cable, Mercer University administrators.

Source: Fanning Family collection.

The sign on the cabin door that greeted hundreds of visitors to the Booger Hill farm.
Source: Gene Younts.

(Left) Road through woods to the cabin on Booger Hill farm. Cora Lee led the bulldozer driver in making his cut.
Source: Gene Younts.

Lake on Booger Hill farm with cabin in the background.
Source: Gene Younts.

Outside Cora Lee's picnic shelter on Booger Hill farm.
Source: Gene Younts.

Dam on Hodge's Creek on Booger Hill farm.
Source: Gene Younts.

Barn on Booger Hill farm.
Source: Gene Younts.

Bill Fanning mowing the meadow that overlooks the lake on Booger Hill farm, 2001.
Source: Gene Younts.

J. W. at the rail of the Captain J. W. Fanning, *a boat named in his honor by the Marine Extension Service.*
Source: Ed Chin.

J. W. and Gene Younts at the Marine Extension Service dock.
Source: Ed Chin.

(Above) J. W. being inducted into the Agricultural Alumni Association Hall of Fame. With him are Cora Lee, Bill and Sandra Fanning and J. W.'s nephew, John Greene, and his wife, Sue.

Source: Fanning Family collection.

(Left) J. W. on the cover of Georgia Trend, the Magazine of Georgia Business and Politics, *July 1996.*

Source: Georgia Trend.

J. W. and Cora Lee celebrating their 50th wedding anniversary, December 22, 1981.

Source: Fanning Family collection.

(Facing page, top) J. W. with Pat Pattillo and Dink NeSmith.

Source: Fanning Family collection.

(Facing page, middle) J. W. with Jane R. Hemmer, Melba Cooper, past director of the Fanning Institute, and Sibyle Jenks.

Source: Fanning Family Collection.

(Facing page, bottom) J. W. and recipients of the J. W. Fanning Humanitarian Award presented by the Athens Regional Medical Center Foundation. Pictured are: Polly Moore, John E. "Buck" Griffin, Mary Beth McDonald, Howard Stroud, J. W., and Louise Boyce.

Source: John Drew, Athens Regional Medical Center.

Phyllis Barrow, J. W., and Upshaw Bentley at Valentine's Day party at the First Baptist Church, Athens, Georgia.

Source: Fanning Family collection.

Celebrating J. W.'s 90th birthday in 1995.
Surrounded by Leadership Georgia alumni and their families.

Source: Dink NeSmith.

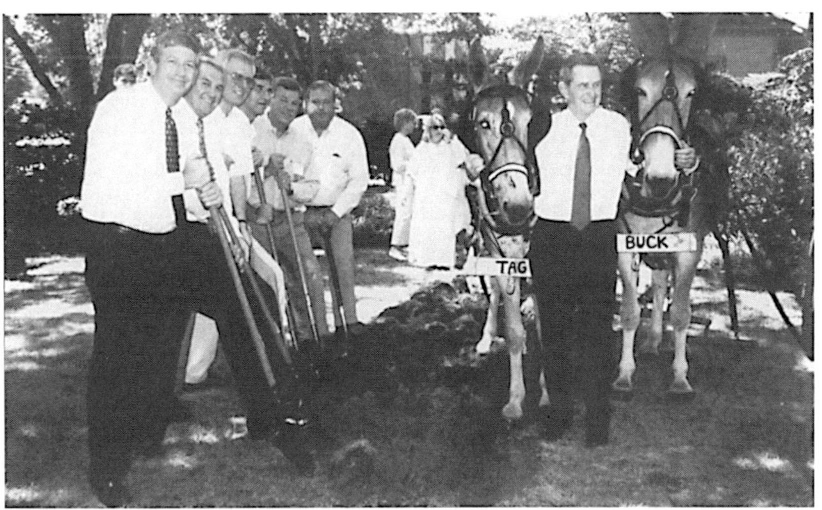

The groundbreaking for the J. W. Fanning Building at 1240 South Lumpkin Street, University of Georgia campus, held on August 14, 1999. Two mules, Tag and Buck, pulled a plow to break ground. Pictured with the mules are alumni of Leadership Georgia.

Source: Pam NeSmith.

Groundbreaking participants, Gene Younts, Sibyle Jenks, Bill Fanning, Dink NeSmith, and Smith Wilson (owner of the mules pulling the plow).

Source: Nancy Evelyn, Georgia Center for Continuing Education.

The First Baptist Church, Athens, Georgia, named this addition to its physical structure in honor of J. W. and Cora Lee Fanning.

Source: Pam NeSmith.

The University of Georgia created the position of vice president for services (now vice president for public service and outreach) in 1965. Three persons have held the position on a permanent basis. Dr. J. W. Fanning, whose portrait is hanging on the wall, was the first, serving from 1965 through 1971; Dr. S. E. Younts, standing, was the second, serving from 1972 through 1999; and Dr. Arthur N. Dunning, seated, began serving in mid-2000. Not pictured is Dr. Thomas F. Rodgers who served as interim vice president for six months in 2000.

Source: Nancy Evelyn, Georgia Center for Continuing Education

Artist's rendering of the J. W. Fanning Building, University of Georgia.

Source: Chapman, Griffin, Lanier, Sussenbach, architects

J. W. Fanning was respected, admired, and loved by people from all walks of life throughout Georgia. Over and over, people mention how he touched and transformed their lives and inspired them to greater accomplishment than they ever thought possible. His unique, motivational style of teaching and advising made him Georgia's pioneer of leadership training; Leadership Georgia, now in its thirtieth year, is Dr. Fanning's continuing legacy to his beloved state. This book chronicles his journey over nearly a century, from his childhood on a large farm to the University of Georgia's first Vice President for Services. I am proud, as a graduate of Leadership Georgia, to occupy that post today and continue the mission of leadership, public service, and outreach that Dr. Fanning held so dear.

ART DUNNING

Vice President for Public Service and Outreach and Associate Provost

The University of Georgia

CHAPTER SEVEN

Leadership Georgia

by Dink NeSmith

In 1960, H. G. (Pat) Pattillo ventured into the backwoods and dirt roads in the shadow of Stone Mountain to assemble 64 parcels to create a 1,000-acre park. With a gutsy plan and a cooperative banker, the young Georgia Tech graduate started cranking out industrial buildings.

In the first twelve years, 150 buildings were built in 144 months. As of 2001, the once fallow farmland had become home to over 200 companies filling more than nine million square feet in his Stone Mountain industrial park.

Today, Pattillo is one of the South's most prolific builders. He has constructed more than 1,000 buildings. The son of a Dekalb County tenant farmer was a leader in helping create new jobs as Atlanta began to flex its economic muscles. On one day in 1963, Governor Carl Sanders clipped the ribbons on nineteen new buildings in the Stone Mountain complex.

Metro Atlanta was on a roll.

So was Pat Pattillo.

But in 1970 as president of the Georgia Chamber of Commerce, he was frustrated. The builder's vision peered beyond the gold glow of Atlanta.

Idea of Two Georgias bothered Pat Pattillo. There were two Georgias —Atlanta and the rest of the state. Patillo fretted because he wanted the other Georgia to experience more of the prosperity Atlanta had been enjoying over the past decade.

During his tenure at the helm of the Georgia Chamber, he was determined to do something about that. The answer, he felt, was leadership. Leaders across the state needed to talk, compare notes and learn from each other.

Pattillo remembers brainstorming with Alma, Georgia, banker, Valene Bennett; Sandersville Railroad owner, Ben Tarbutton; Pen Worden of the Georgia Chamber and his assistant, Rogers Wade, about the need for a leadership development program.

Such a program would cost money.

Who would pay?

The pieces began to fall into place.

Pattillo Construction Company completed a project. The contract came in under budget. Pattillo tried to return $50,000. The customer refused. A compromise was reached. The money would be donated to an educational project. Pattillo recommended a leadership educational initiative spearheaded by the Georgia Chamber of Commerce.

Wade remembered Pattillo walking into the chamber office with a third party check, endorsing it and handing it over. Pattillo remembered that the gift triggered an IRS audit because "they thought the donation was excessive." But he did not complain. He wanted the money put to work soon.

At an Industrial Developers Council meeting at the Kingwood Country Club outside Clayton, more pieces came together in Walter Cates' room. Joining Cates, executive director of the chamber, were Pattillo, Jim Leintz, Jim Topple and Rogers Wade. The group talked about Chatham County's program called Leadership Savannah. Maybe something like that could be started statewide.

Pattillo envisioned business people cross-pollinating with farmers, educators, ministers, government officials and community volunteers. The selection process had to reach into the small communities as well as the large cities.

"We were looking for potential leaders, not those people with eight pages of resume," said Wade. "Walter assigned me to the project and Pat assigned his assistant, Jim Topple. 'Put something together,' we were told."

Soon joining the duo was a vice-president of C&S Bank, Bill VanLandingham. The three continued sketching on the concept.

But who would lead this forum?

As chairman of the state's Board of Regents, Pattillo was privy to Georgia's brightest minds. He had admired one particular college administrator who had helped Chancellor George Simpson guide the university system from 30,000 students to more than 100,000. His name was John William Fanning.

"J. W. Fanning was an immense help in this evolution," Pattillo said. "His reputation was way beyond the University of Georgia. It was statewide. Everyone had respect for him and on that was built appreciation. His number one attribute was his principles. He was low key, but a thinker and a teacher."

Fanning, recently retired vice president for services at the University of Georgia, was known for his quiet style of leadership. His listening skills were legendary. He knew Georgia inside and out.

"The first time I heard J. W.'s name mentioned in relationship to the project, I was sitting in Walter Cates' room at Kingwood," said Wade.

Pattillo asked Fanning to prepare a white paper and develop a theme for the leadership program. "I remember," he said, "Fanning making a deliberate effort to have a mix of gender, race and geography."

Chatham County was finding success with Leadership Savannah. Pattillo asked, "Why not Leadership Georgia?"

Just as he had figured, Stone Mountain was hungry to grow. Pat Pattillo's hunch about Leadership Georgia with Dr. J. W. Fanning as advisor was quick to blossom. Fanning, also the son of a farmer, knew how to nurture the idea. It sprouted into life in 1972. The first class had sixty-three members.

Participants came from Cordele, Athens, Columbus, Brunswick, Cornelia, Sandersville, Rome, Toccoa, Pine Mountain, Atlanta and other towns. The late William J. VanLandingham was the first president. Rogers Wade was program chairman.

Pattillo's idea was put into action on Sea Island as Jim Topple and Rogers Wade led the discussions on The Organization of Government. "We wanted the biggest names we could get," Wade said. "We got Senator Herman Talmadge and Governor Jimmy Carter to be our top speakers. And I'll never forget my wife, Marsha, and Jim's wife, Anne, made name tags in the back seat all the way to Sea Island. Folks may not know, but Jim Topple was one of the real unsung heroes in the formation of Leadership Georgia."

Looking back to 1972, Wade said, "We spent $7,000 on our first meeting. Some people thought I had lost my mind, but I knew if we didn't have a good beginning, the end would come quickly."

Wade and others knew the program's success depended on more than big money and big names. Someone would have to hold it together. "J. W. was the most inspirational, honest and decent leader that I've ever met." Wade said. "I think he touched more lives in a positive way than any other Georgian in the 20th century."

For the second meeting, members of Leadership Georgia traveled to Callaway Gardens where their new advisor, J. W. Fanning, helped them explore Education: Youth, Drugs and Crime. President Bill VanLandingham chaired a program on Criminal and Justice System at Kingwood Country Club. Harry West organized the Stone Mountain meeting on "Delivery of Social Services." The year was concluded in Savannah with Jack Talley's discussion of "Employment and Economic Growth."

In his earliest thoughts on a leadership initiative, Pat Pattillo longed for a stimulus to stir bright minds and help build a framework for better jobs in Georgia. "There's too much rigidity in our education," he said. "What I hoped for in Leadership Georgia was a forum to express different views." He hoped at least five of the sixty participants in each class would go back home and make a difference. "Just five would be great," he said. "Ten would be exceptional."

In the inaugural class was Sam Nunn, a young attorney and state representative from Perry. That forum sparked Fanning's imagination.

He recounted a conversation with Nunn. He said that Nunn left Sea Island excited about Georgia's future. "Sam Nunn," Fanning said, "told me that on the trip home with his wife, Colleen, he decided to run for the United States Senate."

In a 1980s Leadership Georgia filmed documentary, Senator Nunn said, "In his own quiet, but effective way, Dr. Fanning talked with all of us. He helped us find new ideas and solutions to problems we are confronting. Every time I have even a simple conversation with him, I go away with a sense of hope and direction."

That was J. W. Fanning's trademark—listening, asking questions, making subtle suggestions and then standing back to let others lead the way. During his ninety-two years, his work accumulated a stack of honors that would overload any farm wagon. But beyond his family and church, Leadership Georgia was his greatest source of pride.

"Leadership Georgia came at the right time in my life," he said. "Cora Lee and I were enjoying my retirement and the farm, but we needed more. Leadership Georgia kept us young and on the go."

He was not the author of the organization's statement of purpose, but his guiding hand is evidenced in these words: "If Georgia is to achieve its potential, the people in the cities and suburbs of our state must be aware of the social, economic, and governmental need of our rural counties. Likewise, the rural citizens must be knowledgeable and concerned about the problems facing their neighbors in the cities.

"Through representation in Leadership Georgia by their young leaders, these communities are alerted to each other's problems and to their mutual interests in building a better Georgia. Leadership Georgia seeks out the young, recognized leaders in these diverse communities and brings them together. Five hard-hitting programs throughout the year deal with crucial issues facing our towns, cities, suburbs, and rural communities. Together, the participants of Leadership Georgia see mutual understanding of the problems of the state and their solutions.

"The participants in Leadership Georgia profit from getting to know each other and from the formal and informal exchange of ideas and experiences. They gain knowledge and understanding from authorities on a wide variety of subjects such as government organization, education, private enterprise, natural resources, finance, and rural and urban development. Thus, Leadership Georgia prepares them for more active roles in the affairs of our state."

And from the first meeting of Leadership Georgia, one tradition jelled. It continues today. Following the three-day discussions, the advisor gives a wrap-up summary. Almost always Dr. Fanning opened his remarks with, "Well, this is what I heard."

Dave Garrett III is president and CEO of Airis Corporation, the world's largest private aviation facility developer. As member of Leadership Georgia's 1982 class and president in 1984, Garrett still keeps copies of Dr. Fanning's summaries in his desk.

"At least once a month," he said, "I pick out one and read it. Not because I need to know something that day about a particular topic that was covered in the program. I read it for the same reason I read a Bible verse—because of the wisdom contained in it and because of the lesson that he was providing."

Garrett also remembered the time he was at the Fannings' farm on Booger Hill Road in Madison County. A production crew was there to film a Leadership Georgia documentary on J. W. and Cora Lee's thoughts about the organization. "I had the best job in the whole deal," said Garrett. "I was the one who got to ask him questions to which he responded.

"We were down by the pond and he answered a question just perfectly. His answer, as always had a symmetry to it that was amazing. It probably took him one to two minutes, but it told a story, taught a lesson for living and left an impression. Just before he finished, a small breeze came up and rustled the trees. It created just enough background noise that we needed to do a retake. I then asked him the same identical question. Without a moment's hesitation, he delivered a completely different answer, equally well-delivered, possessing a story, a lesson and an impression. When the take was over, I smiled at him and remarked on what had just happened. I asked him if he was aware that he had given two entirely different but equally poignant responses to the same question. He smiled and said, 'I didn't want you to get bored.' No one was ever bored sitting in the presence of Dr. Fanning."

A few years after his Leadership Georgia experience, Garrett walked away from his law practice to begin another career. As a global entrepreneur, he credits the Fannings with a profound impact on his life.

"Other than my mother and father," he said, "there has been no one who meant more to my becoming what I have become than J. W. and Cora Lee Fanning. Though I am, I hope, still a work in process, I will always be thankful to them for inspiring me to demand more of myself and to believe that one person or one group can make THE difference."

Dave Garrett grew up in Atlanta as the son of a powerful airline executive. Two hundred miles down the road, Donnie Morris grew up in the wide-open spaces of Appling County. He followed in his father's footsteps with a devotion to agriculture to become one of America's largest blueberry producers. When Dave Garrett and his wife, Vickie, shop at Kroger's in Atlanta, they are likely to see Donnie's likeness on huge posters promoting blueberries.

Their link is J. W. Fanning—and Leadership Georgia. In 1974, a member of the Leadership Georgia third class was thirty-three-year-old Appling County farmer, Donnie Morris. His parents, the late J. P. and Montene Morris, had befriended the Fannings during the early 1940s. That friendship remained close for the next 50 years. "My daddy thought the world of J. W. Fanning," said Morris. So he wasn't surprised when the elder Morris announced, "Donnie, I'm going to give the best experience and education a father can give his son."

Donnie was 22 years old with a new bride, but his father asked him to ride the state with J. W. Fanning as he presented the area planning and development concept to Georgians.

"I didn't do much," said the young Morris, "but carry bags and listen. I probably learned more during those two weeks than any other time in my life. And ever since my Daddy's statement 'this would be an experience to remember' continues to ring in my ears."

When he and his wife, Jane, participated in Leadership Georgia, they were ready to soak up that experience, too. Among their most prized possessions are numerous hand-written letters from Dr. Fanning.

In 1981, Leadership Georgia created the "Frederick B. Kerr Service Award" to be presented in memory of Rome's Fred Kerr, who died of a heart attack. "The first time I ever heard about Leadership Georgia was from Fred Kerr," said Lynn Dempsey, also of Rome, who served as the organization's president in 1986. "Fred's personality was bigger than life. He was a great guy and he loved Leadership Georgia. He wanted everyone to meet Dr. Fanning and know about Leadership Georgia."

The very first to be honored with the Kerr Award was the blueberry farmer from Baxley, Donnie Morris. A listing of recipients in suceeding years appears in the Appendix B.

Mimi Gudenrath, a Macon educator, was president of Leadership Georgia in 1994. Like Donnie Morris and hundreds of other Leadership Georgia participants, she cherishes the letters received from the co-founder of the program.

"I have two of the many letters he sent me framed and on my office wall," she said.

One letter was dated October 25, 1992. In it he wrote, "The moment is here and I am so glad you will be nominated and elected as president of Leadership Georgia."

Gudenrath said, "The moment was in relation to electing a woman to that office in an organization which had been led almost exclusively by men. He encouraged and celebrated diversity in leadership, and more important, he lived it."

"Honor tradition," Fanning often said, "but don't be a traditionalist." He was pleased to see the emerging role of women in Leadership Georgia. Gudenrath was right. In the early 1970s, much of the leadership had been male. By 1979, however, the group had elected its first female president, Ann Estes Klamon, an Atlanta banker.

During her tenure, the program's theme was "The Challenge of Leadership." Program chairs Horace and Beverly Sibley kicked off the year at Unicoi State Park on the topic of communication. Jim and Karen Pannell invited the class to Savannah to discuss preserving our heritage.

The next step was a big one—to Washington, D.C. Henrietta and Marvin Singletary arranged for the group to travel to the nation's capital to talk about managing government. John and Laura Hardman brought the participants back to Atlanta to examine the issues surrounding cities, suburbs and rural area. Fred and Ann Kerr wrapped up the year in Albany looking at land use.

One woman who had a major influence from the outset of Leadership Georgia was the advisor's wife, Cora Lee Fanning. After attending several meetings, she raised her hand at the conclusion of one of the programs. "I'd like to say something," she said.

She said it was time for spouses and women to be a part of the program. "We want to take part in the discussions, too," she said. And with that change, many believe the program began to flourish. When participants reported to their first meeting, most did not know the nominated participants or their spouses.

"Leadership Georgia gets two for the price of one," quipped Marilyn Marks, a 1982 participant.

Take Calvin S. (Hoppy) and DeAnn Hopkins, for example. In the mid-1980s, both were knee-deep in Upson County civic affairs. Participants for Leadership Georgia are nominated by past participants or a member of the Georgia Chamber of Commerce board of directors. As to who would be nominated, it could have been a flip of the coin. Both Hoppy and DeAnn were being considered.

Mrs. Hopkins didn't mind that her husband's name was submitted. "It didn't matter once we got there," she said. "From the moment I arrived at Unicoi, I was made to feel great. Unless you looked in the book, you couldn't tell who was the participant or the spouse. I'm grateful Cora Lee insisted spouses are an active part of the program."

The Thomaston couple was impressed with the positive attitudes of everyone in the class of 1984. "On Friday morning of the Unicoi meeting, Dave Garrett (chairman of the board) asked for some help to pass out materials," Hoppy Hopkins said. "Eight people must have jumped to their feet. And I was thinking, 'Wow!' Back home you would have had to ask three times for volunteers."

Both agree "getting to do something together outside the home" was special. "Besides having our children, watching them join the church and grow up, Leadership Georgia is the greatest thing we've ever done," said DeAnn. Her husband echoed those sentiments. "Aside from marriage and parenting, "Leadership Georgia was the pinnacle for me," Hoppy said. "It enhanced my awareness of everything we were talking about. Whatever the issues were, we were talking about them at Leadership Georgia. It really gave DeAnn and me a focus and direction in our lives. And we really didn't know how much we missed it until it was over."

He continued, "Everything about Leadership Georgia encouraged me to grow. And Marilyn Marks even helped to show me that some of what I thought were my weaknesses or quirks could be strengths if I used them correctly. Leadership Georgia prepared me for not just the big and important discussions or decisions, it gave me an everyday road map to show me how things ought to be happening. I could always hear J. W. talking about fairness and honesty and how one person could make a difference."

In 1987, Hopkins was president of the organization and his theme for the year was "Commitment to Values—A Better Future for Georgia." As good as the meetings were, he said one of his favorite memories of the experience was the afterglow during the drive home from meetings.

The sentiment has been unanimous among couples. The five meetings during the year took the pair away from their businesses, vocations, families and other civic commitments. Thursday through Saturday noon, they were thrust into a throng of high-energy, can-do personalities who believed Georgia's potential was endless.

But to be nominated for Leadership Georgia, you didn't have to be married. Many single Georgians, such as Ken Callaway of Hamilton and Sherri Davis of Columbus, have participated in the program. Back in 1992, Ken and Sherri didn't know each other even though they were from the same area. She was a senior vice president of Columbus Bank and Trust, active in the community and busy raising a son. Ken was starting a new textile chemical firm based in Newnan and raising his three sons.

"It must have been meant to be," Ken said. During the fourth program in Madison, the two got acquainted. And by the fifth program in Savannah, the romance began.

Former Leadership Georgia chairman Jim Buntin and his wife, Nancy, helped to play cupid in the new relationship. "The Buntins conveniently did not have room for me in their car," Ken said, "so I had to catch a ride home with Sherri."

A year later, Ken and Sherri married and continued their Leadership Georgia involvement while Sherri served on the board of trustees. In 1997, their daughter, Caitlyn Virginia, was born.

Caitlyn's great-grandfather, Cason, founder of Callaway Gardens, was a good friend of J. W. Fanning. Callaway called on Fanning to help shape his visionary "100 Better Farms for Georgia" in the 1940's.

The grandson said, "My grandfather had tremendous admiration for J. W. Fanning. I am thrilled that four generations of Callaways have been touched by the life of Dr. Fanning."

Whether participants were dancing at a sock hop or disco party or engaging in a riveting discussion on at-risk children in urban schools, the electricity crackled among the 120 or so gathered wherever in Georgia. And when Dr. Fanning, or later his successor, Dr. Dale Threadgill, delivered the wrap-up summary, there were hugs, a few tears and for most, a long drive back home.

The ride home was special to couples like the Hopkins. "I remember driving home in 1987 from St. Simons where DeAnn and I had just completed our program," said Hoppy. "For the longest while, we just drove in silence. And then somewhere between Sylvester and Albany, all at once, we both just started crying. Everything had gone perfectly and just the way we had planned. It was wonderful."

Six and a half years before Cora Lee Fanning's death, she and her husband decided to turn over the advisory reins, but they continued their close association with Leadership Georgia.

Three days before Christmas in 1992, tears filled the eyes of the

Leadership Georgia family. On the morning of the Fanning's sixty-first anniversary, J. W. arose early to read the newspaper and prepare a card for his wife. Cora Lee slept late and he heard her coming down the hall around nine. They embraced in the hall, he kissed her and presented the card.

"I'm not feeling too well," she said. J. W. hugged her again and suggested she go back to bed. A few minutes later, he called for an ambulance. By noon on Dec. 22, 1992, Cora Lee had died at Athens Regional Medical Center. On Christmas Eve, hundreds of friends, many from Leadership Georgia, gathered at First Baptist Church in Athens to say goodbye. If J. W. Fanning was the grandfather of Leadership Georgia, Cora Lee has certainly earned the title of grandmother. In the summer of 1993, the organization created an award in memory of Cora Lee. The recipient is a spouse of the current class. Winners are chosen based upon "outstanding participation and enthusiasm." Those two qualities described Cora Lee's role since the outset back in 1972.

On May 15, 1993, Kay Parker of Atlanta, wife of John Parker, was selected as the first winner of the Cora Lee Fanning Award. "It's been almost ten years and I'm still shocked," said Kay Parker. "The Fannings were such wonderful, spunky people. They had the perfect hearts for young people. They wanted to bring them and this state together so everyone could reach their potential. As for Cora Lee, I had a grandmother just like her. You don't meet many angels on earth, but Cora Lee was one of them. She could be sweet and firm at the same time and make the best of everything."

The next year, a husband, Charles Williams, was the recipient. He came to the program with his wife, Charlotte, superintendent of schools in Dodge County. Other winners are listed in Appendix G.

At the organization's fifteenth anniversary celebration at the Waverly Hotel in Atlanta, J. W. Fanning was honored and appointed advisor-emeritus. Co-founder Pat Pattillo addressed the crowd of several hundred. Together, Pattillo and Fanning had seen an idea grow from infancy to reach a network of more than 1,000 people across Georgia. Graduates of Leadership Georgia were in the United States Senate, Congress, the Georgia General Assembly and hundreds of other leadership roles from St. Marys to Dalton and from Columbus to Augusta. As a gift to past and future classes of Leadership Georgia, Fanning penned his now famous "Ten Pillars of Leadership." This is what he said:

> Leaders are doers and leadership does not just happen. It stems from purposes. It grows with involvement. It becomes stronger, more exciting and effective as it makes use of those qualities proven successful by wise and creative leaders over the years—qualities undergirded by 'Pillars' which provide support and purpose for leadership that makes a difference.
>
> Leaders are everywhere. They reside in neighborhoods and communities. They serve at county, state and national levels. They are present in business and industry, and amid the professions. No group, public or private, is without its leaders. The wide dispersal of leadership is one of the great strengths of a democratic society. It was so planned by the founding fathers of this nation.
>
> Some individuals are endowed with leadership abilities. Others behold the value of leadership in human progress and acquire it through diligent effort. Many prefer to be followers, yet, in supportive concern and involvement, there is leadership even in following.
>
> A distinguished Chinese philosopher wrote, "Leaders are best when people scarcely know they exist, not so good when people obey and acclaim them. Fail to honor people, they fail to honor you. But of good leaders who talk little, when their work is done, their aim fulfilled, the people will all say, we did this ourselves."

Using that description of a leader, J. W. Fanning described himself. Quiet. Listening. Asking questions. Listening more. He challenged each class of Leadership Georgia to ask these three questions:

1. What are Georgians saying?
2. What are Georgians not saying?
3. What are Georgians not saying because they don't know how?

"There is no part of Leadership Georgia that doesn't have J. W.'s stamp on it," Rogers Wade said, "He could sit in a small room and guide the conversation around a subject until every person would have input, then sum up in such a way that each participant thought that he or she had originated the idea in the first place."

Former United States Senator Herman Talmadge said, "No son of Georgia has had a greater influence on the destiny of our state than J. W. Fanning." Wade added, "I know for a fact that his counsel was sought and his advice followed by many of our state's highest officials. There is no place in our state where there is not living proof of his influence."

Wade's case is made stronger each year as new classes of Leadership Georgia are selected. Since the participants range in age from twenty-five to forty-five, most have never heard of J. W. Fanning until they enter the program.

"Only words live forever," Fanning often proclaimed.

That's how his legacy of the Ten Pillars of Leadership continues to be interwoven into each new generation of leaders. The words Fanning hoped to live forever are:

1. Custody of Values

"There are values in human endeavors to which people give top priority, and they ask their leaders to hold them in custody. No watering down, no compromises are permitted, even under extreme circumstances, in those foundation values and beliefs which people cherish and cling to. The responsibilities of custodianship are indeed heavy, yet rewarding.

"Walter Lippman once wrote, 'Leaders are the custodians of a nation's ideals, of the beliefs it cherishes, of its permanent hopes, of the faith which makes a nation out of a mere aggregation of individuals.'

"Among basic values in this society are dignity of the individual, privilege with responsibility and freedom to pursue one's own potentials as a creative and responsible individual. Society places these and others in the custody of its leaders."

2. *Willingness to Listen and Hear*

"It is so easy to listen but not hear what is being said. Willingness to listen is an act of respect extending to those who wish to be heard. A willingness to hear is an expression of genuine interest in seeking a full understanding of what those who are heard wish to impart."

3. *Ability to Articulate Heartfelt Concerns and Desires*

"The ability to articulate in simple words the heartfelt concerns and needs of people is a hallmark of effective leadership. It confirms that the leader has truly walked in the shoes of those to be led.

"Helping people to examine their true feelings and search out their real needs is an act of communication which is basic to effective leadership. Communication is always at its best when the chances of understanding are far greater than the chances of misunderstanding. Good communications foster trusting relationships."

4. *Dispensing Hope*

"The future belongs to those who believe in it. Hope brings to life an excitement in conquest of a future that is demanding in commitment, yet rewarding in accomplishment. Without hope, life loses its challenges.

"'Hope is like the sun, which, as we journey toward it, casts the shadows of our burdens behind us.' So wrote a distinguished leader. Hope is progressive and believes strongly in the human will. Leadership searches out hope and shares its challenges and opportunities and visions."

5. *Foresightedness*

"The past has its lessons to teach, and must be respected. The future has rewards to share, and must be embraced. Foresightedness is cautious optimism searching out future meanings in current trends and events. It requires looking through new eyes for new opportunities and challenges, which, when discovered, become goals to be accomplished.

"John Gardner, a distinguished leader, wrote that 'We cannot dream of utopia in which all arrangements are ideal and everyone flawless. It is a dream of death. Life is tumultuous—an endless losing and regaining balance, a continuous struggle, never assured of victory. We need a new hard-bitten morale that enables us to face those truths and still strive with every ounce of energy to prevail. We can ask no guarantee of a secure and happy future. But if we want a future that will demand the best that is in us and lend meaning to our lives, we can have it.'"

6. *Knowledge with Common Sense*

"As the available body of knowledge grows to almost overwhelming proportions, so increases the responsibility to understand its practical use in the affairs of people. There is no substitute for common sense in effective leadership—the coupling of knowledge and understanding into attainable goals and accomplishments for an improvement in human well-being.

"An observer of the 'information explosion' said, 'To know a little less and to understand a little more seems to be our greatest need.' Understanding is where the action is. He who knows and understands what he knows and how to use it for good is a wise and effective leader."

7. Integrity of Character

"Integrity of character is the hallmark of leadership that seeks to make things better without caring who gets the credit.

"George Washington wrote, 'Good sense and honesty are qualities too rare and precious not to merit one's particular esteem. I hope I shall possess fairness and virtue enough to maintain what I consider the most enviable of all titles—the character of an honest man.'

"The truth is not always easy to come by. Facts too often seem to cling to both sides of important issues. It is easy to become confused. Yet, character always speaks to what one is, when and where the truth is at stake."

8. Courage to Think and Act Anew

"Leaders are pioneers who possess great courage to think and act anew. Pioneers have always been individuals of great courage.

"A distinguished journalist wrote that 'without faith the history of man would be no more than a flock of sheep.' Faith is the very essence of thinking and acting anew."

9. Sharing Oneself

"Leadership is generous in sharing time and energy in helping people to a better life, never caring who gets the credit. It ever seeks to wisely and unselfishly invest life in making a difference in how things are. It gives away what it cannot keep to gain what it cannot lose. In sharing of oneself, 'Fragrance remains with the hands that give the rose.'"

10. Motivating People to Act

"Leadership has accomplished its purpose when people become motivated to accept new ideas and new ways of doing things that are elevating in spirit, noble in character, and which result in better living.

"In motivation, there must be understanding, confidence and inspiration. Understanding is to know what is to be done and why and how. Confidence brings trust and resolve. Inspiration strengthens hope and faith and determination to accomplish what seems impossible.

"John Gardner wrote, 'Of all the things that must be renewed, none are more important than the goals and values that move people to action. Leaders must conceive and articulate goals in ways that lift people out of their petty preoccupation and unite them toward higher goals. They must assert a vision of what the nation or community might be and must help the people know what they can be at their best. Leaders have a role in creating the state of mind that is society. They must call for the kind of effort and restraint, drive and discipline that make for great performance.'

"General George Marshall described a leader as 'a person who exerts an influence and makes you want to do better than you thought you could.'"

Lindsay Thomas, president of the Georgia Chamber of Commerce, is convinced J. W. Fanning exerted that type of influence on him. Born in the tiny town of Patterson in rural Southeast Georgia, Thomas attended the University of Georgia, but didn't meet Fanning until years later. In 1973, the illness of his father and the death of an uncle, Lindsay Grace, interrupted the young graduate's career track in Savannah.

Thomas inherited Grace Acres Farm on the edge of Screven, not far from his roots in Pierce County. The investment banker moved his family to Wayne County and traded his silk tie for a pair of work gloves.

As a farmer, he was invited to speak to a 1978 Leadership Georgia program on agriculture. "Dr. Tal DuVall of the University of Georgia Extension Service asked me to tell the story of a modern-day farmer and problems they were facing," Thomas said. "That was, of course, the drought years and the embargoes."

That trip to Tifton opened the door to a close friendship that lasted nineteen years. Since they were both farmers, it was natural for Lindsay Thomas and J. W. Fanning to have plenty to talk about. The next year, Thomas was invited to be a member of the 1979 class of Leadership Georgia.

"It began to get me involved in things outside the scope of my own little world in Screven," Thomas said. "I came away from the program knowing J. W. very well, because, of course, I was a farmer and there was a special place in J. W.'s heart for the land. We all know his deep ties with land and how he felt about agriculture and the rural countryside. He and I corresponded a good bit." Thomas still treasures those letters as some of his most important memorabilia.

Thomas' "little world" cracked open in 1981 when Bo Ginn, longtime congressman from the First District in Georgia, announced he was not running for re-election, but wanted to be governor instead. Through stimulating conversations in Leadership Georgia and the contacts made, the Screven farmer started thinking about going to Washington.

The first two people Lindsay Thomas contacted outside the First District were Dr. DuVall and Dr. Fanning. "I wanted to tell J. W. about what I was thinking about doing and I still remember some of the things that he said to me," Thomas said. "He talked about the importance of agriculture in our state and how I should have a great deal to offer in that area. It was an encouraging note. He, of course, was not the kind of person that would have come out and personally endorsed anyone. And that was not why I was asking him. There were eight other candidates and he knew some of them well."

The first-time candidate beat seven Democratic opponents and a Republican challenger. And he continued to win four more times before deciding to leave Capitol Hill. Lindsay Thomas' ties with Leadership Georgia and J. W. Fanning kept getting stronger. The two men corresponded often, and Thomas continued to speak at programs.

Through Leadership Georgia, Thomas became acquainted with three men—Charlie Battle, Horace Sibley and Billy Payne—who were at the center of the brain trust of something big. By the time the fifth-term congressman was thinking—what next?—these Atlantans were deep into planning for the 1996 Olympic Games.

Thomas shocked his constituents when he walked away from Congress. But Billy Payne was delighted about his committee's good fortune. "Lindsay Thomas has some of the best people and communicating skills I've ever seen," Payne said. And Payne put the freshly retired congressman to work as the director of government relations. His new band of constituents stretched around the globe.

As Don Misher was planning for the opening and closing ceremonies of the Centennial Games, he asked Thomas to introduce him to three or four Georgians who could give him a sense of what the state was all about.

First on Thomas' list was J. W. Fanning.

"Here's a man (Don Misher), a very sophisticated, gifted producer, who has done functions at the Kennedy Center and all over the world," Thomas said. "I will never forget the visit we had in J. W.'s home in

Athens. All others kept quiet as the two of them conversed; and after an hour's conversation, as we were leaving, Don told his driver to stop the car. We sat there at the bottom of the hill and looked back at the house and said, 'There is perhaps the wisest man I have ever met.' That spoke volumes to me and that to me is the way I feel about J. W."

J. W. Fanning got to watch the Olympics when four events came to Athens. And before his death in 1997, he got to see the Screven farmer take on another challenge. When the Games were over, Lindsay Thomas stayed in Atlanta to become president of the Georgia Chamber of Commerce, the sponsoring organization of Leadership Georgia.

"I do not know of a more worthwhile program in the State of Georgia with a statewide scope than Leadership Georgia," said Thomas. In 1998, twenty years after first learning of the program, Thomas was awarded the J. W. Fanning Award as the "Georgian whose state-wide contributions through progressive leadership and service have been broad in scope and rich in achievement."

"The Fanning Award is the one award that I am prouder of than anything that I have ever had the luck to be bestowed upon," Thomas said. "I did not think I was deserving and I still don't today. . . . But it has meant a tremendous amount to me because of the respect that I have for the organization and, like J. W., that award has sort of challenged me to try to do more."

The 2000 recipient of the Fanning Award, James H. Blanchard, was in the first class of Leadership Georgia. Back in 1972, Jimmy Blanchard had just switched career gears. Twelve months earlier, he had gotten a surprise visit from the chairman of Columbus Bank and Trust. Blanchard's father, who had been president of the bank, had just died. The board wanted the 30-year-old attorney to take over the reins of the $200 million bank.

Leadership Georgia was a model for Leadership Columbus.

Thirty years later, Blanchard is chairman of Synovus Financial Corp., which owns thirty-nine banks with assets in excess of $14.9 billion. In 1998, Fortune magazine ranked Synovus as the number one place to work in America. And as a bank holding company, Synovus is consistently one of the top-performing banks in the country.

Looking back to his introduction to Leadership Georgia, Blanchard said, "It was a wonderful experience where we enjoyed the fellowship of proven leaders in our state. We covered subjects that were meaty and relevant. We enjoyed experiences that put meat on our bones. Dr. Fanning's leadership was very important to our experience and our exposure to him was an education in and of itself."

Like Columbus Bank and Trust, Leadership Georgia's growth and influence were rapid. "Leadership Georgia has benefited many young men and women in Columbus and Muscogee County and I believe we are better for that," Blanchard said.

"One of the great secrets to success in our community in the past two decades has been the broadening and deepening of the leadership base. Leadership Georgia was a model for what became Leadership Columbus. The leadership experience is like money in the bank for participants. Our local community and communities throughout our state have been the beneficiaries."

Jimmy Blanchard's walls are filled with accolades, but he treasures the J. W. Fanning Award. "Dr. Fanning was the example of leadership," said Blanchard. "He was able to articulate what leadership really is. He loved to see people grow and develop in their leadership strengths. I will be very sensitive to try to uphold his wonderful reputation and contributions as the recipient of this award named in honor of Dr. Fanning."

"How rich do we need to be?" asked Dr. Fanning.

Back in 1972 when Jimmy Blanchard and others attended the first Leadership Georgia meeting, the organization had the $50,000 gift in the bank. Tuition was charged for participating, but resourcefulness was a key to putting on programs. After ten years of scratching and scrambling, the board of trustees decided to initiate a capital campaign.

"Fundraising for Leadership Georgia was unique," said Dave Garrett. "We had access to the key decision makers at most of the state's leading businesses and foundations. Henrietta Singletary was the best. She chooses her causes carefully and there was never one that she felt more deeply about than Leadership Georgia, and she always had Marvin's support as well."

"Pollard Turman kept telling us to think big," recalled Singletary, Class of 1978. "We all knew we needed to raise some money to help the program be independent, but everyone was always so busy getting their programs together to do anything else.

"Looking back it was amazing how generous people were in giving to the programs. Take the trip to Washington, D.C. That took a lot of money, but people gave willingly." But to ensure long-term stability and affordability to all participants, an endowment was needed. Dr. Fanning believed a scholarship fund should be available to subsidize the tuition of those who could not afford to pay the full price.

If a country preacher or a school teacher needed to participate, the money had to be there to help. The drive was kicked off in the fall of 1983.

"I remember sitting, pregnant with our twins—Duncan and Raymond—and talking for hours on the phone asking people for money," said Henrietta Singletary. "Mr. Turman said to ask for large amounts and we did."

Garrett said, "Ann Estes was another key. She was someone who never took no for an answer. She had a clear vision of the organization and its potential. And she carried that message to prospective donors with great passion."

"I remember going to Pollard Turman with Henrietta Singletary, John Hardman, Mike Barron and Dr. Fanning," said Ann Estes. "Mr. Turman was extremely helpful. The Tull Foundation gave us a challenge grant that made it possible to raise the initial $300,000." The 1979 Leadership Georgia president also remembered "the still, quiet presence of Dr. Fanning" in that meeting with Turman. "Dr. Fanning never said much," she said, "but when he did it was significant.

"And Dr. Fanning always took copious notes. He paid more attention than anyone I've ever known," said Ann Estes. "While most people were running around in all directions, he sat quietly listening and taking notes. And then he'd come back with those great, pithy quotes."

Many alumni like Bill VanLandingham and Bill Bowdoin also helped to raise the initial wave of donations. A second push was made in the late 1980's. On the sidelines, J. W. Fanning listened and answered questions. He also, on many occasions, asked, "How rich do we need to be?" He wanted the program to be financially sound, but he marveled when program chairs used their ingenuity to expand the experience rather than just spend more money to improve the quality. He would be startled to know that by 2001, the foundation's endowment was approaching $2 million. But, he would be proud of the resources available to grant more scholarships.

"Dr. Fanning believed that leadership had no geographical or economic boundaries," said Marilyn Marks. "He emphasized that regardless of someone's socio-economic position, race, color, creed or ethnic origin, everyone should have an equal opportunity to become a part of Leadership Georgia."

Marks explained that Fanning's key question was, "Can the person make a difference" in his or her community? If the candidate was qualified, he felt he should be a part of the program even if he couldn't afford it. And that was a major way to use the endowment, he felt.

"Dr. Fanning had a particular soft spot in his heart for those who came from very small counties where opportunities for effective leadership are great, but where a person's visibility outside of their small town might not have the same 'drum roll' as someone from a more densely populated area," said Marks. "If a person showed the capacity for leading, they should and would contribute to the program."

That's why the scholarship fund was established. The board of trustees reviews each case, quietly and confidentially, to make the grants on an as-needed basis. Tuition for Leadership Georgia started in 1972 at around $600. By 2001, it had climbed to $1,950.

"Dr. Fanning's ultimate goal," said Marilyn Marks, "was to have every Georgia county represented in Leadership Georgia."

Dr. Fanning wanted all Georgians represented in program.

One of Leadership Georgia's vital statistics that was of keen interest to its co-founder was representation. J. W. Fanning wanted alumni from each of the state's 159 counties. Periodically, he'd ask, "Have we had anyone from McIntosh County participate? You know, the small counties need leadership desperately. Let's not stop until we can have participants from all the counties."

During the early 1980's, Bill Rice was knee-deep in Gainesville civic endeavors. Many people thought the Milliken executive would be a prime candidate for Leadership Georgia. One of his friends, Sam Dunlap, 1983 president of Leadership Georgia, submitted Rice's name. Others did, too. Not once or twice, but three times before he was selected.

Later when Bill and his wife, Helen, attended their first meeting in 1985, he joked, "I had to get transferred to Alma before I could be picked."

Sam Dunlap and others were right about Rice. He was a good choice. In 1987, he was elected president of Leadership Georgia.

"One of the highlights of mine and Helen's experience," said Rice, "was the afternoon we spent with Cora Lee and Dr. Fanning in their home planning for our year of programs. We just marveled at his insight."

By 2001, Gainesville had forty-eight alumni and counting the Rices who moved to LaGrange, Alma had four.

According to 2001 president Andy Davis, a Rome attorney, Dr. Fanning's dream of claiming 159 counties is within a few years of becoming true. He said that with each new class, the trustees try to chip away at the remaining counties. According to advisor, Dr. Dale Threadgill, only thirteen counties—Dade, Echols, Jenkins, Jones, Lanier, Long, Marion, Quitman, Taliaferro, Union, Walker, Wheeler and Wilcox—are not represented.

Back in the 1980's, Davis got to meet Dr. Fanning. Leadership Rome traveled to Athens for a retreat. Katie Dempsey, Lynn's wife, made sure Davis got to spend some time with Fanning. But he regretted, "I am the first Leadership Georgia president to not have had a sit-down meeting with Dr. Fanning."

Since J. W. Fanning's death, each new class has been presented the overview of the original advisor's legacy through a variety of films and speakers. "As Leadership Georgia matures." said Davis, "it could be easy to lose its heritage and founding." He said it was important for those alumni who knew Fanning to continue sharing their remembrances so each class could "be aware of the impact Dr. Fanning has had on this state and its leaders."

Fanning's life spanned all but eight years of the 20th century. He often marveled at the advances made from horse and buggy to airplanes to space exploration to the Internet. Even though he still relied on a manual typewriter, the computer age fascinated him. He loved hearing experts explain the possibilities of the Internet.

Davis believes Fanning would be pleased with the board's March 2001 decision to create a Leadership Georgia web page. "Our intent is to create a data base with information about participants and alums," said Davis. "The nomination and application process will be on-line. Necessary fire-wall protections will be included."

As for the thirtieth year of the organization, Davis said, "The Class of 2001 is one of the most diverse groups we have ever had." Diversity was a big issue with Dr. Fanning, too. Marilyn Marks recalled the way Leadership Georgia's advisor worked hard with each class to develop a "kinship among the chicken farmers, entrepreneurs, doctors and ministers." He wanted them to sit down and informally find out what they had in common. "It worked like a charm," she said.

Through those chats, they discovered their concerns were the same—better public schools, cleaner water and decent medical care. But the conversations and relationship plowed deeper, Marks noted. Soon the talks bored into topics such as "our heritage, our family tree, our values and beliefs."

"We learned that an immigrant grocery store owner's daughter, an undertaker's son and a minister's son had a lot in common," she said. "We learned that these common core values would keep us close long after our active Leadership Georgia participation was over. Dr. Fanning's belief that diversity was more than gender, religion or race was in practice long before the term 'diversity' was a corporate buzz word."

Before Fanning's death in 1997, he knew that Ed Tarver was on his way to becoming the first African-American president of the organization. The Augusta attorney remembers the first time he and his wife, Beverly, met Fanning. It was at Unicoi State Park where the ninety-year-old advisor emeritus addressed the Class of 1994 on a Saturday morning.

"Beverly and I were thrilled and somewhat overwhelmed by our first Leadership Georgia experience," Tarver said. He was also impressed by Dr. Fanning's eagerness to talk with individual members of the class. "We were amazed," he said, "by his recollections about Augusta and his ability to call many Augusta alumni by name. It did not take much to see that, even in his later years, his vision for Georgia reached farther than that of any of the young 'hot shots' in the class."

At the end of that year, Ed and Beverly Tarver were asked to be program chairs for 1995. "Dr. Fanning was one of the first to congratulate Beverly and me," Ed Tarver said. "He shared in our joy and did not hesitate to assure us that we would do well."

When Tarver began to move through the chairs to become president, he said, "Dr. Fanning discussed ways to make Leadership Georgia more inclusive. He also shared his opinion that we should not be overly concerned with accumulating a large treasury."

Fanning recounted to him the success stories of the early years of Leadership Georgia when limited money was available. He also insisted, "No one should be prevented from participating in Leadership Georgia because of the inability to pay tuition."

Tarver said his favorite memory was a brainstorming session attended by Fanning. President Doug Carter had invited the group to his Gainesville home. "Beverly and I joined Ted Lawrence, Jimmy Allgood, and Doug to discuss a strategic planning session with the board of trustees. We talked for several hours and Dr. Fanning took time to consider each one of our questions before providing his response. Two days after the meeting, my wife received a hand-written thank-you note from Dr. Fanning. He told her Cora Lee would have been happy to know that she was there."

Tarver said he was pleased his wife got the note, but he was disappointed he didn't get one. He said they still laugh about the two weeks he frantically searched the arriving mail for "his Dr. Fanning letter."

After seven years of active Leadership Georgia involvement, January 2001 came hard for the Tarvers. "It was extremely difficult to accept that we would not be traveling to, and participating in, the first Leadership Georgia program for the new class," he said. "With the help of our memory of Dr. Fanning, we were able to make it by recalling that he never treated Leadership Georgia as if he owned it. He was a tremendous man of enormous intellect. Through our association, I have gained the experience and confidence that will enable me to offer myself for further service to my community and our great state."

J. W. Fanning would be proud of Ed Tarver. As Tarver released the reins as chairman of the board of Leadership Georgia, he accepted the chairmanship of the Richmond County Chamber of Commerce.

Leadership Georgia now seeing second generation participants.

In 1972, Sam and Colleen Nunn were active participants in Leadership Georgia's first class. Their daughter, Michelle, who is executive director of Hands on Atlanta/City Cares, was in the group's thirtieth class. Hugh Tarbutton, president of the Sandersville Railroad, was a 1972 classmate of Sam Nunn's. Thirty years later, his son, Charles, served as the 2001 chairman of Leadership Georgia. No official records are kept on how many second-generation participants there have been.

"Next to faith and family," Charles Tarbutton said, "Leadership Georgia has been the most enriching experience of my life. It is clear to me that the potential for progress in Georgia is as immense as the need for progress is immediate. I truly believe that participants of the Leadership Georgia will play a large part of that progress. And I know of no other Georgian who has had a greater impact than J. W. Fanning in communities all over our state through the people he inspired to further service."

His father, Hugh, after thirty years still feels connected to the spirit of Leadership Georgia. "I have always felt honored to be a member of the first class," he said. "The program was developed through the vision, effort and support of Pat Pattillo, Walter Cates, Rogers Wade and others, but the heart and soul of the program has always been J. W. Fanning.

"In 1972, there were no corporate CEOs, presidents or senior politicians in our class, but there was, as a group, a tremendous capacity for achievement. It was Dr. Fanning and the Leadership Georgia experience that served as a catalyst for each of us to redouble our efforts in our respective communities."

Exposing emerging leaders to a "cadre of like-minded people" through a series of thought-provoking programs to explore opportunities and challenges is the "enduring power of the Leadership Georgia experience," explained the elder Tarbutton.

In 1986, Vicki Adams Davis was sixteen years old and remembers her parents, James Lee and Sue Adams, coming home from their first Leadership Georgia meeting. "They were excited," she said. Fifteen years later, she could understand. Vicki is one of a growing number of second-generation Leadership Georgia participants. She and her husband, Kip, also a Georgia Tech graduate, attended their first meeting in January 2001 at Brasstown Valley near Young Harris in Georgia's mountains.

"Kip thought the meeting was incredible," Vicki Davis said. "He had heard my parents talk about their experience, too. And I'm so glad he could participate, because you only get half the picture of me without him. We're a team. Leave him out and you leave out half of me."

She also remembers the impact the program had on her folks, too. "You could tell Dad began to think more globally and less locally," Vicki Davis said. Both generations felt the impact of J. W. Fanning.

"When I look back at the last century," said James Lee Adams, the Farmer of the Year for the Southeast in 2000, "outside of public office, there were some real giants in Georgia. Four people come to mind: Robert W. Woodruff, John Sibley, Martin Luther King Jr. and J. W. Fanning.

"Those four sum up the verse 'where there's no vision, the people will perish,'" he said. "Vision was Dr. Fanning's real contribution to Georgia. He could almost see around corners and expect what was going to happen."

His daughter didn't get to meet Dr. Fanning personally, but she took notes when she heard him speaking on film at her first Leadership Georgia meeting. "The biggest thing that impressed me was the video about Dr. Fanning," she said. "When he said, 'There is no such thing as a hopeless situation, only apathy,' that really hit me between the eyes. I went straight home to Camilla and shared that with my board of directors." As the chairman of the chamber of commerce, she was ready to put the co-founder's words into action.

Her father, James Lee, could relate. "J. W. Fanning was an encourager. He had tremendous character, judgment and vision, but he had a way of putting his confidence in people and that made them feel as if they could do anything. Being in his presence was a real learning experience. It was like osmosis, you feel yourself absorbing from him."

Fresh from one meeting and a video "pep talk" from Fanning, Davis got her board to rolling on improving Mitchell County's public education system. "That first meeting was a catalyst for us to create an initiative to tackle something many people thought was hopeless," she said.

At Brasstown Valley, she met some inner-city school principals who explained how many people had written off their students and schools as hopeless causes. Their startling turnarounds further ignited Vicki Davis.

"Those people proved you can make a difference," she said. "Too many people think that things can't change. I'm ready for South Georgia to get over that and let's get on with improving our schools."

At 31, she had already witnessed improvements coming from a bad situation. At midnight on Valentine's Day 2000, a tornado swept through Mitchell County, displacing 1,200 people and damaging 280 homes. Vicki Davis saw black and white citizens working together like never before. "We can use that same positive spirit of cooperation to make our schools better," she said.

Fanning was an encourager, a mentor to many. Among Marilyn Marks' most prized possessions are two big cardboard boxes of letters from Dr. Fanning. The correspondence spans over a dozen years. "They are all hand-written, mostly on blue lined paper, positive, inspiring, and jammed with quotable quotes," she said. "He was always accessible, patient, humorous and gave us courage during the more trying times in our lives. He was tremendous resource for strength when our own strength was faltering a bit."

Marks, like many other Leadership Georgia participants, would drive to Athens to visit with Fanning. He was a mentor to hundreds, probably thousands over this ninety-two years. And he always had time to listen.

On her trips from Atlanta to Athens, Marks would make mental notes of questions about important decisions she had to make. "I was always in hopes of getting Dr. Fanning to answer them for me. He never answered one," she said. "Instead, he asked me even more questions. Then, he'd tell me to go home and think about what we talked about.

"Once I made a decision, I'd tell him what course of action I was going to take," she said, "he'd write back quickly and encourage me to go forward. Unknowingly to me, Dr. Fanning helped me to focus and put a decision in perspective."

Marks, a business consultant and professional speaker, said, "Moreover, he made sure I was the one to take the journey and that I had to own the decision. Now, years later, I find myself trying to emulate that same mentoring technique."

Asa Boynton, the University of Georgia's director of public safety, echoed Marks' sentiments. In 1969 soon after he arrived in Athens, Boynton began hearing J. W. Fanning referred to as the person who "could straighten the mess out." Wherever he went, with whatever the discussion of problems—social, civic or economic—Boynton soon learned the community knew it could call on J. W. Fanning to listen and offer ideas.

Disagreements did not faze Fanning. "J. W. Fanning insisted on dealing with you as an individual, not a person with titles that afforded certain privileges," said Boynton. "He met every human being where he found them in life and worked to help them achieve the goals that were important to them."

In 1980, Boynton was selected to participate in Leadership Georgia. During that year, he got an even closer look at J. W. Fanning. "Dr. Fanning," he said, "treated every Leadership Georgia participant as a special person who warranted his time and energy in shaping ideas and formulating strategies to make Georgia a better place in which to live."

He enjoyed watching the advisor mingle with the participants. He moved around listening, answering questions and engaging in conversations. And then Boynton remembered the unusual touch Fanning had in recapping what he had heard.

"It was somewhat comical," he said, "to watch as participants presented ideas to Dr. Fanning only to have him rephrase them and make them more acceptable by saying, 'what I think I heard you say is. . . .' Of course, he went on to point out to us, without making it any issue or embarrassing us in any way, how to phrase questions and make statements in a way which did not alienate the people whom you were attempting to address."

Boynton's association with J. W. Fanning was different compared to the Leadership Georgia participants who did not live in Athens. For within Clarke County, Boynton saw Fanning's untiring work in community affairs and his church. "There are many ideas that have been attributed to great leaders of the State of Georgia that came directly from the mind of J. W. Fanning," he said. "It was not uncommon for statewide leaders to consult with Fanning before going public with their action plan."

Boynton said he thinks a line from Kipling's "If" best described J. W. Fanning—"If you can talk with crowds and keep your virtue, or walk with kings and not lose the common touch." "Dr. Fanning," he said, "felt at ease dealing with issues of race and prejudice, rich and poor, the powerful and the disenfranchised. He was never ill at ease regardless of the topic or setting.

"He believed," said Boynton, "that dealing with problems with the best interest of everyone in mind is the way to achieve the greatest potential success. J. W. Fanning planted a seed of hope in everyone he dealt with. That seed of hope opened our eyes so that we could see from a different vantage point."

Asa Boynton thought J. W. Fanning was a giant. So did Dr. Fred Harrison, dean of the College of Agriculture at Fort Valley State University.

"Dr. Fanning was a giant of a man," said Harrison. "And, by all measures, a very decent human being. His visionary influences had an impact on my life."

The two knew each other through agriculture education circles; they became friends through Leadership Georgia. "Leadership Georgia and J. W. Fanning are synonymous," said Harrison. "Had the lexicographer Webster known Dr. Fanning when he published his first iteration of his dictionary, Fanning's picture would have been published alongside the definition of leadership."

Like Boynton, Harrison was inspired by the way Fanning navigated turbulent waters. Complex issues and heated debate did not deter J. W. Fanning. And like James Lee Adams, Fred Harrison believed Fanning could "almost see around corners."

"I sincerely believe," he said, "that Dr. Fanning—like my grandfather—could accurately predict the future. He could do so by following the footsteps of budding young leaders and in a very special way, assist these individuals in discovering how to hone their God-given talents."

Leadership Georgia pondered: "Who could fill Fanning's shoes?"

In 1986, the inevitable surfaced. At age eighty-one, J. W. Fanning believed the time had come for him to step aside. Leadership Georgia was celebrating its fifteenth anniversary. He and Cora Lee promised they would always be available, but it was time to pass the torch to a new advisor.

The board of trustees conducted a successor search that eventually turned them inside the organization to an alumnus of Leadership Georgia, Dr. Dale Threadgill. Dr. Threadgill, a native of rural Alabama and a graduate of Auburn University, and his wife, Patsy, were members of the Class of 1981. He had served as a program chair, vice president and a trustee. Threadgill, like Fanning, was an agriculture professor at the University of Georgia and today serves as director of Faculty Engineering. The two men first met in 1976 at Pineland Plantation near Newton, Georgia.

At thirty-two, Threadgill was a department head at the University of Georgia and had the responsibility of seeking a $1 million grant from the Richard King Mellon Foundation to irrigated agriculture research and development in South Georgia.

He recalled, "I was told that a representative from the governor's office would join us in the session. When I entered the room at Pineland, I wondered who the 'old man' was sitting at the end of the table." Threadgill quickly learned the "old man" was J. W. Fanning, who was there negotiating on behalf of the governor.

Within no time, the young college professor learned why Fanning was in the room. "When Dr. Fanning spoke, everyone listened," he said. "It was clear J. W. Fanning understood agriculture and its needs.

He understood the state of Georgia's agenda and could speak the language of the private sector as well as the public sector."

Looking back, Threadgill said, "As Yogi Berra said, 'You can observe a lot by just watching.' I learned a lot that day. UGA was awarded the $1 million grant which was, at the time, the largest private grant ever awarded for production agriculture research in the U.S."

Fast forward five years to 1981.

Dale and Patsy walked into the banquet hall of Unicoi State Park for their first meeting of Leadership Georgia. Standing in the room was J. W. Fanning. "That was the first time that I was aware he was advisor to Leadership Georgia. I didn't really observe him doing anything during the meeting other than taking a few notes. But then at the end of the meeting, he gave a wrap-up summary."

Hundreds of Leadership Georgia participants agree, the best part of the always excellent programs was last on the agenda—Dr. Fanning's summaries. Newcomer Dale Threadgill was doubtful at first, but quickly changed his mind.

"My first thought was why do we need someone to summarize meetings. I've been here all the time," he said, "and I've heard everything said and I participated in the discussions myself. But after he had completed the summary, I realized that this had not really been just a summary, but rather an insightful analysis of the comments of both speakers and participants. It focused on the theme for the weekend's program and presented it in such a way that you felt a call to action, an urge to go out and make a difference."

Precisely the impact Pat Pattillo had envisioned back in 1970. Programs started on Thursday evening and concluded at noon on Saturday. "His summaries always brought this clearly into focus," said Threadgill. "He very effectively used quotations, both his own and those of famous people, to emphasize key points and he always injected a little humor."

The Threadgills were invited back to Leadership Georgia in 1982 to serve as program chairs for the Athens meeting: Opportunities for Leadership in Agriculture. The first thing Dale and Patsy Threadgill did was to develop a list of topics and potential speakers. Next, they drove from Tifton to Athens to visit J. W. Fanning for their first one-on-one interaction.

"As I asked questions of him, I began to realize that he wasn't answering my questions; instead he was asking questions of me or simply making a comment," said Threadgill. "He never once suggested that I should do this or that I should not do that."

What Fanning was doing was his trademark brand of mentoring. He was guiding his guest through his own thought process and letting him make up his own mind about what was best.

"As I left him," Threadgill said, "his concluding remark about the program content was, 'Fill it, but don't pack it.' He made that same remark to many other program chairs who were struggling to include too much material, too many speakers in the agenda."

In 1983, Dale Threadgill got another chance to work closely with J. W. Fanning. As vice president and member of the board of trustees, he saw the same style of leadership that Fanning exhibited in the first meeting at Pineland Plantation. And in that class was Heywood Parrish, general manager of the Mellon Family's plantation.

"When Dr. Fanning was asked for advice by the trustees or others," said Threadgill, "he didn't suggest what should be done but instead he asked questions and made comments that facilitated others in arriving at their own conclusions."

Threadgill said he was amazed at the advisor's knowledge of history, current events and issues. "In terms of breadth and depth, it was incredible," said Threadgill. "He also understood the politics of the state and nation. He could integrate all of his knowledge into ideas and approaches for addressing a broad range of problems." J. W. Fanning was also ahead of most of his generation, said Threadgill.

"He understood the value of diversity and embraced diversity long before it became the popular thing to do."

So when the board of trustees asked Threadgill to fill Fanning's shoes as the next advisor, he said, "I went straight to see Dr. Fanning. We spent a long afternoon of discussion out at Booger Hill, his farm north of Athens." Again, Threadgill was loaded with questions and eager for answers.

"I had a million questions and he really wouldn't answer any of them," said Threadgill, "but the wisdom he shared with me that afternoon has had a huge impact on my decision and my life. As we ended our discussion, I told him that I would only agree to become advisor to Leadership Georgia if he agreed to be the advisor's advisor. He agreed. He was the advisor's advisor until his death and he still is my advisor in a very special way."

In his fifteenth year as advisor, Threadgill reflected on the success of Leadership Georgia. He explained that Fanning had told him that in the early stages, the organization felt it needs an executive director. He repeatedly declined the offer to fill that type of job.

Why?

"He believed that an executive director would put his own personal stamp on the organization and it would then become the director's organization which would constrain Leadership Georgia from achieving its potential," said Threadgill.

As the fledgling organization struggled in the early years, the request was made of Fanning several times. Each time, he declined. "I strongly believe," Threadgill said, "that one of the primary reasons Leadership Georgia has succeeded beyond the wildest dreams of its founding fathers was J. W. Fanning's steadfast refusal to become its director. He recognized the value of a group of dedicated volunteers in all endeavors of Leadership Georgia."

What about Leadership Georgia's next 30 years?

If J. W. Fanning and Pat Pattillo could have one more conversation about the organization they launched in 1972, both founders would be impressed by the quality of the almost 4,000 people touched by the program. As Dave Garrett said, "Look at Georgia's Who's Who of leadership today and it's for the most part a roll call of Leadership Georgia alumni."

Fanning would be proud, but he would also be reflective. And he would have a story to express his sentiments. He especially liked the tale told by his friend, Cason Callaway of Blue Springs.

When the West Georgia cotton mill magnate sold his company, he turned his energy and money toward altruism. The 100 Better Farms for Georgia, directed by J. W. Fanning, was one of his favorite pet projects. Another was the creation of Callaway Gardens.

Fanning said Callaway was driven to transform an over-farmed, eroded area into a beautiful oasis. His vision called for a huge lake. The locals watched with curiosity and skepticism. Finally, one resident approached Callaway and said, "Mr. Cason, others have tried to dam Mountain Creek and failed. I don't think God wants Mountain Creek dammed up."

The warning did not dampen Callaway's spirits. He hired engineers to study the situation. They conducted a 100-year flood survey and advised the dam could be built. And the bulldozers started pushing earth.

When the lake filled, Callaway planted lush grain fields below the dam. He was proud of his accomplishments.

And then came the rains and more rain—a 200-year flood. There was a knock on Callaway's door. A worker said, "Mr. Cason, I think you should come and see what's happened over at the lake." Callaway got in his truck and drove over. Sure enough, the dam had burst and the flood had ravaged the fields below.

As the great Georgian stood there on the hills overlooking the disaster, he felt a tap on his shoulder. When he turned around, it was the Lord looking at him.

"Cason," God said, "I hated to do this to you . . . but I just had to."

"But why, God?" asked Callaway.

"Because you got too big for your britches."

At least fifteen classes heard J. W. Fanning chuckle as he delivered that punch line. And then he would rub his chin and add, "Well, it seems to me that is a pretty good question: are we getting too big for our britches? I think not."

As Leadership Georgia begins its second thirty years, would J. W. Fanning think the organization is getting too big for its britches?

No, it's just adapting to change and getting better.

To begin the thirty-first year, president Andy Davis passed the torch to Tavia McCuean, state director of The Nature Conservancy of Georgia, who looks ahead to the next thirty years.

"I would hope that Leadership Georgia would continue," said McCuean, "to be in a position to groom leadership for Georgia, adapting itself according to the landscape. We are in an era of great change because of technology, probably more rapid change than the last thirty years."

The key she predicts is keeping the programming in touch with Georgia's needs. "Georgia must remain competitive in this country and the world," she said. "We need dynamic leadership to do this; generating risk takers and innovators is something we should continue to try to do in our programming."

Advisor Threadgill saw a common thread in all of his discussions with Dr. Fanning. "He had a strong belief that education and leadership are the underpinnings of civilization and society," said Threadgill. "He felt that education and leadership are inseparable qualities."

Marilyn Marks recalled the conversations about the essence of Leadership Georgia. "The real impact does not occur while going through the program," she said. "Dr. Fanning and I talked about that often. You leave with the idea that there is much to be done, much I can do, and much is expected of me. You leave not with a burden but a mission to continue your best and to go about figuring out how you can leave a legacy.

"It is not a legacy of position power, but one of a personal nature. It is not a building named for you, but for people that will remember you and repeat some of your words and deeds when it is all said and done. Leadership Georgia asks you to leave a legacy. Dr. Fanning did-and he was our bridge builder.

"He helped us to begin our journey on the right foot. Now, the torch has passed to all of us and our journey continues. And along my travels, I still hear in my ear his words as he closed each summary—'May you stay alive as long as you live.'"

CHAPTER EIGHT

The J. W. Fanning Institute for Leadership

Community-leadership programs conducted by the University of Georgia and supported by Georgia Power Company bolstered the important work of Leadership Georgia. The programs—run by the Institute of Community and Area Development (ICAD)—would become the catalyst for a remarkable new force in leadership development in the state. The university, officials had decided, needed to expand its services in leadership development.

So in 1982, the university created an independent leadership development center and named ICAD's Walter A. Denero as director. Three years later, the center was renamed the J. W. Fanning Community Leadership Development Center in recognition of J. W.'s reputation as "Mr. Leadership in Georgia," his visionary contributions to the field, and his forty-three years of teaching, research, and service at his alma mater. It would be a lasting memorial to his contributions.

In 1991, public service initiatives in leadership development and training at the university were consolidated within the center, and the name was shortened to the Fanning Leadership Center. Melba G. Cooper succeeded Denero as director, and as the twenty-first century began, following further restructuring in public service and outreach, the name became the J. W. Fanning Institute for Leadership. In her decade of service, Cooper built the program from a start-up crew of a few members to a staff of fifteen. She was an eloquent and impassioned spokeswoman for J. W.'s work in leadership until her retirement at the end of 2000.

Norma Q. Reed served a dual role—program leader and interim director—as the newly named director, David P. Mills, prepared to join the institute in July 2001. She underscored the strong connection of the institute to J. W. Fanning. "Dr. Fanning believed in people; so do we," Reed said.[1] The institute's work reflects his desire to encourage all Georgians to grow and develop—not just the privileged, but also people with fewer advantages.

In case you are worried about what's going to become of the younger generation, it's going to grow up and start worrying about the younger generation.

J. W.

"Some of our most exciting work now is in inner-city neighborhoods, helping prepare people who are not usually given the chance to have a voice in community betterment," Reed said.[2] J. W.'s love for the state's rural areas is also reflected in the institute's work. With funding from the Robert Wood Johnson Foundation, the institute worked with Mercer University and the Georgia Department of Community Health in developing leadership programs for rural residents interested in improving access to health care in their communities.

For a very different audience, the institute implemented a three-year, four-phase program for the state's U. S. Department of Agriculture Rural Development staff, touching almost every one of its employees in Georgia. As its core, the institute works to expand program planning and instructional resources in local communities to strengthen their ability to provide ongoing leadership development for their citizens. Partner in these efforts include USDA, the Cooperative Extension Service, the Georgia Department of Community Affairs, and the Georgia Department of Industry, Trade, and Tourism. Dozens of traditional community, youth, and organizational clients are served annually along with new clients to keep the mix fresh."[3]

The institute's staff members had a personal relationship with J. W. Fanning. They met with him at lunch at least three times a year. In fact, Reed had set the date for his birthday celebration the week before he died. She remembered that Walt Denero would deftly ask a question of J. W. that "would set him to musing, reflecting aloud." His audience always listened to him closely. "How vital that brilliant mind was," Reed marveled. "Still in his nineties."[4]

J. W.'s legacy is the core of the institute's purpose and mission. Melba Cooper's frequent interchanges with the institute's namesake allowed her to articulate the underlying principles or tenets of his philosophy that focus the institute's efforts in organizational, community, and youth leadership. They are that: every person has leadership potential; no one person or group possesses all of the knowledge, skills, talents, and experience required of leadership today; leadership should be dispersed throughout all segments of society; leadership development is an ongoing process to maximize individual potential; leaders have a responsibility to prepare future leaders; and with leadership training comes the responsibility for action.[5]

"J. W. Fanning's legacy is the development of a culture which understands the importance of surfacing and nurturing young leaders," said Laura Meadows of Atlanta, an alumna of Leadership Georgia. "It is a culture that understands and cherishes the fact that true leaders come from all parts of the state and from all races and genders and from all socioeconomic levels."[6] Tim Maund of Augusta, who worked with J. W. in regional development, saw the culture as building a "platform for future leaders to follow so that we can expect children to be exposed to the right way to lead."[7]

Today, the Fanning Institute focuses on developing effective leaders for Georgia communities. It serves people who want to develop leadership abilities within themselves and others. The institute's emphasis is on the potential positive impact that sustained leadership-development programs can have on a community or organization. Programs address mastery of self, mastery of relationships, and mastery of action as key components of the balanced leader.

It is easy to tell when you have found a smart man.
He is going to think like you do.

J. W.

While the J. W. Fanning Institute for Leadership enjoys considerable outside support, one group in particular has been steadfast in its work: the board of directors, made up of twenty alumni of Leadership Georgia who represent all congressional districts in the state. The members include W. H. "Dink" NeSmith (chair), Dorothy Beasley, John Bell, Asa Boynton, Nancy Buntin, Ken Callaway, Melba Cooper (emeritus), Lynn Dempsey, Dave Garrett, Calvin "Hoppy" Hopkins, Maxine McNutt, Donnie Morris, Ross Pittman, W. Louis Sands, Henrietta Singletary, Zelda Tennenbaum, Lindsay Thomas, Rogers Wade, Philip Wilheit, and Gene Younts. The board was charged to review the institute's work, alert communities that need leadership training, and promote and seek support for leadership training in general. When the board was formed in 1993, the institute was housed in limited space and getting a new building was a top priority. So the board and the University of Georgia Office of Development launched a campaign to raise money for a new building that would bear J. W. Fanning's name.

They received about $1 million in private donations and pledges, and in 1998 the Georgia General Assembly appropriated $4 million.[8] The building would be a two-story, twenty thousand-square-foot structure with a state-of-the-art instructional room, boardroom, administrative and data technology areas, faculty and staff offices, a program development collaborative center, and other work and meeting areas. The funds would also build a memorial honoring the late Chappelle Matthews, who dedicated years of service to higher education as an

Athens representative in the General Assembly. Two years earlier, the university had designated a group of buildings as the Chappelle Matthews Complex, and the J. W. Fanning Building would be the first to be added to the complex.

A ground-breaking ceremony for the J. W. Fanning Building was held on August 14, 1999, at 1240 South Lumpkin Street in Athens. It would have been J. W.'s ninety-fourth birthday. Two mules, named Tag and Buck for the occasion, pulled the plow that turned the soil—a whimsical and appropriate addition honoring a man who loved to plow with mules. Gathered were administrators of the University of Georgia, faculty for leadership and community development, retirees who had worked directly with J. W., representatives of twenty-six classes of Leadership Georgia since 1972, and others who knew of and respected the quiet and influential man. The keynote speaker was a longtime friend and colleague, H. G. "Pat" Pattillo of Decatur, President of Pattillo Construction Company. Pattillo shared J. W.'s vision for leadership development and helped establish Leadership Georgia. Excerpts from his speech point out the distinctive characteristics and strengths of the man whose ideas and work would be carried on by those he had inspired:

> *Life for J. W. was an adventure* . . . One of his first adventures must have been the mystery of how a cotton seed became a cotton shirt: the wonder of it became a reality of practical ways to understand, to use, and to improve. From early days, his curiosity led him to try to know that a good seed was apt to grow a good cotton stalk. If the culls were chopped out and the weeds removed, a good stalk would make good bolls of cotton.
>
> *Life for J. W, was an opportunity* . . . You and I, and our predecessors, and ten thousand others became good cotton stalks in the beds of agriculture, of business, and of public service. . . . His

> words were energy that made healthy persons, encouraged healthy principles, sold thoughts and extra effort. One hundred fifty-nine counties in our state have opportunity from his programs, through groups he organized, or with a person that J. W. encouraged to be a leader.
>
> *Life for J. W. was a blessing* . . . And oh, how he appreciated the beginning of each day. J. W. was thankful from the heart to his God, to the complexity of nature, the divergence of thought, and for the opportunity in the state of Georgia and the United states of America. Dr. Fanning was a blessing to the University System of Georgia during its days of enormous change in the late sixties . . . Dr. Fanning was a blessing to the state of Georgia for over forty years during a transition from agriculture to a blend that includes finance and industry. By example, J. W.'s blessings became our blessings.
>
> In 1972, Dr. Fanning was looking ahead to retirement from a remarkable career at the University of Georgia. Somehow, he sensed a new adventure, a different and expanded blessing . . . It was that year, with risk and courage, with vigor and wisdom, J. W. founded Leadership Georgia . . . Among you shielded by this tent, you are the fulfillment of these dreams—no, these expectations. About ten minutes ago, I imagined J. W. saying, "Enough about the past. The future is the main thing." Certainly, it is the main reason for this magnificent facility. J. W.'s tens of thousands will become your hundreds of thousands. The adventures, the opportunities, and the blessings will reach beyond our imagination.[9]

Shortly after her retirement, Melba Cooper reflected on the impact J. W. Fanning had on her personally and on the evolution of the institute during her ten years as director:

Sparkling eyes, overly optimistic belief in people, and big dreams-this was Dr. Fanning to me. Oh how I miss those numerous afternoon chats filled with insight and wisdom! I always left Dr. Fanning's presence feeling rejuvenated and able to "take on the world," for he would convince me that I could. These were the challenging days of restructuring the institute, of opening a significantly expanded mission, of increased demands for service, and of limited resources. It was a time when neither the unit nor most of the state actually understood what leadership development could become to the University of Georgia and, even more importantly, to the state. Dr. Fanning would remind me, "But this is what leadership is all about, Melba." When asked to choose how he would like his name used in perpetuity at UGA, Dr. Fanning said leadership. "This is how I want to be remembered," he would say. After many years of working in local communities, he was convinced that leadership development was the one factor that could make the greatest difference for both individuals and communities statewide. It was with equal fervor that the Fanning Institute embraced his leadership beliefs and concepts and applied them throughout its community and youth leadership curriculum materials and instruction. During this time, the Fanning Institute attempted not only to model his leadership beliefs externally but to live them internally as an organization. This was the awesome power of Dr. Fanning's Ten Pillars of Leadership. Undeniably, this power gave the institute the capacity to be more and do more than it ever thought possible. Reflecting on the accomplishments of the J. W. Fanning Institute for Leadership, I have no doubt that Dr. Fanning's rich leadership legacy is laced throughout the organizational being of the public service and outreach unit that bears his name. Thank you, Dr. Fanning, for enriching our lives in so many ways. The humor and wit, the contagious enthusiasm and wise counsel . . . oh, how I miss those afternoon chats, Dr. Fanning.[10]

As the institute moved into its next phase, fueled by new enthusiasm and a permanent director with considerable experience, Reed saw that J. W.'s influence would continue to affect all kinds of people—grassroots leaders, emerging and established leaders, young people, educators, and others throughout the state. "The future is so bright," she said.[11]

I have loved few men in my lifetime as much as I loved J. W. Fanning. To me he is not dead, gone forever. His spirit lives on in the memories of dozens of people like me whose lives he profoundly touched. As I write this, it is as if he were still in Athens and I in Auburn and I am about to write him a letter or go there to see him. I can recall his face and watch his eyes light up as he greets me. I can see the movement of his hands as he makes a point, the half-grin as well as his more serious expressions. And best of all, when I have a problem or idea I would like to talk over with him, I know with considerable clarity the kind of advice he would give me. That comes from over thirty-five years of being associated with him.

GENE A. BRAMLETT,
University of Georgia colleague

Nobody I know better lived their motto than J. W., which was "Stay Alive As Long As You Live."

JOEL GIDDENS,
next-door neighbor

Life is very short and very uncertain; let us spend it as well as we can.

J. W.

Epilogue

All my life I carried a secret longing
to be just a plain dirt farmer, one who makes his living
from the land.

J. W.

J. W. Fanning's feet were planted firmly in the rich, red Georgia soil, when the hot sun beat down so hard that the air shimmered before him. His family's Wilkes County farm in the early 1900s provided fertile ground for dreaming. He sometimes ached for the farm life he left, but he found a way to participate in the growth of people and communities.

In his own quiet way, J. W. Fanning achieved greatness, which he believed comprised three elements: the desire to excel, the ability to accept change, and a genuine concern for one's fellow beings. A cornerstone of his thinking was that development—of communities and human beings—is an unending process that requires catalysts in order to achieve movement from existing plateaus to those a level above, just out of reach. These insights, and his Ten Pillars of Leadership, have withstood the test of time. They are likely to endure.

It is inconceivable that John William Fanning Sr. will be all but forgotten in a few more years. His legacy will survive the rapid rush of time passing, not only because of the tangible structures and programs named for him and the annual awards given in his honor. Perhaps even more important are the intangibles: warm, personal remembrances of J. W. in the minds of so many Georgians in whom he planted fertile ideas and gave encouragement. Traces of J. W.'s impact on people remain: in the stories, told with profound respect, admiration, and even love; in the cherished letters, framed and hung on office walls; and in the illogical but compelling sense that he will somehow turn the corner on an Athens street and appear, armed with a humorous one-liner and the ever-present kind word.

Maturity is knowing that security is not how much you can get, but how much you can do without.

J. W.

His professional mark on the state was significant. His programs succeed him: the Fanning Institute for Leadership, and the community and regional development work at the Vinson Institute of Government, which he created, at the University of Georgia; and Leadership Georgia, conducted through the Georgia Chamber of Commerce. Two monuments were erected: one, the Fanning Building at the First Baptist Church in Athens, honors J. W. and his wife, Cora Lee; the other, the J. W. Fanning Building on the University of Georgia campus on South Lumpkin Street, celebrates J. W. the catalyst. Both structures stand as constant reminders of the Fannings' accomplishments and of J. W.'s integrity, wisdom, and service to others.

No less important are annual honors associated with him: the J. W. Fanning Lecture Series, conducted by the Department of Agricultural Economics at the university; the J. W. Fanning Award, given by Leadership Georgia; and the J. W. Fanning Humanitarian Award, granted by Athens Regional Medical Foundation and the Athens community. J. W. was about improving the quality of life for all people; the awards recognize those who follow in his footsteps.

Personally, he was loved by a diverse group of people. He was a friend's friend and a loyal and wise confidant. He was a fine companion for hiking a foothill, singing a song, digging a ditch, attending a play, visiting a cathedral, traveling across Georgia, plowing Piedmont soil with a red mule named Buck—or examining a complicated economic theory. J. W. talked to people with respect and interest—regardless of their gender, color, socioeconomic class, or political power. He was quick with a quiet word of praise, and he helped others find a way to discover their own strengths. To know J. W. Fanning was to enhance your life.

Life is a confrontation
between circumstances and character.

J. W.

Will Georgia ever produce another leader with as much depth, influence, and vision as J. W. Fanning? The state needs such a catalyst as it enters the twenty-first century. During J. W.'s lifetime, the cracker state moved from being a backwater of the South to being the fastest-growing region of the country. Georgia could use J. W.'s instinctive ability to unravel complex situations into discrete, manageable elements that, once identified, could be understood.

More important, perhaps, Georgia could use J. W.'s charismatic yet simple belief in others. He was a man to whom others were attracted; once they walked beside him, they were constantly challenged to go the second mile. They were made to believe they could. Finally, J. W.'s goodness was infectious. Grounded in a religious environment that enabled him to develop his own spirituality, J. W. never wavered in his beliefs and values. He never forgot selling Bibles to the poorest families in South Alabama; the experience taught him what was truly useful and needed in life.

He found inspiration, also, from his rock-solid family, particularly in the determination of his brother, Wootten. The brothers stayed close after their beginnings at the family farm. There they both dreamed. J. W. held tenaciously to his vision: a Georgia that would be infinitely better than the one he knew as a boy. During his life's journey, he gathered around him, from the four corners of the state, disciples of that dream. Together they hammered out a new community of cities and counties enriched by people who made too much progress ever to turn back.

APPENDIX A

Three Eulogies

The first of the eulogies reprinted below was written by the Reverend Jon Appleton, pastor of the First Baptist Church of Athens, and delivered by him at J. W.'s funeral on July 30, 1997. The second, written by Dink NeSmith, was published in the *Press Sentinel* on July 30, 1997. It is a tribute to the life of J. W. The third, which eulogizes Cora Lee Fanning, was also written by Dink NeSmith and appeared in the *Athens Daily News/Athens Banner-Herald* on January 1, 1993.

Funeral Eulogy for J. W. Fanning

THE REVEREND JON APPLETON

He was " . . . like a tree planted by the streams of water,
which yielded its fruit in its season,
and the leaves will not wither.
. . . the Lord watched . . ." (Psalm 1:3, 6)

J. W.'s days.

J. W. was the precedent epitome of Scott Peck's "road less traveled," echoing the poetical genius of Robert Frost:

"Two roads diverged in a wood, and I—
I took the one less traveled by,
And that . . . made all the difference."
The vision of the prophet Isaiah foresaw heroes
for the people who possess a land—
bereft of economy,

dismantled by war's fury,
depleted by constant overuse,
wasted by famine's depravity,
ravaged by flood's inundations,
pillaged by the blights of locusts.
Amid the travesty, suffering and agony in such a land,
the heroes are to arise to sing melodies of expectancy
and to lift the wary people
toward God's wondrous provision.
Listen to Isaiah:
"Enlarge the size of your tent,
and let the curtain of your habitation be stretched out;
do not hold back;
lengthen your cords;
strengthen your stakes.
For, you will spread out to the right and to the left,
and your descendants will possess the land,
and will establish from desolation . . ." (54:2–3),
the land fertile to farm; the village centers in which to gather;
the towns teeming for trade, the cities alive for commerce.
This vision, twenty-eight centuries young,
has been a boon for generations, ancient and recent.
Many have been the hero voices, raising people strapped by inequities,
leveled by plagues,
despondent in poverty.
In mid-twentieth century Georgia
such a hero traversed this state—
from the Hills of Rabun to the wiregrass of Donalsonville,
from the marshes of Glynn to the headwaters of the Etowah.
He came not with trumpet sound,
nor by legislative decree;

but, out of the university's astuteness and his own awareness
of what had been,
was
and could become.
He came with ears, to every county seat,
assembling farmers and bankers,
merchants and landholders,
the whites and the blacks,
the rich and the poor;
rural Georgia and urban Georgia;
not so much, to give direction,
but to create a forum in which his questions
incited the awareness of common identity
and communal necessity.
He came with a voice to encourage all voices
to declare their thoughts;
and, he came with a genius, urging the people
to declare what before, they had not known they could say.
He came with gumption,
compelling Georgians to enlarge their tent sites,
lengthen their cords,
strengthen their stakes.
And Georgians have!
We could be pridefully possessive of our hero;
however, his vision, call, ministry and gumption
were not to be self-contained, just for us.
His savvy and gracious demeanor moved others,
across the nation and into international arenas,
to sing his praise,
to follow his steps,
to look beyond.

Our hero, J. W., who was so humbly audacious,
has brought us to the portal of the twenty-first
century, having encouraged an ensuing leadership
who will, indeed, spread far and wide,
inclusive of all dimensional persuasions,
so that our descendants will possess this land
accountable to potentiality,
with ears to listen,
with eyes to see,
with gumption to dare.
Some would claim this as a fearful day.
Our hero lies dead!
The question is raised—
"Who will take the hero's place?"
In the tradition of our hero, he would answer:
"Did you not hear me?
My time has been spent,
my season is awash in the out-tide.
It is not to be one who must step forward to take my place.
No! No!
It is the time, a season anew,
simply for others, each to take his or her place.
You would not honor me by imitation;
my place is dated,
yours is yet to be.
You will honor me by being who you are."
That is a mentor's calling—
not to fashion robots, but to encourage
singularity.
Losing him as we do is a test of the spirit:
Yes, we will miss his being, but not his presence;

his words, but not his inspiration;
his calm, but not his peace;
his vision, but not his indomitable spirit;
his hope, but not his faith;
his availing love, but not his joy.
Our loss takes a selfish turn
should we too despair;
our loss takes an eternal turn
should we trust the mercy of God.
For this church, this community,
the university, the state of Georgia and beyond—
I am honored to address our hero's family:
Thank you for your daddy, grandfather, great-grandfather.
It cost you dearly, in that we so often called him
away from you.
We came to depend upon him—
requiring his time, counsel and attention,
when you needed him for the same reasons.
Together, we caught him between presence and absence—
for as great as he was,
he could only be in one place at a time.
That really was a burden for him
and he spoke of this, in reflection, as a great loss—
his absences from you.
However, in his parenting of you, you must understand.
He was also a parent for us—
therefore, we know how you felt, when he was away,
for we felt the same, ourselves.
Your daddy, our hero, was
a parent's answer to prayer;
a brother of affectionate care;

a husband in union with your mother, Cora Lee,
in and of herself a heroine of endless energy,
salty advice,
and consummate love;
a father to you, proud, expectant, available, loving;
a grandfather of considerable pride;
a great-grandfather of wonder;
a friend, whenever, for whatever;
a man, gentle, genteel, generous.
And, the wonder of you is that you knew all of this
about your dad, our hero; and, you were found
in him, among all his honors, to be his most
cherished joy.
Thank you—!
A final note of infinite worth—how come?
How comes to be such a son, husband, father?
How comes to be such a hero, tree, road-traveler, mentor?
This response: John William Fanning Sr., with all
his concerns, wisdom and counsel
relative to the things of this world,
was first and foremost a spiritual
man, one of faith, of hope, of love.
This most human man of uncommon
gifts was spiritually alive, with exceeding, great joy.
Benediction: Lord,
Our tears bespeak our sorrow.
Lord,
Our laughter will bespeak our joy.

As a "Teacher, Preacher and Farmer," J. W. Fanning Left a Legacy of Leadership

DINK NESMITH

Since Sunday, Georgia has been awash in tears.

Because Dr. J. W. Fanning is gone, there are tears of sadness.

Because he died at home in his sleep, there are tears of thanksgiving.

Because he enriched so many lives, there are tears of celebration.

Because he is now back in the arms of his beloved wife, there are tears of joy.

Cora Lee died on their 61st anniversary in 1992. Lately, J. W. had been dreaming about his bride. And now, I can hear that lovable, sassy lady saying, "J. William, what took you so long? I've been missing you. You're still the most handsome man I ever saw. Come on, I want to show you something I've been working on. J. William, you're gonna love heaven."

J. W. and Cora Lee Fanning came into my family's life in 1983.

Pam and I were asked to participate in Leadership Georgia. Our bond began at the first meeting on a brisk January day. We spotted J. W. and Cora Lee walking hand-in-hand on their way back from Anna Ruby Falls at Unicoi State Park. We offered them a ride and before we reached the lodge on the hill, we became friends forever.

They came to see us in Jesup. We visited them. When we moved to Athens in 1990, they made certain we were happy in our new home. Our children, Alan, Emily, and Eric, adopted the Fannings as the great-grandparents they would never have known.

I cannot imagine the past 14 years without the Fanning impact on our lives.

J. W. reminded me often, "Words are the only thing that live forever." He encouraged me to write. He challenged me to read. He wanted me to slow down. He admonished me to listen.

"Listen for the answers to these three questions," he said:

"1. What are Georgia's people saying?

"2. What are Georgia's people not saying?

"3. What are Georgia's people wanting to say and cannot?"

God gave us a gifted listener and leader in J. W. Fanning. In his humble, quiet way he knew the right questions to ask. He inspired you to reach deep into your soul and sift through your thoughts.

He blushed when you bragged on his wisdom and vision. Still, he could not escape General George Marshall's description of a leader: "a person who influences you to do better than you thought you could."

I cannot envision Georgia without his influence.

This year marks the 25th anniversary of Leadership Georgia. Thousands of men and women across this state have benefitted from the legacy begun by J. W. Fanning and Pat Pattillo. The distinguished results are epitomized in Sam Nunn. Driving home from the very first meeting of Leadership Georgia, Sam decided to run for the United States Senate.

Ask scores of leaders, "Who is your mentor?" Their response will be the same as Sam Nunn's: "Dr. J. W. Fanning."

When J. W. Fanning spoke, Georgia listened.

Often we heard his advice, "May you stay alive as long as you live."

J. W. Fanning did more than just preach that motto. For 91 years, 11 months and 27 days, he embraced it.

When J. W. Fanning was a boy growing up in Wilkes County, his father wanted him to be a teacher. His mother hoped he would be a preacher. His dream was to be a farmer. Before he died, the retired vice president of the University of Georgia mastered all three.

A prized pastime was to ramble the back roads with J. W. Fanning. He was a stranger to nowhere and had a story for everywhere.

Once we were driving back from Washington where he had just

spoken to his hometown Kiwanis Club. He said, "One of my favorite memories as a boy was riding in the mule wagon from Tyrone to the cotton gin. On the way back, I would sit on the tailgate, drink a Coke, eat a tea cake and drag my feet in the dusty road. I never had a worry, because the mules knew the way back home."

Many have asked me, "Why in the world did you want to be a mule farmer?" J. W. Fanning gave me the idea. Last fall, I hitched up Ruby and Rose. Together, we sat on the tailgate as Smith Wilson drove us around my farm.

"There's a lot of things that have come along in my life that I didn't always understand," he said. "But I can relate to these mules."

This fall, we were planning a Leadership Georgia Cotton Pickin' Day. The J. W. Fanning Patch was planted and he wrote me regularly to say, "I'm praying for you . . . and your mules."

I had invited some past presidents of Leadership Georgia and their families. The thought of J. W. Fanning's missing the fun made me want to cry.

But then I remembered.

Not only will J. W. be there. Cora Lee will be, too.

I can't wait for us to look up and listen for their laughter.

And that will make us shed more tears of joy.

Cora Lee Fanning Made Her Mark!

DINK NESMITH

How long has it rained? Most would have reported, "Forty days and 40 nights." On December 24, the clouds parted and a clear blue sky beckoned the arrival of Christmas Eve in Athens.

Happenstance? Not hardly if you knew Mrs. J. W. Fanning. She insisted you call her Cora Lee. The minute she arrived in heaven, she made a request, "St. Peter, I am glad to be here, but you need to talk to the Lord. I don't want my funeral to be on a rainy day. Please have Him send some sunshine."

Since May 29, 1905, this spunky lady spread her own brand of sunshine. Make no mistake, Cora Lee could cause thunder and lightning too. Her feisty nature was just as notorious as her hugs and kisses. She showered her family and friends with affection. With equal vigor, she unabashedly let you know where she stood.

Perhaps her preferred stance was by the side of her husband of 61 years, J. William. She was his constant companion hooking her hand around his arm. Dr. J. W. Fanning, retired vice president of the University of Georgia, is a legendary statesman and leader. His vision has enhanced the quality of life in all 159 counties. Cora Lee was evidence that if a good man is lucky, there is a great woman in his life, too. Together, the Fannings were a remarkable team and one of Georgia's most respected couples.

In 1983, we met the Fannings through Leadership Georgia. Two years later when I was asked to serve as president, it was Cora Lee and J. W. to whom I turned for guidance and counsel. Our friendship became an adopted kinship. For a decade, Pam, Alan, Emily, Eric, and I have basked in the warmth of a wonderful relationship with the Fannings.

J. W. Fanning is the person who made Pat Pattillo's dream of Leadership Georgia come true. Since 1972, almost 4,000 men and women have nurtured themselves and their communities, seeking the answers to three questions often asked by Dr. Fanning: 1. What are Georgians saying? 2. What are Georgians not saying? 3. What are Georgians wanting to say, but cannot?

Today, Leadership Georgia is America's flagship program of its kind. One significant reason Leadership Georgia has endured is a demand made by Cora Lee. In the early days, women were not as involved. The wives stayed home. That bothered Cora Lee, so she stood up at a meeting, put her finger on the problem, and espoused her views. She said, "It is time the wives got involved and we had more women participants." She did not sit down or hush until change was assured. Ever since, women have played a key role in shaping the future of Leadership Georgia.

"There was little arguing with Cora Lee. When she made up her mind, that was it. Plain and simple. Many times, I would say, 'Okay, Cora Lee, you have heard my last objection . . . now just tell me what you want to do' and we would go ahead and get it done." recalled her husband.

A good example was her devotion to the "Dawgs." If they were in the Sanford Stadium, she was going to be there. Dr. Fanning tried to keep her from going to the Georgia Tech game. The cold night air would not be good for her. "Just get my warmest coat, J. William," she said heading for the door.

Growing up on a southeast Georgia farm, she quipped, "Mamma and Pappa had just us three girls, so I had to be Pappa's boy." She died believing if you went to bed without being weary-to-the-bone tired, you were sinning.

Cora Lee loved her family, church, university, community, and friends. She also loved her Madison County farm that she insisted they buy 27 years ago. Her children, Bill and Sibyle, are certain she rearranged every rock on the 75 acres. With the help of her family and "volunteers," she transformed the Booger Hill Road retreat into a miniature kissing cousin to Callaway Gardens. The stone cottage with its mammoth fireplace, the exposed log beams, the picnic shelter overlooking the lake, and every other inch were designed to her exact specifications.

Once Dr. Fanning planted the meadow by the lake in pines without telling Cora Lee. On her next trip, she promptly pulled up every seedling. She saved two to transplant in their backyard on Parkway Drive.

"I don't want to mess up the view when you are driving into Booger Hill," she announced. When the thousands of mountain laurels and azaleas bloom each year, they will be a floral memorial to one who adored nature's beauty.

That was the lady loved by thousands. John Wayne starred in the movie, "True Grit." Cora Lee could have taught the Duke a lesson or two about grit. Despite failing health, her pace never slowed. The night before she died, she was stirring in the kitchen. She was determined to host one more holiday party.

When the ambulance arrived the next morning, the guest list and menu were on her bedside table. In the refrigerator was a freshly made family favorite, a "soggy" coconut cake.

She only knew two speeds: wide open and off. Cora Lee drew her last breath churning to make this another memorable Christmas for family and friends. That is the only way she would have had it.

None of us were ready to say "good-bye." Nonetheless, she leaves a legacy of Cora Lee anecdotes that will keep us loving her and laughing forever. Cora Lee Fanning used every moment of her 87 years to make this world a better place.

Now, she has another challenge. I know she already has her sleeves rolled up and ready to go to work in heaven. I can hear her saying, "Lord, I sure do thank you for the sunshine during my funeral. Now, do you reckon you could tell St. Peter to get me some soap and water? I want to polish up those Pearly Gates."

APPENDIX B

Selected Honors and Awards

J.W. Fanning received numerous honors and awards for his contributions to his community and profession. Following is a partial list of these recognitions.

Alpha Zeta Proficiency Medal. Gold medal on chain, Alpha Zeta honor fraternity, 1924.

Man of the Year in Service to Georgia Agriculture. *The Progressive Farmer Magazine,* December 31, 1960.

1963 Key Citizen Award. Georgia Municipal Association, June 21, 1964.

The degree Doctor of Laws. Mercer University, August 15, 1969.

Lay Award. Georgia Recreation and Park Society, November 17, 1969.

Award for outstanding service as president of the Georgia Planning Association, 1970–71. Georgia Planning Association, Inc.

Award in adult education. Georgia Adult Education Council, May 12, 1971.

Service Award, "For more than 10 years of service to Georgia Agriculture." Georgia Development Authority, July 21, 1971.

Award of Merit. College of Business Administration, University of Georgia, 1971.

Silver Beaver award for distinguished service. Boy Scouts of America, February 28, 1972.

Great Georgian Award. Georgia Chamber of Commerce, April 7, 1972.

Special Alumni/Faculty Service Award. University of Georgia Alumni Society, April 15, 1972.

"God's servant. Master of little words, with deep real meaning. Your friends, The J.P. Morris Families." Morris family, 1972

Great Athenian Award. Athens Chamber of Commerce, January 23, 1973

Distinguished Service Award. Northeast Georgia Area Planning and Development Commission, 1974.

Georgia Development Service Award, for more than 15 years of loyal and devoted service to Georgia Agriculture. Georgia Development Authority, June 25, 1975.

Award for more than ten years of service to the Forum Sunday School Class. First Baptist Church, August 14, 1975.

Blue Key Award for outstanding service to the University of Georgia. Georgia Chapter of the Blue Key National Honor Fraternity, October 15, 1976.

J. W. Fanning Day proclamation. State of Georgia (presented by Governor George Busbee), May 1977.

Aghon Award for aid to worthy students. University of Georgia College of Agriculture, School of Forestry, and College of Veterinary Medicine.

Distinguished Service Award. Georgia Society of Farm Managers and Rural Appraisers.

Award for National Service to Regional Councils, for pioneer efforts to develop regional councils in Georgia.

Recognition for outstanding service. Soil Conservation Districts Program in Georgia.

APPENDIX C

Selected Speeches Delivered by J. W. Fanning

During his lifetime J. W. Fanning gave hundreds of speeches, through which he conveyed his aspirations and dreams for a better Georgia. The four reproduced in this appendix were given to audiences of different interests.

The first speech was delivered to the Cotton Producers Association (now Gold Kist, Inc.), which had asked him to address the annual meeting of its membership in 1965. The purpose of the speech was to envision the characteristics of agriculture ten years hence.

The second reflects J. W.'s interest in leadership development. The city of Athens, Georgia, conducts a leadership training program for emerging leaders annually. J. W. was asked to give the kickoff speech for the 1988–89 participants.

In the third speech J. W. challenged his audience to consider the concept of regionalism as an opportunity for economic progress and development.

The movement to establish Area Planning and Development Commissions (now Regional Development Centers) throughout the state of Georgia occurred in the 1960s, and counties were grouped regionally according to similar economic and geographic characteristics. Meetings were held in each region, with J. W. leading the discussions to help the local citizens grapple with the concept of counties working together for common good. It was largely through his persuasiveness, region by region, that the movement succeeded. The remarks reproduced here were delivered in the West Central Georgia Region.

J. W. served as the advisor of the Leadership Georgia program from 1972 to 1986. When he handed this responsibility to Dale Threadgill, the Leadership Georgia family honored him at a reception and dinner at the Waverly Hotel in Atlanta. His address to the gathering that evening is the fourth and final speech reprinted in this appendix.

Agriculture in 1975

COTTON PRODUCERS ASSOCIATION, NOVEMBER 23, 1965

I am highly honored to be among this distinguished group and to appear on the program of the Cotton Producers Association.

There is an old house about ten miles from Athens standing on a hill facing south.

This old house was constructed in 1801—164 years ago.

It stands strong and erect and seems to blend into the hills like it means to be around for another 164 years.

This old house was the home of a man who owned 10,000 acres of land with 1,000 head of cattle and 500 head of sheep.

It has survived five wars including the war between the states.

The great depressions of 1873, 1892, and 1932, to say nothing of five-cent cotton in 1914, have come and gone.

But the old house stands.

It has been a part of prosperity and depression, inflation and deflation, argument and quiet conversation, joy and sorrow, war and peace.

Yet the old house stands.

But all around the house has changed.

People have come and gone—and now they seem to have gone never to return.

The mules which once pulled the plows have gone on to mule heaven.

And giant mechanical monsters—coldly impersonal—have come to take their place.

I guess the old house often wonders about all the change and ponders the way of mankind in the 1960s as compared to the 1860s.

I talked to a man a few days ago who is 87 years of age—and spry enough to play nine holes of golf every day.

He and I talked about his life and how interesting it has been.

And we both remarked that probably no other generation within the history of mankind had seen or would ever see the contrasts that he had seen in his lifetime.

He grew up with oxen as the source of power,

Yet today he turns on his TV and observes a rocket of many tons hurled hundreds of miles into space.

All in one lifetime has this happened.

Actually you and I have observed miracles, actually we have performed miracles—all the time saying we did not believe in miracles.

Have you ever watched an electric light come on where only darkness existed—a miracle.

Or a bale of cotton produced per acre?

Even 45 bushels of corn per acre in Georgia.

One man tending 100 acres of cotton.

5,000 food items in one store to select from.

A giant cooperative grow from a net worth of $2,100 to more than $30,000,000 in just 30 years.

Miracles—sure—this is the age of miracles.

And you and I haven't seen anything yet.

The greatest of all miracles is a nation feeding itself well with only 7 percent of its labor force engaged in basic raw product production.

This is fantastic—a story much of the world refuses to believe—yet true.

Change is truly the order of the day

New knowledge
New technology
Increasing efficiency
Narrower margins
Shifting market demand
Shifting cost structures
Big gets bigger
The simple gives way to the complex
Agriculture finds itself in a great, big, changing world.
A world of bigness
A world of complexity
A world of intense competition
A world of unparalleled government activity
A world of dependence upon each other—yet a world of conflict
A world that cries out for understanding

Now we peel eyes to the future—wondering what will come next—and how we will handle it when it comes.

May I suggest to you at least eight characteristics of the Agriculture of 1975.

1. Managing money and machines will be more demanding.
Dollars and machines will plague the daylights out of farmers.
The right place for the right dollar will cause head-scratching.
The right machine for the right job will require figuring.
Busy dollars and busy machines will test the managerial skills of the farmer.

2. Science will press harder for understanding.
The formula has come to the farm
The balanced feed
The balanced fertilizer
The correct pesticide
The vigor of the hybrid

To know and understand the correct formula is fast becoming more important than how to plow a straight furrow.

The answer by computer is no longer a laughing matter.

Neither are the profits by science rather than art to be laughed off.

The "what" will come to outrank the "how."

3. Farmers will follow their dollars to town in greater numbers.

Bird-dogging their dollars will become the normal practice of farmers.

Farmers used to brag about their city cousins and go to town to see them.

It's not people farmers are sending to town now.

But dollars . . .

And farmers will follow those dollars with more interest and concern than they did their cousins.

One billion dollars leaving Georgia farms become four billion in town.

That productiveness deserves more attention at the place of productiveness—and will get it.

Those $500,000,000 Georgia farmers spend in towns for goods will be investigated at the source.

4. The world will become the farmer's market place.

The cotton farmer of the Old South looked around the world for his market,

And so will the cotton and all other farmers in 1975.

D. W. Brooks is leading them to this point of view and effort.

He has done more to stir the natural competitive instincts of the farmer for a market for his product than any other man.

The private enterprise system does not give or guarantee a market.

It simply provides the freedom and opportunity and motivation to go and get your market,

And that market for food and fiber is anywhere in the world where a demand exists.

There the American farmer and his representative will go.

"Gold Kist," guard of a great, private enterprise institution is in the vanguard—and will stay there.

5. Cooperatives will grow stronger and more influential.

Organization will increasingly become a way of life for the U.S. farmer—and that includes the Georgia farmer.

Through organization will the farmers of 1975 search for solutions that in years past they have delegated to government.

Farmers will increasingly feel an economic relationship with and dependency upon their cooperatives.

Farmers will peel their eyes across the years and consider the career of managing a cooperative one of the chosen positions—and one for which there must be preparation.

Cooperatives will become increasingly honored among the great American business institutions whose counsel and influence are sought.

For cooperatives will grow big without losing the common touch,

And serve a cause that must be served.

The young farmer and his pretty wife and five children of 1975 will be a great American businessman—large yet small—who will be both student and practitioner of organization.

6. U.S. farmers will tote a bigger world load.

The real problem of the world is slowly but surely coming into clearer focus.

Man must have good food—or else he dies.

For most of the world the rate of population increase is faster than the rate of food production increase.

This will eventually lead to chaos.

There either must be fewer people or more food.

There will not be fewer people in the foreseeable future.

Sure the rate of increase in the number of people may slow down,

But not the total world population—and especially among the most underdeveloped nations of the world.

In this country food production is running at a rate faster than population.

We are in a favored position,

But this very favored position brings a world responsibility we cannot shun,

For if we do, we will leave to our children and their children an unbearable burden of tragic consequences.

So to the U.S. farmer we look for the answer,

And on his shoulders place a bigger world load,

Which is to provide food where there is dire hunger,

And to extend his skills to those who don't know how to feed themselves much above starvation levels.

Truly this is a big job.

7. Farmers will get deeper in politics.

There is no one on the face of the globe who believes stronger in democratic government than the farmer.

No one feels the need for a government providing the basic opportunities for growth more than does the farmer.

No one is more social minded without being a Socialist than the U.S. farmer.

No one believes more strongly in sound local government than does the farmer,

And to achieve desirable goals and live by their beliefs, farmers must study government, become knowledgeable in the art of government and engage in the politics of democratic government.

Sure, more farmers will become practitioners in holding office in government,

And this will be good.

But I am talking about something else.

I speak of activity in influencing the passage of legislation by the councils and legislatures and the Congress.

And the formulation of administrative regulations and procedures,

And the operations of government at all levels.

The farmer can no longer depend upon his vote alone to influence government.

He must look to organization,

And participation on commissions and authorities,

And study and the application of skill in politics.

The farmer of 1975 will be much farther down this road than we are today.

And it will be good.

8. The Faith of our Fathers will rest more heavily upon the shoulders of the farm family.

I am sure there is inherent virtue in urbanization,

But I am doubly sure there is virtue in the soil and the open country and a fireside out alone under the stars.

When a man wants to think, he tries to go where there is quietness and serenity and an environment that brings a sense of closeness to his God.

The Faith of our Fathers carved out a great nation dedicated to certain great principles—and based upon certain great moral and spiritual values.

Those principles and values grew out of a closeness to the soil and a quietness and serenity and a challenge that have already produced great independence of the spirit and strong and moral fiber and driving determination.

Upon the relatively few people who will tend our lands in 1975, this nation will look more and more for an expression through word and action that the Faith of our Fathers still lives and proposes to move this nation ever forward as a land of the free and a home of the brave.

The U.S. farmer will stand in 1975, as he does today, in a world of mixed emotions and frustrations, as a living demonstration of the accomplishment of a good life which freedom brings to a people who are willing to assume its privileges as responsible men and women.

Leadership Athens Kickoff

HIGHLANDS COUNTRY CLUB, AUGUST 16, 1988

I am glad to be here.

1. A Mother said to her 20 year-old daughter, "I don't want to be liberated." The daughter said, "I don't want to be liberated either at least not until I know how it feels to be captured."

I like being captured by you for it feels so good.

You are a very special group of wonderful people.

You are not here to study the skills of leadership, for you have demonstrated your skills in leading.

You are here to get to know each other better and to study and discuss and come to a better understanding of the opportunities and challenges calling for effective leadership to make the good community better.

General George Marshall once said that "A leader is a person who exerts all influence and gets people to want to do more than they would."

You have demonstrated your concern for your community—and your desire to make it better.

2. On Leadership Athens, you are embarking on a very delightful and fruitful journey.

A journey of new experiences

New friendships

Broader associated relationships

Examination of crucial issues—economic, social, political, educational, etc.

Embrace new ideas—a broader vision
Becoming more sensitive to your leadership responsibilities.

3. "Things aren't like they used to be—and never wuz."
We are encountering wonders in our way of life. "Life is now in session. Are you present?"

4. Leaders in our kind of society are amateurs.
Not born to lead in all aristocracy
Not born to dictate as in a totalitarian society
But born to lead for the love of it.

5. In our society, leadership is widely dispersed.
A president
A congress—wide representation
A state government—wide representation
City and county government
Boards
Commissions
Committees
Volunteer groups

6. Never, never say no to any opportunity to exert your influence
Public office
Appointed office—Board of Commissioners
Committees

7. "Why don't somebody do something" Then I realized that I am somebody.

8. "Blessed is he who has learned to admire but not envy, to follow

but not imitate, to praise but not flatter, and to lead but not manipulate."

9. The American Dream is called the newest thing in the history of nations.

I have the opportunity to attain my full potential—and my government honors the individual and opens the doors of opportunity.

10. You will help build a new Athens within a future that will be exciting, demanding, fearsome, and challenging.

11. Stay involved—stay sharp—stay concerned. Exert a noble influence—help people to build a new Athens

"A leader is best when people barely know he exists,
Not so good when people obey and acclaim him,
Worse where they despise him,
But of a good leader who talks little
When his work is done
His aim fulfilled,
They will say,
"We did it ourselves."

12. Old Job of the Bible said:

"Where he has tried me, I shall come forth as gold."
You, too, will be tried as leaders
But in the end, you shall come forth as gold.
"May you stay alive as long as you live."

Challenge to an Area Planning and Development Commission

ELLAVILLE, GEORGIA, CA. 1963

You have created a Commission with representatives from each county to get on with the job of building a plan for development of this great region, providing the framework of a regional plan for growth and progress and development—a plan for backing up the front-line agencies and organizations actively promoting and securing industrial and agricultural and business growth—those ingredients of economic progress.

You are doing a work that must be done for West Central Georgia for this region to be numbered among the choice and most desired areas of America.

A work that will ensure it's being pointed to as the area in which to locate and prosper.

For it to be singled out as a community of eight counties that is balancing agriculture with industry—rural with urban—good living with jobs—beauty of landscape with income.

Yes, you are building a new community—one that must be built—one that will require a lot of sweat to build—but you are on your way.

Abraham Lincoln said, "I will study and get ready and perhaps my time will come." You too can make this statement.

Sure you have work to do on the new community but . . .

1. You Have Work to Do at Home Also

Back home is your rural-urban community within the boundaries of your county and city limits.

You want to develop—to go forward—to stir economic activity.

And this takes work—

Because economic activity goes along with . . .

Sound and efficient government
Top quality education
Attractiveness
Adequate housing
Recreation
Transportation arteries
Community planning
And a host of other essentials.

These come with hard work.

And the right kind of help from those who can assist.

The staff of your Area Planning and Development Commission stands ready to help with this job also.

For while the Commission is striving to put together the big picture of potentials for the region and striving to get the new community on its way, it also has the responsibility to assist your individual communities, set up plans for sound and progressive development and carry them out.

Here is a partnership you can't lick for getting a job of economic development done.

So, that is my reason for saying that.

2. Cooperation Is the Key to Your Success

Never has economic growth depended so much upon the continuing work and cooperation of so many people, groups and organizations.

That's what area development is for.

To set goals.

To stimulate growth.

To motivate action.

To solve tough problems which the individual community can't solve—but which must be solved before the individual community can move forward as it should.

To create an image of progress that ongoing folks want to be associated with.

These jobs require cooperation . . .

Between Boards of County Commissioners.

Between Mayors and City Councils.

Between City and County governments.

Between Chambers of Commerce.

Between Industrial Development Corporations.

Between Civic Organizations, Clubs and Groups.

Between School Boards and Superintendents.

Between Rural and Urban groups.

Between Farmers and Businessmen.

Between your Members of the State Legislature.

Between your Area and State Government.

Yes, cooperation is the key.

And may I say with all possible emphasis that the kind of cooperation you are establishing and stimulating between and in these eight counties to create this new community and strengthen your individual communities is the most powerful force yet turned loose in Georgia for the development of one of the great sections of America.

A section that belongs to you.

A section that can be made whatever you wish it to be.

A section with growth potentials beyond the comprehension of most of us.

A section that must feed upon cooperation for its growth.

3. You Are Asking Much of Your Board of Directors

You have a unique organization.

You have a Board of Directors with a charge to plan and bring about development in the big community and in each of the counties and municipalities.

Each Director has been honored by appointment from either a city government or a county government.

Nowhere in America is there a better example of city-county government cooperation in planning and development.

And with the support of your state government, a three-way team approach is created.

Directors have a great responsibility.

One which they cannot hand to anyone.

Not even to the executive director and his staff as employees.

Directors are policy makers.

Directors are supporters.

Directors are guides in operations.

Directors are the "spike" that makes the punch taste good.

Directors are the strategists who figure the roads to travel for maximum returns.

It is a big job, sure.

But big men have been appointed to handle the big job.

May I urge that you stay with it.

Attend meetings.

Keep informed.

Stimulate interest.

Keep pushing.

Your concern and participation are those needed ingredients to get the job done.

Many years ago, Abraham Lincoln said, "Die when I may but let it be said of me by those who know me best that I plucked a thistle and planted a rose where a rose would grow."

You are plucking the thistle of indifference and planting the rose of concern.

Plucking the thistle of decline and planting the rose of growth.

The New Community Is Your Responsibility

1. The privilege of citizenship in this country is the finest of all treasures, but the greatest of all responsibilities.

The finest of all treasures because of the opportunity it offers each of us to do and to become as individuals and the freedom it gives to live a full and useful and productive life.

The greatest of all responsibilities because of the responsibility which freedom places upon you and me to protect and insure that freedom shall belong to all persons and shall be desired more than silver and gold.

I tip my hat to you who are assuming the responsibilities of citizenship in a society that places its hopes in the individual—competent, capable, intelligent, honorable, and responsible individuals.

I am convinced that "Freedom rests and always will on individual responsibility, individual integrity, and individual effort, individual courage, and individual religious faith. It does not rest on Washington, it rests on you and me."

2. You are what your choices make you. Your choices are mighty important.

I read the other day of a banker lending a young man a 100 percent loan to enter farming.

The young man had made four wise choices:

a. He had been a 4-H Club member of long standing, revealing the wisdom of associating with that which is uplifting.

b. He married a fine girl who gave promise of being a fine wife, thus establishing the hope of a happy home and wonderful family.

c. He had saved enough money to buy a tractor—and in so doing he demonstrated that fine quality of thriftiness.

d. He was active in his community giving of himself to building a better place in which to live—thus revealing the qualities of good and unselfish citizenship—a jewel greatly to be desired.

3. Your job is cut out for you. You must build a new community which we grown folks are shaping up today.

We are in the process of building a new community.

The people of your new community will largely live in cities.

Your community will possess all the problems that arise when a people concentrate themselves on small areas of land.

The income of this new community will be higher than we have known in our farm communities.

Jobs will go mainly to those supplying services to others.

This new community will cry out for understanding of social problems like crime, delinquency, slums, high taxes, adequate education. It will beg for leadership to bring discipline and compassion and the embrace of the great moral and spiritual values given to us by our forefathers.

But this is the community you must build and make live.

It is a big job and to you is handed the responsibility of getting it done.

It is the job of building and thinking anew—not tearing down.

"I watched them tearing a building down
A gang of men in a busy town
They pulled a beam and a whole wall fell.
I asked the boss, "Are these men skilled
And the kind you'd hire if you were to build?"
He laughed and said, "Why, no indeed
Just common workmen is all I need
They can easily wreck in a day or two
The work it took builders years to do."
So I said to myself as I went on my way
What part in the role of life do I play?
Am I shaping my deeds to a well-made plan

Patiently building the best I can?
Am I a builder whose work will last
And serve as a shelter against life's blast?
Or am I a wrecker who walks the town
Content with the work of tearing down?"

4. Keep your eyes glued on four big jobs in this new community.

a. It is your responsibility to understand the economic system which provides you with such an abundance of goods and services—and work to protect and strengthen it.

Money is a good thing and greatly to be desired, but it must never become more than a tool for a full and abundant life.

You will hear many false prophets proclaim the doom of the American economic system.

There will be those who will try to convince you that the problem is sharing wealth not producing wealth.

Yet, I say to you that no nation shares its wealth among others more than the United States.

There must be wealth produced before it can be shared.

And a responsible people who produce great wealth will out of compassion voluntarily share its wealth.

Profit is an honorable objective in our society.

And must ever be.

For in profit we have a motivation to build and create and produce.

So I say to you, understand the economic system which is so good to you—and work to make it better.

In the words of one who came 2000 years ago—

"Beware of false prophets."

b. The opportunity to learn is a privilege of exceptional value.

Strive to strengthen our educational system—and give to every person young and old the opportunity to learn—to know—to understand—to seek wisdom.

Abraham Lincoln said, "I will study and get ready and perhaps my chance will come."

This world is intolerant of ignorance.

Mediocrity has no place in a world of precision.

"Lord, Grant that I may always desire more than I accomplish."

The blue-collar job is on the decline.

The while-collar job is on the increase.

The machine must be mastered or it will become our master.

This new community needs individuals who can think for themselves—who can take the grain and sift out the chaff—who develop their convictions on the basis of study.

"Education is what's left over after you have forgotten all the facts." Thinking is hard work—but think you must.

c. Develop a strong and efficient government that offers no easy life but demands our very best for our community.

A government that doesn't lull me into thinking that someone owes me a living.

That someone owes me more than an opportunity to develop into a strong, self-reliant capable and responsible individual.

A government that gives us liberty and does not take it away from us by spreading among us bounties, donations, and largeness.

You and I are asking much of our government.

More than any people have ever asked of their government.

Study and understand the function of government in a democratic society.

Study and understand our political system and take part in it. From politicians, statesmen grow.

Study the art of good government and insist that we have the best.

Vote in every election. This is your privilege.

So to you comes the challenge to have the kind of government in the new community that builds a people—builds strong individuals—provides an environment in which private enterprise can flourish and give to responsible members of our society the challenge to make, to save, and to share.

d. Be sure your new community is underlain by strong moral and spiritual values.

Mud sill values

Dignity of the individual

Privilege commensurate with responsibility

Reward for excellence

Freedoms: To own property, to make a project, to state my views but reply as a responsible person.

Build your life strong and useful and dedicated to those values that uplift a person and the community in which he lives.

Mr. Dag Hammarskjold said, "He who wants to keep his garden tidy doesn't reserve a plot for weeds."

So keep out of your life the weeds of ignorance, and prejudice, and hate, and doubt, and selfishness and unconcern.

With Abraham Lincoln, say also, "Die when I may, but let it be said of me by those who know me best that I plucked a thistle and planted a rose where a rose would grow."

Pluck the thistle of doubt and plant in deep and fertile ground the rose of hope

and faith of your fathers and their fathers and a community of free and responsible and intelligent men and women, boys, and girls.

Fifteenth Anniversary of Leadership Georgia

WAVERLY HOTEL, ATLANTA, GEORGIA, AUGUST 9, 1986

Cora Lee and I are honored to be with you on this Fifteenth Anniversary of Leadership Georgia.,

We can say, as did Walt Whitman, "I feel about fame as the fellow did who found himself in heaven. He didn't ask himself whether he deserved it. He just kept quiet and stayed."

We have enjoyed every moment you have permitted us to be with you in Leadership Georgia.

You have brought an added dimension to our lives.

You have made us think young at a time we were flirting with thinking old.

You have caused us to embrace a vibrant vision instead of settling into dreams of yesterday.

You have called us friends and granted to us the privilege of calling you our friends.

You have confirmed our belief that "all the way to heaven is heaven."

Thank you for these and all other favors you have extended to us.

You are very special people.

You have Georgia on your minds and its future deep in your hearts.

You have expressed your hope and demonstrated your faith that things can be changed for the better.

You are builders who are toiling today with a vision of tomorrow.

The sparkle in your eyes and the enthusiasm springing from your hearts speak of your determination and dedication.

The twenty-first century beckons. You are accepting its challenges and responsibilities.

Life is a journey with many never-to-be-forgotten experiences scattered along the way. Leadership Georgia is one such experience.

Leadership Georgia can be neither explained nor described, it must be experienced. One must feel and revel in its spirit.

Leadership Georgia is the creation of the creative and perceptive mind of Pat Pattillo, who served as president of the Georgia Chamber of Commerce fifteen years ago. He set a goal at that time of at least 500 young leaders from every nook and cranny of this state to broaden their associations and embrace a vision of Georgia and its potentials as it moves onward into the twenty-first century.

That goal has been reached and exceeded. At the end of this year, 869 selectees together with their spouses will have experienced Leadership Georgia. Spouses are full-fledged members actively engaging in all study, discussions, and other aspects of programs. Thus, almost 1,800 young leaders have been influenced by this program in its fifteen years of existence.

Leadership Georgia is now an institution that is strong and abiding with an honorable and influential tradition. It is a do-it-yourself program with members accepting responsibilities for organization, programming, member selection, financial planning and management, and other required functions. It is governed by a Board of Trustees with a rotating membership. It is now sponsored by the Business Council of Georgia, a successor of the Georgia Chamber of Commerce, its first sponsor.

General George Marshall described a leader as "one who exerts an influence and makes you want to do more than you could."

Georgia has come from where it was to where it is because there were leaders who exerted influence and caused people to want to do more than they could. As it has been so shall it be as we move onward into the twenty-first century.

A leader with vision, conviction, and courage is a resource of immeasurable value in our society.

Daniel J. Boorstein, of the Library of Congress, refers to leaders in a democracy as amateurs possessing what he terms as "Amateur Spirit." He defines an amateur as one who does something for the love of it. He says, "The progress, perhaps even the survival of our society, depends upon the vitality of the 'Amateur Spirit' in the USA today and tomorrow."

John Gardner, a national leader of great understanding and vision, wrote, "In our society leadership is more than ordinarily dispersed. Leaders are scattered around at every level and in all segments of our national life. If it weren't for this wide dispersal of leadership, our kind of society couldn't function."

The great wisdom and perception of these two leaders cause us to more clearly understand that Georgia's future will be largely influenced by well informed and dedicated leaders scattered all over this state.

North and South
East and West
Big city and little town
Urban and rural
Suburban and open country

and from a cross-section of all occupations—truly a wide dispersal of leadership with one aim in mind, to help people make a difference in the quality of their life—under the banner of one Georgia striving to build a greater Georgia for all its citizens.

You believe, with Justice Oliver Wendell Holmes, who said, "It is required of a man that he should share the passion and action of his time at the peril of being judged not to have lived."

Truly, "he is no fool who gives away what he cannot keep for that which he cannot lose."

Let me ask three questions which I often ask of myself:

Are we listening to what Georgia is saying?

Are we listening to what Georgia is not saying?

Are we listening to what Georgia is trying to say and can't?

An effective leader is a good listener—and seeks earnestly to interpret what he hears. Then puts into words—simple words—what he comes to understand from the voices and events and trends and pressures that constantly ask to be heard and interpreted.

We of my age are experiencing a new Georgia far different from the Georgia of our birth. We helped to bring about this new Georgia which you now inherit. This new Georgia will soon become the old Georgia to you as you strive to create another new Georgia.

Change is fascinating and exciting—and one special quality of leadership is a willingness to accept change and to change.

Presently, signs point to a future that will be exciting—demanding—fearsome—challenging—a future that speaks of a new Georgia which you will help build.

Embrace that future—strive to understand it—hold fast to its creative processes.

It promises to be a future in which

Attitudes will come under stress

Cherished traditions will be dealt hard blows

New lines will replace old boundaries

In the search for new answers to old questions and problems

New communities will evolve with more effective local governments and stronger Educational, social, and economic bases

Thinking anew and acting anew will be the order of the day

Excellence will be demanded

Courage will be required

Challenges will accompany exciting opportunities

The urgency of decision—the right decision—the correct action—will issue the clarion call, "Life is in session. Are you present!"

Former President Harry Truman said, "Men make history and not the other way around. In periods where there is no leadership, society stands still. Progress occurs when courageous, skillful leaders seize the opportunity to change things for the better."

H. G. Wells, a distinguished historian, writes of a dialogue between God and Peter.

> "Why do you suffer all these cruel and unclean things?" asked Peter.
>
> "You don't like it," said the Lord God, without any sign of apology or explanation.
>
> "No," said Peter.
>
> "Then change it," said the Lord God, leaning back with the weariness of one who had to argue with each generation from

Job onward, precisely the same arguments.

The Lord God in His great wisdom gave us the gift of choice,
With all privileges and responsibilities that accompany it,
Yet, we seem to persist in saying, "Why don't somebody do something."
Then, a quiet voice says, "Change it yourself."
And only then do we come to realize that "I am Somebody."
We ask of you to help us help ourselves to make life better.
We have full confidence that you will do it.
My prayer is that Leadership Georgia will even grow stronger—and that all whom it touches will stay alive as long as they live.

APPENDIX D

Tribute to J. W. Fanning on His Ninetieth Birthday

The Reverend Jon Appleton,
First Baptist Church, Athens, August 14, 1995

Originally for most of us is the fine art of remembering what we hear but forgetting where we heard it. But not the honoree on this occasion: He is—Original: in ways that paint with clarity vistas which were present all along; but, of which we had not seen. Creator: of forms, images and/or impressions from which we find meaning, understanding, comprehension. Prototype: a means by which perceptions in their complexities are broken down into bite-sized nuggets, making the irrational rational; the irrelevant expendable; the relevant a necessity.

Precursor: a herald anticipating what is to be as though it already were; because he sees so well what he sees, he gives good direction to what is yet to be. Forerunner: a generating cause, introducing light, launching projects, ushering in new days with a grateful nod to yesterdays. Spring: from which the business community, industry, educators, legislators, theologians, planners, developers, revisionists, sinners in need, and saints with hope have drunk. . . . He possesses the gift of putting into short sentences lessons distilled from long experiences. . . . However he resides with us as a man of mystery: whose word is bond, whose reputation is noted, whose character is flawless, whose respect is renown, whose mind is accessible, whose trust is limitless, whose faith is contagious, whose hope is confident, whose love is genuine. And mystery of the man is, was, and will be—his absolute, gracious congeniality, and his audacious gumption. . . . I have known him at grand moments and through bad experiences; I have laughed with him and, together, we have wept; I have been in groups divided and befuddled, only to hear the lucidity of his suggestion clear the air and unite support; I have watched him face disappointment and beheld his strength; I have seen him at tables of honor and beheld his humility; and still this man, mysterious, is simple, so real. That's your name J.W.—Real!"

APPENDIX E

Handwritten Letters

J. W. was a prolific letter writer, corresponding with his many friends and colleagues; especially during the later years of his life with participants of Leadership Georgia. The recipients treasured the letters not just because they came from J. W., but because they were instructive, descriptive, and inspirational. Examples of two such letters penned in his own handwriting follow: the first to Hoppy and DeAnn Hopkins, Thomaston, Georgia, and the second to Jim and Nancy Buntin, Columbus, Georgia.

Dear Hoppy and DeAnn-

Your letter is a delight and comes like a cool breeze on a hot day- so refreshing. Thank you very much for remembering us in such a nice way.

You unlocked my memory box- hidden deep in my brain- and out poured images of past days- the Sunday afternoon you came to our house and we talked together about Program themes- and the many times we were together at Leadership Georgia- and especially as we laughed over the witticisms of Hoppy.

Well, I guess that is why the Good Lord saw fit to place "memory boxes" in brains so that as we grow old we can live again the fun times of yester years.

Cora Lee and I visited with the 1990 Class of Leadership Georgia at Unicoi. We had a good time as we always do. The 1990 Participants are very special as all have been in prior years. Larry Sanders has planned well around the general theme of A Quality Environment for a Quality Life. I hope we can make another, but to be perfectly frank when you are pushing 85 that is fast becoming a right heavy load to handle!!!

It is interesting to observe the many comments regarding the need for rethinking and recapturing the moral and spiritual values around which we established this Society. You were ahead of the pack in your program and set a lot of people thinking straight. Now, even there is a strong movement to teach values in schools. Well, I hope the teachers know how to teach values. The job isn't easy. One of the best — in my judgment — is through biography — the study of individuals who are living examples of portraying the values we hold dear.

Cora Lee and I are "holding". She is not in good health but keeps on her feet; I feel good most of the time and exercise a lot. One thing I am learning is that I can sit down easier than I can get up!!

You two are wonderful people and I know you are enjoying your children. Sometimes when you come our way, extend to us the privilege of being with you once more to talk, to laugh - to remember.

Best always from Cora Lee and me -

2/9/90

JW

Dear Jim and Nancy-

You brought great joy in my heart when you came to the Birthday Party, bringing your two beautiful daughters, on Sunday afternoon.

And for the gift, I am very thankful for it shall be used.

You two wonderful friends are very special to me and enrich my life so very much - more than words can express. You dedication to what is right and good is a shining light in my life. Your philosophy of life is so sound and strong. Thank you for your friendship which I shall always cherish.

And, Jim, my congratulations upon your selection as Superintendent of the Public Schools of Columbus. Muscogee. That is a

Position requiring great Courage, solid Values about life, appreciation for the Worth of every individual and a dedication to first class educational opportunities. These qualities you possess and I wish for you the best. God never puts on the Shoulders of any person More than he can bear for as the old man said "Me and God is a Majority".

I will follow with abiding interest your journey in leading the Schools to a Better day.

You are so fortunate to have Nancy by your side. She is truly a great lady - the great wife of a great Man - an incomparable partnership.

My best always - Thank you so much for your friendship

[signature]

?/16/94

APPENDIX F

Leadership Georgia Programs, 1972–2001

Presidents of Leadership Georgia are elected on a yearly basis, and they assume major responsibilities, the largest of which is arranging programs. The president enlists alumni to help him or her develop agendas for five regional meetings. Following is a list of presidents, program themes, and regional meeting leaders since Leadership Georgia began in 1972.

A Georgia Odyssey, 2001
J. ANDERSON DAVIS, PRESIDENT

Brasstown Valley
A Journey into One's Self—Peter and Emily Hjort

Dublin
All Systems Green—Bill and Mitzi Linginfelter

St. Simons
An Environmental Exploration—Bruce and Vickie Williamson

LaGrange
Our Mission—Duncan and Angie Moore

Augusta
Our Search for Life—Tony and Avia Calloway

Georgia's Vision, 2000
CHARLES K. TARBUTTON, PRESIDENT

Brasstown Valley
But I Am Only One—Fred & Malinda Bergen

Douglas
Rural Healthcare: The Prognosis—Dan & Susannah Sisson

St. Simons Island
Ecology and Commerce: Striking a Balance—Warren & Kelly Turner

Forsyth
Equal Protection under the Law—Anthony & Sandra Parker

Gainesville
From Sesame Street to Main Street—Davis & Kay Stewart

The Value of One—The Power of All, 1999
EDWARD J. TARVER, PRESIDENT

Brasstown Valley
One Together—Gregg & Nancy McDougal

Vidalia
Georgia's Tomorrow—Today—Pope & Evelyn Langdale

Jekyll Island
Leading Georgia into the New Millennium—Bill & Cecilia Verner, Laura Reid

Tifton
Cultivating a Better Georgia—Bob & Karen Ray

Savannah
Reconciling Our Past—Securing Our Future—Joseph & Theresa Roseborough

---

Building Relationships for a New Millennium, 1998
DOUGLAS A. CARTER, PRESIDENT

Brasstown Valley
The Self—John & Tracy Vardeman

Thomasville
The Child—Bill & Jill Clark

St. Simons Island
The Environment—Phillip & Jennifer Abshire

Statesboro
The Government—Fred & Brenda Head

Dalton
The Community—Ken & Caryl Smith

A New Georgia: The Dreams . . . The Realities, 1997

TED E. LAWRENCE, PRESIDENT

Unicoi
My Time, My Turn—The Leader Must Lead!—Allen & Anne-Knox Hodges

Atlanta
My Brother's Keeper?—Laurie & Rick Amerson

St. Simons Island
Man and the Environment—Can One Survive Without the Other?—
Jerry & Cindy Fulks

Albany
Knowledge—Power for the Twenty-first Century—Powell & Caren Jones

Callaway Gardens
The World Came to Georgia—Will They Ever Come Back?—
Wayne & Michelle Edwards and Abbe Hockaday

Values and Visions, 1996

JAMES L. ALLGOOD JR., PRESIDENT

Unicoi
Mastery of Self—To the Best of Our Knowledge—Charles & Debbie Cauley

Sandersville
Protection/Production—The Balance of Nature—David & Connie Waller

Washington, D.C.
Principles of Leadership—Sallie Daniel & Molly Dye

Rome/Cartersville
Adapt—Educate—Survive—John Grant & Rhonda Wilcox

Americus
A Firm Foundation—Rick & Brenda Bradshaw

Together We Can, 1995

WARREN A. RAGSDALE, PRESIDENT

Unicoi
Leadership in Different Ways—Charles & Charlotte Williams

Newnan
High Tech, High Touch—Bill & Elizabeth Todd

Jekyll Island
Cultural Diversity: Comprende?—Ed & Beverly Tarver

Bainbridge
Education—We Can't Afford To Fail—Hugh & Emelyn Hunter

Macon
Law Enforcement—To Serve and Protect—Doug & Sandy Carter

Life Changers,1994
MIMI D. GUDENRATH, PRESIDENT

Lake Lanier
Change is Inevitable: Growth Is Optional—Kenny & Janie Coggins

Dublin
Uncle Sam, M.D.: Your Health Matters—Laura Meadows

St. Simons
The 1996 Summer Olympics: The World Drops In on Georgia—
Henry & Debbie Whitfield

Valdosta
Freedom for All: Mission Impossible?—Jack & Beth Sullivan

Athens
Education: An Odyssey of the Mind—Bob & Marla Nelson

Building the Future One Block at a Time, 1993
CHARLES W. WHITNEY, PRESIDENT

Unicoi
Leadership and the Leader—Gordon & Jane Smith

Waycross
The Environment—A Strong Foundation—Doug & Tavia McCuean

St. Simons Island
The Private Sector—An Engine Moving Us Into the Future—
Buck & Patti Ruffin

Carrollton
Education—The Keystone—Lester & Salyon Johnson

Augusta
The Public Sector—Tying It All Together—
Mike Gaymon & Sherri Davis Callaway

The Georgia Family: An Ever-Widening Circle, 1992
THOMAS E. FITZGERALD III, M.D., PRESIDENT

Unicoi
The Family: The Foundation of the Community—Buddy & Rita Bumgarner

Moultrie
The Earth: Sustaining the Family—Bill & Jessica Barrick

St. Simons Island
Cultural Diversity: The Family Around Us—Dean & Dee Scarborough

Madison
Education: The Family Widens the Circle—Michael & Annette Short

Savannah
The Family of Man: A Broader Perspective—Henry & Linda Dickerson

A Better Georgia beyond 2000: If We Build It, It Will Come, 1991
JAMES E. BUNTIN, PRESIDENT

Unicoi
Staying Alive As Long As You Live—Pillars of Leadership—
David & Mary Varner

Columbus
Examining Georgia's Role—National Defense—
Mike & Leah Sumner

Jekyll Island
Exploring Georgia Resources—The Environment—Wales & Lynn Barksdale

Statesboro
Educating Georgia's Youth—Ordinary People Can Do Extraordinary—
Warren & Terri Ragsdale

Decatur
Understanding Problems & Seeking Solutions:
Crime, Drugs and the Homeless—J. J. & Sandra Jackson

Quality of Life for the Twenty-first Century, 1990
LARRY E. LANDERS, D.D.S., PRESIDENT

Unicoi
Brave Leadership For a Preferred Future—Bryan & Beth Bell

Thomasville
Crimes, Drugs and Morality: Is the Damage Already Beyond Repair?—Ray & Jean Chadwick

St. Simons Island
Of Neighbors and Neighborhoods: Comprende?—Guy & Merry Jo Whidby

Dalton
What Then Education?—John & Missie Raudabaugh

Callaway
Our Physical Environment: Who's In Control?—Duane & Carol Harris

Bridging the Gap: The Two Georgias, 1989
PHILIP A. WILHEIT, PRESIDENT

Unicoi
Leadership, The Link Between the Two Georgias—Marva & Cecil Carter

LaGrange
Strategy for the Future, Managing Georgia's Natural Resources—Chris & Emily Joseph

St. Simons Island
Georgia's Endangered Species—Responsible Youth, What is Their Future?—Gene & Lynne Kernaghan

Marietta
Georgia's Health Care in the '90s. What is the Diagnosis?—Tom & Brenda Fitzgerald

Tifton
Education in Georgia. Equal Opportunities for All?—Willie Paulk & James Pleydell-Bouverie

Georgia 1990—The Challenges and Opportunities of a New Decade: Are We Prepared? 1988
WILLIAM C RICE, PRESIDENT

Unicoi
The Link Between Yesterday and Tomorrow—Dave & Bev Brown

Warner Robins
Georgia's Increasing Role in National Defense—John & Janie Maddox

St. Simons Island
Economic Growth Influenced by International Trade—Bob & Bambi Berry

Rome
Educational Challenges and Opportunities—Jim & Nancy Buntin

Jesup
Do We Have Adequate Resources To Meet The Future With Certainty?—Pat & Gaile Allen

Commitment to Values: A Better Future for Georgia, 1987
CALVIN S. HOPKINS III, PRESIDENT

Unicoi
Why Does It Matter?—Harry & Jane Yeomans

Americus
Where Are We Failing Our Children?—Bill & Mary Olive Cribbs

St. Simons Island
Is Government Serving or Hindering?—Sherman & Mary Ann Dudley

Macon
Are We Forgetting Liberty and Justice For All?—David & Janet Hudson

Gainesville
Custodians of Values—Philip & Mary Hart Wilheit

Effective Leadership: The Road to Georgia at Her Best, 1986
LYNN DEMPSEY, PRESIDENT

Unicoi
Qualities of Leadership—Bill & Helen Rice

Atlanta
Which Path—Government—Chris & Toni Jones

Savannah
Tourism: All Roads Lead to Georgia—Larry & Valery Landers

Albany
Which Way to the Farm—Robert Jr. & Joy Williams

Augusta
Advances in Medicine—Where Are They Leading Us—
Edward & Beverly Simpson

Accepting the Challenge of Georgia's Growth, 1985
W. H. NESMITH JR., PRESIDENT

Unicoi
Developing Leadership for Today and Tomorrow—Charlie & Carol Harman

Valdosta
Why Are We Growing—Hoppy & DeAnn Hopkins

Jekyll Island
Quality of Life: That's the Difference—Jones & Stephanie Hooks

Madison
Coping with a Growing Crime Rate—Asa & Evelyn Boynton

Perry
Seeking and Managing Growth—Dave & Marty Green

Leadership for Georgia's Future, 1984
DAVID C. GARRETT III, PRESIDENT

Unicoi
The Attributes of Leadership—Dink & Pam NeSmith

Athens
Georgia and the World—John & Susan Gornall

St. Simons Island
The Georgia of Tomorrow—Tom & Janice Faircloth

Tifton
Our Physical Environment—Lynn & Katie Dempsey

Columbus
Georgia's Role in National Defense—Tricia Rogers

Two Hundred Fifty Years of Georgia: Understanding Our Potential, 1983
SAMUEL R. DUNLAP JR., PRESIDENT

Unicoi
Understanding Ourselves—Morris & Marilyn Benveniste

Moultrie
Understanding our Natural Resources—Sam & Dusty Wellborn

St. Simons Island
Rediscovering Georgia's Heritage—John & Anne Jurgensen

Rome
Understanding Georgia's Economic Strength—Charles & Janelle Whalen

Atlanta
Understanding Georgia's Higher Educational Strength—
Alex & Janet Patterson

Opportunities for Leadership, 1982
ALFRED R. ROACH JR., PRESIDENT

Lake Arrowhead
Challenges for Personal Involvement: A Look into Ourselves—
Sam & Charlotte Dunlap

Athens
Opportunities for Leadership in Agriculture—Dale & Patsy Threadgill

Savannah
The Cities and Towns of Georgia—Richard & Martha Kessler

Macon
Opportunities for Leadership in Government—Martha Hazelton

Augusta
Opportunities for Leadership in Medicine—David & Kay Hogg

Leadership in a Changing World, 1981
MICHAEL S. BARRON, PRESIDENT

Unicoi
Communication—Al Roach

Thomasville
Challenges and Opportunities for Public Education in the '80s—
Ed & Linda James

Sea Palms
Challenges Facing Our Free Enterprise System—David & Juliet Lindholm

Valdosta
Challenges to Land and Water Resources in an Urbanized Society—
Mac & Jane McLane

Dalton
The Changing Roles and Responsibilities of Government for the '80s—
Will Ball

Challenges of the '80s, 1980
JOHN B. HARDMAN, M.D., PRESIDENT

Unicoi
Rediscovering Our Humanness—Jerry & Jane Howington

Douglas
Energy—Bond & Virginia Almand

Jekyll Island
International Trade and the World Economy—Kit & Betsy Weitnauer

Rome
Communications—Media—Chuck & Judy Farrell

Columbus
The Military—Mike & Patti Barron

The Challenge of Leadership, 1979
ANN ESTES KLAMON, PRESIDENT

Unicoi
Communication—Horace & Beverly Sibley

Savannah
Preserving Our Heritage—Jim & Karen Pannell

Washington, D.C.
Managing Government—Marvin & Henrietta Singletary

Atlanta
Cities, Suburbs, and Rural Areas—John & Laura Hardman

Albany
Land Use—Fred & Ann Kerr

The Challenge of Change, 1978
WILLIAM T. GREER JR., PRESIDENT

Unicoi
The Family—Carl & Pat Swearingen

Augusta
Healthcare—Ann Estes Klamon

St. Simons Island
Government and Business—Skip & Frannie Hilsman

Waycross
Natural Resources—Jeff & Liz Savage

Rome
Crime—Guy & Melanie Eberhardt

Directions in Georgia Development, 1977
ROBERT L. REARDEN JR., PRESIDENT

Lake Lanier Islands
Energy and its Impact on Georgia—George & Honey Edwards

Savannah
Tort Liability Confrontation: Society's Demands vs. Ability to Pay—Sam & Rochelle Smith

Jekyll Island
Government and Community Development in Georgia—Tom & Faith Willis

Tifton
Rural Development and the Georgia Economy—Ray & Carol Bragg

Athens
Human Interrelations in Georgia's Development—Lester Strong

Horizons at Bicentennial, 1976
H. INMAN ALLEN, PRESIDENT

Unicoi
Freedom: Its Privileges and Responsibilities—Gene & Ruth Younts

Five Regional Alumni Meetings
Wesley & Pat Johnson

Milledgeville
Moral, Spiritual and Ethical Values—William & Fann Greer

Savannah
Environmental Objectives and Resources—Edwin & Jane Feiler

Callaway Gardens
Educational Challenges and Opportunities—Philip & Sandy Goff

Jim Newman, Program Chairman, 1975
JAMES R. NEWMAN, PRESIDENT

Unicoi
Natural Resources

Berry College
Educational Resources

St. Simons Island
Natural Resources

Milledgeville
Human Resources

Savannah
Economic Resources

Joel C. Williams, Program Chairman, 1974
ROBERT F. HATCHER, PRESIDENT

Callaway Gardens
Influence on Government and How to Become Involved

Kingwood Country Club
Honesty, Integrity and Morals in Business, the Press, Government, and Religion

Sea Palms
Economic Goals and Conflicts and How They Relate to Inflation, the Energy Crisis, and the Environmental Question

Lake Lanier
The Problems of Social Services:
Welfare, Penal Reform and the Parole System, and Education

Savannah
Georgia and Its Place in the World

B. Harry West—Program Chairman, 1973
J. W. TALLEY JR., PRESIDENT

Callaway Gardens
Our Society and How It Relates to Us as Individuals—Rogers Wade

Stone Mountain
The Effect of the Social Delivery Services System—Harry West

St. Simons Island
Criminal—Richard Harden

Helen
The Educational System—Richard Huseman

Savannah
Economics & Taxation—Jim McIntyre

T. Rogers Wade—Program Chairman, 1972
WILLIAM J. VANLANDINGHAM, PRESIDENT

Sea Island
Organization of Government—Jim Topple and Rogers Wade

Callaway Gardens
Education: Youth, Drugs, and Crime—J.W. Fanning

Kingwood Country Club
Criminal and Justice System—Bill VanLandingham

Stone Mountain
Delivery of Social Services—Harry West

Savannah
Employment and Economic Growth—Jack Talley

APPENDIX G

Leadership Georgia Award Recipients

Leadership Georgia presents three awards of distinction each year: the J. W. Fanning Award, the Frederick B. Kerr Service Award, and the Cora Lee Fanning Award. Below are listed the individuals who have been honored in these special ways.

J. W. Fanning Award

Presented in honor of J. W. Fanning to a Georgian whose state-wide contributions through progressive leadership and service have been broad in scope and rich in achievement.

2002 President Jimmy Carter
2001 Congressman John Lewis
2000 James H. Blanchard
1999 Governor Roy Barnes
1998 Congressman Lindsay Thomas
1997 Governor Zell Miller & Shirley Miller
1996 Ambassador Andrew Young
1995 U.S. Senator Paul D. Coverdell
1994 William P. Payne
1993 Dr. Fred C. Davison
1992 Joseph D. Tanner
1991 S. Truett Cathy
1990 Millard Fuller
1989 Honorable Griffin Bell
1988 Deen Day Smith
1987 Governor George Busbee
1986 Ivan Allen, J.
1985 Dr. Glenn Burton
1984 Professor Dean Rusk
1983 J. Pollard Turman
1982 Harley Langdale Jr.
1981 William R. Bowdoin
1980 Jasper Dorsey
1979 H. G. Pattillo
1978 U.S. Senator Sam Nunn

Frederick B. Kerr Service Award

Presented in memory of Frederick B. Kerr to Leadership Georgia members who have demonstrated enthusiastic and active support of Leadership Georgia on a continuing basis.

2002 T. Rogers Wade, Atlanta
2001 Dale Threadgill, advisor, Leadership Georgia
2000 James L. Allgood, Dublin
1999 Woody Woodside, Duane and Carol Harris, Brunswick
1998 Lynwood Hall, Moultrie
1997 Sam R. Hunter Jr., Americus
1996 Mimi and Allen Gudenrath, Macon
1995 Alfred W. Jones III, Sea Island
1994 Mary Louise Hill, Athens
1993 William H. Cribbs, Valdosta
1992 Philip and Mart Hart Wilheit, Gainesville
1991 John L. Gornall, Atlanta
1990 Hoppy and DeAnn Hopkins, Thomaston
1989 Dink and Pam NeSmith, Athens
1988 Marilyn Benveniste-Marks, Atlanta
1987 David C. Garrett, Atlanta
1986 John B. Hardman, Atlanta
1985 William R. Bowdoin Jr., Atlanta
1984 Henrietta McArthur Singletary, Albany
1983 Joseph A. Buck III, Savannah
1982 Robert F. Hatcher, Macon
1981 Donnie Morris, Baxley

Cora Lee Fanning Award

Presented in memory of Cora Lee Fanning to the spouse of a current class member for outstanding participation and enthusiasm. This award was established at St. Simons Island on Saturday, May 15, 1993.

2001 Kim Chavez, Tifton
2000 Ned Blumenthal, Atlanta
1999 Donnie Chapman, Atlanta
1998 Celia Walker, Dallas, Texas
1997 Emily Hjort, Rome
1996 Nancy McDougal, Raleigh, North Carolina
1995 Anna Burns, Griffin
1994 Laura A. Dunwoody, Macon
1993 Charles Williams, Eastman
1992 Kay Parker, Atlanta

APPENDIX H

Magazine Articles

For most of the decade of the nineteen fifties, J. W. Fanning wrote an article each month for *The Progressive Farmer Magazine*. Following are the complete texts of two articles that were referenced in Chapter Three: *The Agriculturist*.

"Six Steps to Farming," July 29, 1958

For most families, owning a farm is a step-by-step proposition over a good many years. The Earnest Blakeys of Barrow County, Georgia, vouch for this statement. Within twelve years, they have come a long way in farming.

As I talked with Earnest and his wife, it seemed to me that they had taken six steps. Each step was forward. Today they own and rent land—and have a good system of farming. They like what they are doing. They have reason to be proud of what they have accomplished.

Let me line up for you the six steps taken by the Blakey family.

Step one was taken when they made up their mind to farm. Actually, this was probably the most important step of all. Earnest was a town boy with a good job. He didn't have to farm. He went to the farm because he wanted to make a living in that kind of work. Mrs. Blakey was ready and willing to go, too. After serving in the Army for three years, Earnest and his wife moved to the farm in April of 1946.

There used to be a saying that "since he can't do anything else, let him farm." That kind of situation doesn't make good farmers. It probably never was true for good farming—and it sure isn't today. Good farmers love to farm and choose this way of making a living. So step one is mighty important. The Blakey family is satisfied with their decision.

Step two is starting to farm with the best possible arrangement. Without money, you either have to hire out as a laborer or go in on shares. Under the latter, a person can put up labor against capital. Earnest chose this way of going in. His uncle had a farm with some cows, mules, and machinery. He needed a partner. They got together. Here were the terms of their first agreement:

The owner furnished land, buildings, milk cows, mules, and machinery.

Earnest furnished all labor.

Both parties shared the operating expenses, other than labor, on a fifty-fifty basis. (Capital expenses like taxes, insurance, and major repairs were paid by the owner.) All calves would be jointly owned. (This arrangement would provide a jointly-owned milking herd after a few years.) Profits above current operating expenses were shared equally.

These terms were placed in a written agreement. This was properly executed by both parties.

At the beginning of this share arrangement in 1946, this farm had 130 acres. They have twenty-one milk cows. Two tenants grew six to eight acres of cotton each and some corn. There was one tractor and a pair of mules. Grade A milk was sold.

Step three was taking advantage of every opportunity to get ahead. Earnest enrolled in the Veterans Farm Training Program. He learned a lot and the extra money came in handy. He says this helped him to become a better farmer.

He bought a little land next to the farm. On this thirty-eight acres, he and Mrs. Blakey built a house. He kept his eyes open on the credit question, and he began establishing a basis for credit with the North Georgia Production Credit Association. He borrowed money to build a broiler house on his thirty-eight acres. This loan was paid in a short period. Then another broiler house was built on credit. A three-year loan was paid off in thirteen months. You must take advantage of the breaks to succeed in farming. The Blakeys did their share of this—and they are still at it.

Step four was working toward the ownership of "working" capital. Within a few years, Earnest came into one-half ownership of the milking herd. Through a good breeding program, he and his owner improved the quality of the cows. Milk production increased. As his uncle was agreeable to selling his interest in the herd, Earnest borrowed money from the North Georgia Production Credit Association to buy him out. At about the same time, a loan was secured from the same institution to buy all machinery and equipment. Earnest was now sole owner of all "working" capital—cows, heifers, calves, machinery, and equipment.

So, after a period of about six years, the Blakeys moved from no capital and no credit basis to the ownership of considerable capital and a good credit base. They now had in hand the real essentials of good modern-day farming experience, a desire to learn more, working capital, and the ability to borrow money.

Step five came with the renting of "fixed" capital—land and buildings. Earnest now has a five-year lease on the 130-acre farm. This makes sense. He possesses what it takes to handle land for largest profit.

Without money or "working" capital, you can't do much with crop and pasture land. But you can most always rent land—if you have what it takes to work it. The Blakeys own a little land—and they are in the position now to become full-fledged owners of much land. This will be the final step—when they wish to take it.

Step six came along during their twelve years of farming. It was the desire and the effort to increase their efficiency in farming. They did a lot of things. Here are some of them: A breeding program improved the milk-cow herd. Earnest thinks he will get a 9,000 pound milk production average per cow this year. He now milks thirty cows.

Cotton went off the farm. So did the tenants and mules. A feed program went in. Alfalfa and oats are cut for hay. More alfalfa is going in. There are twenty-four acres of winter grazing, well fertilized. This is followed by summer temporary grazing. Permanent pasture has Bermuda and Fescue, mostly Bermuda grass, with plenty of chicken manure on pasture—plus mixed goods and nitrogen. Some grain produced—but main effort directed toward plenty of high quality hay and grazing.

Blakey family does the work. With the right equipment in the milking barn and on the farm, the load is not too heavy. Earnest does all milking.

A poultry program provides added income. Grows out one brood of pullets for layers to ten weeks of age on a per-head basis. Then three broods of broilers of 10,000 each.

This family has made progress in farming. They have planned well and acted wisely. Some folks say opportunities to go to farming are gone. The Blakeys don't agree with this statement. They say the road is open, but you've got to climb some hills to travel it. Do you agree?

"Six Ways to Judge Efficient Farming," November 1, 1953

You have wondered why you hear so much talk lately about efficiency in farming? Past records certainly don't cause any concern over inefficiency in farming. Today one farm worker feeds from fifteen to twenty others. Not so long ago, he fed only five others besides himself. In the past forty years, farm production has gone up sixty-nine percent—even though we lost ten million people from our farms. That's a great record of efficiency.

It could be that folks are getting kind of worried about their food supply thirty years from now. By then, we will have about 235 million people to feed—around seventy-five million more than we have today. Can we furnish each of those people 406 eggs, thirty pounds of chicken meat, eighty pounds of beef and thirty pounds of cotton? Can we do this and still have plenty to ship to other nations? Our past record says we can. But we are about to run out of new land. This means that we've got to get more through higher yields—per acre, per animal, and per man. Most folks say that this is going to require far greater efficiency than we have even today.

A problem closer to home to farmers right now is a price-cost squeeze. During the past year, farm prices went down twelve percent—but prices paid by farmers didn't change much. That hurt. Two years ago, farm prices were ten to twelve percent above parity. Today they are six to seven percent under parity. It takes mighty good farming to live with a situation like that. Do you agree that efficient farming is about the only way out of this bad spot?

One thing for sure is that the more you depend upon dollars, the more efficient you've got to be. A lot of Georgia, Florida, and Alabama farmers have gone "commercial" in the past ten years. Today they find themselves "high cash cost" farmers. They are handlers of big dollars. One slip in this kind of farming and the "show" may be all over. A sharp drop in income can leave a debt too large to overcome. Maybe it's this kind of thing that's got us talking about efficiency. You can't live with this "commercial" farming without high efficiency.

There are lots of ways of looking at "efficiency" in farming. Maybe we ought to see if we can agree on how to judge it then we can see what makes for greater efficiency. Probably the best way to start is to take a look at how a certain 160-acre Georgia farm came out in 1953.

This farm has the "new look." It's a grain-grass-livestock farm. It has ninety-two acres of crop land and thirty-four acres in pasture. A tractor does most of the work. One family tends the farm. The 1953 production was greater than that of 1952—but the drop in cattle prices hurt mighty bad. Fortunately there were some hogs to help out.

Now, let's take this farm apart and see if we can agree on how to go about measuring farm efficiency.

1. Receipts must be greater than expenses:

This farm took in $3018.13 in 1953 and spent $1515.33—leaving a balance of $1502.80. Modern day farming must show a profit. Folks used to say that a farm was the only business that could lose money year after year and continue to operate. That may have been true in the past—but not today. Farmers are managers of capital. Anybody who handles lots of capital has got to show a dollar profit or he goes broke. Anyway you look at it, dollar profits are one way of measuring farm efficiency. Do you agree?

2. All resources must be fully used:

Most of the land on this farm is at work—but it isn't working hard enough. Almost ten percent of the entire 160 acres was idle in 1953. This kind of practice pulls efficiency down. All acres at work is a sure sign of efficient farming.

About seventy-five percent of the productive labor on this farm was used in 1953. The twenty-five percent not used was a twenty-five percent "leak" in efficiency. If either land or labor is under-employed, dollar profits are not what they ought to be. The chances are good that this 160-acre farm has got to add another cash crop or make its hog enterprise larger to use all of the available labor.

This farm carries one tractor on its 135 acres of open land—which isn't bad especially since most of the crops can be easily handled with machinery, but there are two mules, also. The chances are that some power went unused. Partly used capital is pretty expensive capital. Hard-working capital is a sure sign of efficiency. Can we say then that efficient farming calls for working every acre, using every hour of labor, and keeping machines?

3. *Yields must be above average:*

The per-acre yields on this farm were about average. Corn turned fifteen bushels per acre, wheat twenty, and oats forty. Around two tons of hay were saved per acre. As a general rule, average yields mean about average profits, and average profits aren't good enough anymore. We've got to have profits much above average to get along. This means yields must be well above average. Have you ever figured your break–even point in per unit yields? A lot of folks say it takes more than one-half bale of cotton, twenty bushels of corn, twenty bushels of wheat, one-half ton of peanuts, and fifty bushels of oats per acre to make any money. If that is true, there are a good many people going in the hole every year. It's pretty well established that four pigs per litter, 150 eggs per hen, 450 gallons of milk per cow will barely break even on ordinary costs. High yields and top-notch efficiency go hand in hand. Here's another good measure.

4. *Volume turnout per man must be large:*

This one-family farm had a gross income in 1953 of $3018.13. Another way of figuring volume is on a per "man" basis. This family had the equivalent of two full-time workers. Which means the $3018.13 was produced by two "men," and the volume per man was $1509.07.

Maybe you don't agree with this measure of farm efficiency. Well, let's take a look. Commercial farming takes dollars and a lot of them. There are large operating cash costs to cover, and living costs are pretty high, too. Which means that gross income per farm and per man must be high to take care of these costs—and give a good living. When dollar income per man is low, trouble starts. When it's high, it's not so bad. How much have we got to have in gross income per man to get by in the future? $3,000? $5,000? Maybe $10,000? Not a bad thing to think about. But one thing is sure, large gross income per man comes only with efficient farming.

5. *A high return must be made on the investment:*

This farm made about four percent on its capital investment. That's pretty low. Most types of farming turn money pretty slow. A lot of farms have a hard time paying management. If they get labor paid—they've done pretty good. This has got to be changed one way or another—through better practices on more fertile soil, higher paying enterprises, less labor on more land, or by some other means. A high rate of return on investment is a pretty good indication of farm efficiency.

Let's look at some other returns on this farm. For each dollar spent on fertilizer, $5.50 came back in sales. That's about twenty percent. Better sow animal unit came to $69.80. This might have been all right for beef cattle but it was far too low for hogs. Sales per acre of open land came to $22.57. Quick judgment says that is too low for a good living. Shouldn't it be about three times this figure to give the dollars needed? That would have given a gross farm income of $8,840. A good goal to shoot for is $10,000—about three times what it actually was. Getting a lot of dollars back for each dollar spent is a sure sign of efficiency.

6. *Capital investment must be protected:*

Efficient farming is "money-making" farming and not "tearing-down" farming. The land on this farm is mostly in conserving crops. The machinery and equipment are housed and greased regularly. The animals are pretty well protected against disease. One thing for sure—the dollar income is not coming from tearing-down capital—in land or labor or machines. The problem on this farm is to make the present farming system work harder and turn out more stuff to sell.

When you sell off your soil fertility and call it profit—things are getting in a bad way. When the cows are sold and the dollar returns are considered profits—it won't be long before you are out of the cow business. Efficient farming builds the farm capital strong while it is making money. Not easy, but isn't it a good way to measure farm efficiency?

Notes

Chapters 1–7 have lead-in pages with quotes by persons who knew J. W. personally. Quotes were received in surveys from the authors in March 2000.

Prologue

1. *Chronicle of the 20th Century*. New York: Kindersley. 1995. J. W. Fanning was born in the year of 1905. The first four references are cited to give the reader a better understanding of some of the interesting events of that year from an international, national, state and local perspective.
2. *Time Lines of the Twentieth Century*. Boston: Little Brown,1996
3. *The Gazette-Chronicle*. Vol.1, no.33, 16 August 1905.
4. *The Gazette-Chronicle*. Vol. 1, no. 32, 2 August 1905.
5. *The Atlanta Journal*. Vol. XXII, no. 176, 14 August 1905.
6. Saggus, Charles Danforth. "Anglo-Virginia Planter of Wilkes County, Georgia in the 1850's." *Agrarian Arcadian*, (1996):76–79.
7. Saggus, Charles Danforth. "Anglo-Virginia Planter of Wilkes County, Georgia in the 1850's." *Agrarian Arcadian*, (1996):76–79.
8. *The Atlanta Journal*. Vol. XXII, no. 176, 14 August 1905.

Chapter One: The Formative Years

1. Fanning, J. W. Personal taped interview by doctoral student, Sherry LaBoon. Athens, Georgia. 18 April 1997. J. W. Fanning agreed to participate in a number of interviews conducted by Sherry LaBoon, a graduate student in the College of Education, The University of Georgia. The interviews were held during a period beginning April 4, 1997 and concluding July 13, 1997. Sherry LaBoon shared the tapes of nine interviews, and the information on the tapes provides many of the details of his early and professional life. For all succeeding quotes that come from more interviews, the JWF/SLB designation will be used.
2. *Augusta Chronicle*. 8 August 1909.
3. Fanning, J. W. Unpublished handwritten notes. Personal papers. Ca 1996.
4. Fanning, J. W. "My Life." Unpublished. Autobiography, Ca 1996.
5. JWF/SLB. Athens, Georgia. 18 April 1997.
6. JWF/SLB. Athens, Georgia. 18 April 1997.

7. JWF/SLB. Athens, Georgia. 5 May 1997.
8. JWF/SLB. Athens, Georgia. 18 April 1997.
9. Chester, R. J. Carson and Associates, registered investment advisor. Athens, Georgia. November 2000.
10. JWF/SLB. Athens, Georgia. 5 May 1997.
11. JWF/SLB. Athens, Georgia. 5 May 1997.
12. JWF/SLB. Athens, Georgia. 5 May 1997.
13. JWF/SLB. Athens, Georgia. 18 April 1997.
14. JWF/SLB. Athens, Georgia. 18 April 1997.
15. JWF/SLB. Athens, Georgia. 18 April 1997.
16. JWF/SLB. Athens, Georgia 18 April 1997.
17. JWF/SLB. Athens, Georgia. 5 May 1997.
18. JWF/SLB. Athens, Georgia. 18 April 1997.
19. Willingham, Robert, E., Jr. *No Jubilee, The Story of Confederate Wilkes.* Washington, Georgia. Wilkes Publishing Company, 1976.
20. JWF/SLB. Athens, Georgia. 18 April 1997.
21. JWF/SLB. Athens, Georgia. 5 May 1997.
22. JWF/SLB. Athens, Georgia 8 May 1997.
23. Fanning, J. W. Unpublished handwritten notes. Ca 1996.
24. JWF/SLB. Athens, Georgia. 5 May 1997.
25. Bachtel, Douglas. Family and Consumer Sciences Department, University of Georgia. Personal communication. June 2000.
26. Fanning, J. W., Jr. Personal taped interview by author. Madison County, Georgia. 28 August 2000.
27. JWF/SLB. Athens, Georgia. 18 April 1997.
28. "Fanning: Keep Basic Values Constant." *The News Reporter.* Vol. LXXVI, No. 45. 7 November, 1985.
29. JWF/SLB. Athens, Georgia. 5 May 1997.
30. JWF/SLB. Athens, Georgia. 8 May 1997.
31. JWF/SLB. Athens, Georgia. 8 May 1997.
32. JWF/SLB. Athens, Georgia. 5 May 1997.
33. JWF/SLB. Athens, Georgia. 5 May 1997.
34. JWF/SLB. Athens, Georgia. 18 April 1997.
35. JWF/SLB. Athens, Georgia. 13 May 1997.
36. JWF/SLB. Athens, Georgia. 19 May 1997.
37. JWF/SLB. Athens, Georgia. 19 May 1997.
38. JWF/SLB. Athens, Georgia. 18 April 1997.
39. Fanning, J. W. Personal communication with author. Ca 1990.
40. Younts, S. E. Historic marker at Phillips Mills Baptist Church. June 2000.
41. JWF/SLB. Athens, Georgia. 5 May 1997.

42. JWF/SLB. Athens, Georgia. 18 April 1997.
43. Fanning, J. W. Personal communication with author. Ca 1980.
44. JWF/SLB. Athens, Georgia. 8 May 1997.
45. JWF/SLB. Athens, Georgia. 8 May 1997.
46. Fanning, J. W. Personal communication with author. Ca 1975.
47. JWF/SLB. Athens, Georgia. 5 May 1997.
48. JWF/SLB. Athens, Georgia. 8 May 1997.
49. Fanning, J. W. Unpublished handwritten notes. Ca 1996.
50. JWF/SLB. Athens, Georgia. 5 May 1997.
51. JWF/SLB. Athens, Georgia. 5 May 1997.
52. JWF/SLB. Athens, Georgia. 5 May 1997.
53. JWF/SLB. Athens, Georgia. 5 May 1997.
54. Fanning, J. W. "My Life." Unpublished autobiography. Ca 1996.
55. Fanning, J. W. Unpublished handwritten notes. Ca 1996.
56. McMillian, Lawrence. *The Schoolmaker.* Chapel Hill: The University of North Carolina Press, 1971.
57. JWF/SLB. Athens, Georgia. 8 May 1997.
58. Fanning, J. W. "My Life." Unpublished autobiography. Ca 1996.
59. Fanning, J. W. "My Life." Unpublished autobiography. Ca 1996.
60. Bullock, Henry Morton. *A History of Emory University.* Atlanta: Cherokee Publishing Company, 1972.
61. "J. W. Fanning: A Great Georgian." *Great Georgians Film Series*, Georgia Center for Continuing Education, The University of Georgia. 1977.
62. JWF/SLB. Athens, Georgia. 8 May 1997.
63. JWF/SLB. Athens, Georgia. 8 May 1997.
64. JWF/SLB. Athens, Georgia. 8 May 1997.
65. JWF/SLB. Athens, Georgia. 8 May 1997.
66. Fanning, J. W. Contents of a letter to grandson, Dan Cook. 17 September 1979.
67. Fanning, J. W. Unpublished handwritten notes. Ca 1997.
68. JWF/SLB. Athens, Georgia. 18 April 1997.
69. JWF/SLB. Athens, Georgia. 18 April 1997.
70. JWF/SLB. Athens, Georgia. 18 April 1997.

Chapter Two: University Studies

1. Fanning, J. W. "My Life." Unpublished autobiography. Ca. 1996.
2. Bachtel, Douglas. Personal communication. University of Georgia. November 2000.

3. "Boll Weevil Cost Growers of Cotton up to $400,000,000." *The New York Times*. 1 July, 1921.

4. Dollar values based on cotton harvested and price per pound received. Calculations by author. November 2000.

5. Fanning, John Wootten. Business Records for 1920. 1 January 1921.

6. Fanning, J. W. Personal communication with author. Ca 1975.

7. Fanning, J. W. Response to student questions in Dr. Joseph Hammock's class. Psychology Department, University of Georgia. 5 August 1980.

8. Dyer, Thomas, G. *The University of Georgia, A Bicentennial History, 1785–1985*. The University of Georgia Press, 1985.

9. Dyer, Thomas, G. *The University of Georgia, A Bicentennial History, 1785–1985*. The University of Georgia Press, 1985.

10. Dyer, Thomas, G. *The University of Georgia, A Bicentennial History, 1785–1985*. The University of Georgia Press, 1985.

11. Reed, T. W. *The History of the University of Georgia*. Vol. VI, (1956) 425. Unpublished.

12. Fanning, J. W. Transcription of tape on selling Bibles in 1925. Athens, Georgia. 1993.

13. "J. W. Fanning: A Great Georgian." *Great Georgians Film Series*, Georgia Center for Continuing Education, The University of Georgia, 1977.

14. Fanning, J. W. "My Life." Unpublished autobiography. Ca 1996.

15. Fanning, J. W. "My Life." Unpublished autobiography. Ca 1996.

16. Fanning, J. W. "My Life." Unpublished autobiography. Ca 1996.

17. *The Pandora*. Vol. XL. Athens, Georgia, University of Georgia publication, 1927.

18. Fanning, J. W. Personal communication with author. Ca 1975.

19. Fanning, J. W. Transcription of tape on obtaining Master's Degree 1927–28. Athens, Georgia. 1993.

20. Fanning, John William. "Negro Migration." Phelps-Stokes Fellowship Studies No. 9. *Bulletin of The University of Georgia*, Vol. XXX, No. 8b. June 1930.

21. Fanning, John William. "Negro Migration." Phelps-Stokes Fellowship Studies No. 9. *Bulletin of The University of Georgia*, Vol. XXX, No. 8b. June 1930.

22. Boatright, Susan R. and Douglas C. Bachtel. *The Georgia County Guide*. Eighteenth Edition, 1999.

23. Fanning, J. W. Transcription of tape on obtaining Master's Degree 1927–28. Athens, Georgia. 1993.

24. Fanning, J. W. Transcription of tape on obtaining Master's Degree 1927–28. Athens, Georgia. 1993.

25. JWF/SLB. Athens, Georgia. 18 April 1997.

Chapter Three: The Agriculturist

1. Fanning, J. W. "My Life." Unpublished autobiography. Ca 1996.
2. Smith, Clarence Bearman and Meredith Chester Wilson. The Agricultural Extension System of the United States. New York: John Wiley & Sons, Inc. 1930.
3. Smith, Clarence Bearman and Meredith Chester Wilson. The Agricultural Extension System of the United States. New York: John Wiley & Sons, Inc. 1930.
4. Annual Report of the Cooperative Extension Service, College of Agriculture. Athens, Georgia: The University of Georgia. 1 July 1928–30 June 1929.
5. Fanning, J. W. Response to student questions in Dr. Joseph Hammock's class. Psychology Department, The University of Georgia. 5 August 1980.
6. Bramlett, Gene A. "Some Recollections of the Wit and Wisdom of J. W. Fanning." Ca 1990.
7. Fanning, J. W. "My Life." Unpublished autobiography. Ca 1996.
8. JWF/SLB. Athens, Georgia. 5 May 1997.
9. Fanning, J. W. "My Life." Unpublished autobiography. Ca 1996.
10. Fanning, J. W. Personal communication with author. Ca 1975.
11. Fanning, J. W. Personal communication with author. Ca 1975.
12. Fanning, J. W. "My Life." Unpublished autobiography. Ca 1996.
13. Nelson, Bobbe. *A Land So Dedicated: The History of Houston County.* 1999.
14. Chandler, F. C. "County Agent's Newsletter," Houston County, Georgia. 1931.
15. Chandler, F. C. "County Agent's Newsletter," Houston County, Georgia. 1931.
16. Nelson, Bobbe. *A Land So Dedicated: The History of Houston County.* 1999.
17. "J. W. Fanning: A Great Georgian." *Great Georgians Film Series,* Georgia Center for Continuing Education, The University of Georgia. 1977.
18. Fanning, J. W. "My Life." Unpublished autobiography. Ca 1996.
19. Fanning, J. W. "My Life." Unpublished autobiography. Ca 1996.
20. Fanning, J. W. "My Life." Unpublished autobiography. Ca 1996.
21. Fanning, J. W. "My Life." Unpublished autobiography. Ca 1996.
22. Fanning, J. W. "My Life." Unpublished autobiography. Ca 1996.
23. Bramlett, Gene A. "Some Recollections of the Wit and Wisdom of J. W. Fanning." Ca 1990.
24. Evans, Aurelia. Personal interview by author. Perry, Georgia. 29 March 2000.
25. Fanning, J. W. "My Life." Unpublished autobiography. Ca 1996.
26. Fanning, J. W. "My Life." Unpublished autobiography. Ca 1996.

27. Fanning, J. W. "My Life." Unpublished autobiography. Ca 1996.

28. Rhodes, Edgar. Personal interview by author. Bremen, Georgia, 28 March 2000.

29. Cheek, Earl. Personal interview by author. Perry, Georgia. 29 March 2000.

30. Rhodes, Edgar. Personal interview by author. Bremen, Georgia, 28 March 2000.

31. Marshall, Joseph. Response to survey from authors. Athens, Georgia. March 2000.

32. Marshall, Joseph. Response to survey from authors. Athens, Georgia. March 2000.

33. Fanning, J. W. "My Life." Unpublished autobiography. Ca 1996.

34. Fanning, J. W. "My Life." Unpublished autobiography. Ca 1996.

35. JWF/SLB. Athens, Georgia. 8 May 1997.

36. Harrison, Carlyle. Response to survey from authors. Athens, Georgia. March 2000.

37. Morris, Donnie. Personal communication with author. Baxley, Georgia. June 2000.

38. Morris, Donnie. Personal communication with author. Baxley, Georgia. June 2000.

39. Morris, Donnie. Personal communication with author. Baxley, Georgia. June 2000.

40. Fanning, J. W. "My Life." Unpublished autobiography. Ca 1996.

41. Fanning, J. W. "My Life." Unpublished autobiography. Ca 1996.

42. Fanning, J. W. "My Life." Unpublished autobiography. Ca 1996.

43. Fanning, J. W. "My Life." Unpublished autobiography. Ca 1996.

44. Shubert, Paul. *Cason Callaway of Blue Springs.* Atlanta, Georgia. Foote and Davies. 1964.

45. Fanning, J. W. "My Life." Unpublished autobiography. Ca 1996.

46. Fanning, J. W., W. T. Fullilove, and L. M. Awtrey, Jr. *The Business of Farming.* Ida Cason Callaway Foundation. Hamilton, Georgia, 1948.

47. Fanning, J. W. "My Life." Unpublished autobiography. Ca 1996.

48. Fanning, J. W. "Six Steps to Farming." Article for *The Progressive Farmer Magazine.* 29 July 1958.

49. Fanning, J. W. "Six Ways to Judge Efficient Farming." Article for *The Progressive Farmer Magazine.* 1 November 1953.

50. Fanning, J. W. Personal papers. The University of Georgia. March 2001.

51. *The Progressive Farmer Magazine.* Vol. 76, no. 1, January 1961.

52. "About Berry College." Web page. www.berry.edu. 2 August 2000.

53. Dodd, D. R., J. W. Fanning, and Charles N. Stephardson. "An Appraisal

of the Berry School's Program with Particular Reference to the Agricultural Activities." Report presented to the College president. August 1958.

54. Fanning, J. W. "My Life." Unpublished autobiography. Ca 1996.

Chapter Four: Community Development (1954–1956; 1961–1965)

1. Bonniwell, Hilton T. *A Historical Analysis of Non-Credit Adult Education Program Development at The University of Georgia, 1804–1968.* Doctor of Education Thesis. Athens, Georgia: The University of Georgia, 1969.

2. Carter, Jimmy. Response to survey from authors. Atlanta, Georgia. March 2000.

3. Fanning, J. W. "Rural-Urban Balance." Article prepared for *The Progressive Farmer Magazine.* November 1958.

4. Healan, Hill R. Response to survey from authors. Atlanta, Georgia. March 2000.

5. Fanning, J. W. "My Life." Unpublished autobiography. Ca 1996.

6. Coan, Gaylord. Taped interview by author. Atlanta, Georgia. 24 May 2000.

7. Younts, Sanford E. "John William Fanning, The Most Widely Accepted Person in Georgia During the 20th Century." J. W. Fanning Lecture. 5 November 1997.

8. Hardwick, Clifford III. Response to survey from authors. Savannah, Georgia. March 2000.

9. "Georgia General Planning Enabling Act." Passed by the General Assembly of Georgia. 1957.

10. "Georgia General Planning Enabling Act." Passed by the General Assembly of Georgia. 1957.

11. Thomas, Sidney F., Jr. Personal interview by author. Savannah, Georgia. 11 August 2000.

12. Tanner, Joe D. Personal taped interview by author. 18 August 2000.

13. Tanner, Joe D. Personal taped interview by author. 18 August 2000.

14. "J. W. Fanning: A Great Georgian," *Great Georgians Film Series*, Georgia Center for Continuing Education, The University of Georgia. 1977.

15. Fanning, J. W., "Community Planning," Georgia Municipal Journal. Vol. VII. July 1958.

16. Fanning, J. W. "A New Georgia in the Making." Coosa Valley Regional Conference. Rome, Georgia. 7 May 1959.

17. "A Prospective for the Total Development of Northwest Georgia." Coosa Valley Area Planning and Development Commission, 1960.

18. Thomas, Sidney F., Jr. Personal interview by author. Savannah, Georgia. 11 August 2000.

19. Fanning, J. W. "My Life." Unpublished autobiography. Ca 1996.

20. Fanning, J. W. "My Life." Unpublished autobiography. Ca 1996.

21. The University of Georgia Annual Report. Administrative Section. 1961.

22. Fanning, J. W. "My Life." Unpublished autobiography. Ca 1996.

23. Fanning, J. W., "The Institute of Community and Area Development." Georgia Municipal Journal. Vol XI, no. 11, 1961.

24. Boatright, Susan R. and Douglas C. Bachtel. *The Georgia County Guide.* Eighteenth Edition. 1999.

25. Bachtel, Douglas C. Personal communication with author. November 2000.

26. Sparer, Burt. Response to survey from authors. Athens, Georgia. March 2000.

27. Maund, Tim. Response to survey from authors. Athens, Georgia. March 2000.

28. Maund, Tim. Response to survey from authors. Athens, Georgia. March 2000.

29. DuVall, Tal C. Response to survey from authors. Athens, Georgia. March 2000.

30. Verner, Ann. "Savannah's Young Leaders." *The Georgia Alumni Record.* Summer 1966.

31. Burgess, James V. Jr. and Howard A. Schretter. Personal interviews by author. Social Circle, Georgia. 1 August 2000.

32. Burgess, James V. Jr. and Howard A. Schretter. Personal interviews by author. Social Circle, Georgia. 1 August 2000.

33. Schretter, Howard. A. Personal communication. Athens, Georgia. July 2000.

34. Schretter, Howard. A. "Central Savannah River Area, Economic Condition and Trends." Institute of Community and Area Development. The University of Georgia. 28 May 1962.

35. Schretter, Howard. A. "The Area Planning and Development Commission and Local Planning." Institute of Community and Area Development. University of Georgia. 18 October 1963.

36. Bramlett, Gene A. "Memories of J. W. Fanning." Unpublished. Ca June 1998.

37. Schretter, Howard A. Response to survey from author. March 2000.

38. Hill, Robert J. and Howard A. Schretter. "Guidelines for an Over-All Development Program." Institute of Community and Area Development. The University of Georgia. 18 October 1963.

39. George, Elmer W. Personal communication. Griffin, Georgia. 10 February 2000.

40. Glenn, Hazel. Personal communication with author. Athens, Georgia. December 2000.
41. Bramlett, Gene A. "Memories of J. W. Fanning." Unpublished. Ca June 1998.
42. Morris, Donnie. Personal interview by author. Baxley, Georgia. June 2000.
43. Morris, Donnie. Personal interview by author. Baxley, Georgia June 2000.
44. Fanning, J. W. Portion of a speech delivered in Tifton, Georgia. September 1971.
45. Bramlett, Gene A. "Memories of J. W. Fanning." Unpublished. Ca June 1998.
46. JWF/SLB. Athens, Georgia. 5 May 1997.
47. JWF/SLB. Athens, Georgia. 5 May 1997.

Chapter Five: Vice President for Services (1965–1971)

1. Dyer, Thomas G. *The University of Georgia, A Bicentennial History, 1785–1985*. Athens: The University of Georgia Press, 1985.
2. Dodd, Lamar. Letter of congratulations to J. W. Personal papers. 8 January 1965.
3. Cook, Sibyle Fanning. Letter of congratulations to her father. Personal papers. 1965.
4. Fanning, Bill. Letter of congratulations to his father. Personal papers. 1965.
5. The University of Georgia Fortnight. "J. W. Fanning, New Vice President for Services." Vol 1, no. 7, 13 January 1965.
6. An opinion of fact by authors on the situation of the times.
7. Burke, John D. Response to survey from authors. March 2000.
8. Fanning, J. W. "My Life." Unpublished autobiography. Ca 1996.
9. Fincher, Cameron. Taped interview by Sherry LaBoon. June 1997.
10. Blueberry Growers Association. Personal communication. June 2000.
11. Values mentioned by the news media for several years.
12. Chin, Edward. Personal interview by author. Athens, Georgia. July 2000.
13. Chin, Edward. Personal interview by author. Athens, Georgia. July 2000.
14. Davison, Fred C. Personal interview taped by author. Augusta, Georgia. 22 May 2000.
15. Fanning, J. W. Invocation for Inaugural Dinner for President Fred C. Davison. Summer 1967.
16. *The Athens Daily News/Athens Banner-Herald*. 3 August 1969.
17. Fanning, J. W. "The American Dream." Commencement Address. Mercer University, Macon, Georgia. 15 August 1969.

18. Younts, S. E. Collection of J. W. Fanning quotes. Unpublished. December 2000.

19. "Service Career to End." *The Athens Daily News/Athens-Banner Herald.* 31 December 1971.

20. "Fanning Services Will Remain Much in Demand." Editorial. *The Athens Daily News/Athens-Banner Herald.* 31 December 1971.

21. Davison, Fred C. Comments at J. W. Fanning's retirement dinner. 6 April 1972.

22. Fanning, J. W. Comments at his retirement dinner. 6 April 1972.

23. Davison, Fred C. Personal taped interview by author. Augusta, Georgia. 22 May 2000.

24. Younts, S.E. Collection of J. W. Fanning quotes. Unpublished. December 2000.

25. Fanning, J. W. Letter to Ralph Griffin. Haralson County, Georgia. 9 August 1996.

26. Boynton, Asa. Personal taped interview by author. Athens, Georgia. 16 October 2000.

Chapter Six: The Personal J. W.

1. Bramlett, Gene A. "Memories of J. W. Fanning." Unpublished. Ca June 1998.

2. Jenks, Sibyle Frances Fanning. Taped interview by Sherry LaBoon, Athens, Georgia. 16 June 1997.

3. Fanning, J. W., Jr. Personal taped interview by author, Madison County, Georgia. 28 August 2000.

4. Fanning, J. W., Jr. Personal taped interview by author. Madison County, Georgia. 28 August 2000.

5. Fanning, J. W. "My Life." Unpublished autobiography. Ca 1996.

6. Fanning, J. W. "The Art of Human Living." Sunday school lesson plan. Athens, Georgia. 26 August 1955.

7. Best, Edward E. Jr. "J. W. Fanning, 1905-1997." Tribute presented to J. W. July 1997.

8. Cave, Julian. Response to survey from authors. Radisson Beach, Florida. March 2000.

9. Bentley, Upshaw. Personal communication with author. Athens, Georgia. 11 October 2000.

10. Appleton, Jon. Response to survey from authors. Athens, Georgia. March 2000.

11. Appleton, Jon. Response to survey from authors. Athens, Georgia. March 2000.

12. Appleton, Jon. Response to survey from authors. Athens, Georgia. March 2000.

13. Culpepper, E. H. Personal communication with author. Athens, Georgia. October 2000.

14. Bramlett, Gene A. "Memories of J. W. Fanning." Unpublished. Ca June 1998.

15. Appleton, Jon. Response to survey from authors. Athens, Georgia. March 2000.

16. Fanning, J. W. Comments at memorial service for Margaret Beasley Broun. Athens, Georgia. Spring 1981.

17. Fanning, J. W. Speech to Northeast Georgia Council of the Boy Scouts of America. Undated.

18. Fanning, J. W. "Wisdom." Presentation to congregation of First Baptist Church. Athens, Georgia. Undated.

19. Fanning, J. W. Prayer sent to daughter Sibyle. Spring. 1986.

20. "First Baptist to Dedicate Today." *Athens Daily News/Athens Banner-Herald.* 28 August 1994.

21. Jenks, Sibyle Frances Cook. Taped interview by Sherry LaBoon. Athens, Georgia. 17 June 1997.

22. Fanning, J. W. "Temptation." Sunday school lesson plan. Athens, Georgia. 27 July 1997. Lesson was never taught due to his death on the morning of July 27, 1997.

23. Bramlett, Gene A. "Memories of J. W. Fanning." Unpublished. Ca June 1998.

24. Fanning, J. W. "My Life." Unpublished autobiography. Ca 1996.

25. Bentley, Upshaw. Personal communication with author. Athens, Georgia. 11 October 2000.

26. Jenks, Sibyle Frances Cook. Taped interview by Sherry LaBoon. Athens, Georgia. 17 June 1997.

27. Fanning, J. W., Jr. Personal taped interview by author. Madison County, Georgia. 28 August 2000.

28. Jenks, Sibyle Frances Cook. Taped interview by Sherry LaBoon. Athens, Georgia. 17 June 1997.

29. Jenks, Sibyle Frances Cook. Taped interview by Sherry LaBoon. Athens, Georgia. 17 June 1997.

30. Jenks, Sibyle Frances Cook. Taped interview by Sherry LaBoon. Athens, Georgia. 17 June 1997.

31. Jenks, Sibyle Frances Cook. Taped interview by Sherry LaBoon. Athens, Georgia. 17 June 1997.

32. Davison, Fred C. Personal taped interview by author. Augusta, Georgia. 22 May 2000.

33. Morris, Donnie. Personal interview by author. Baxley, Georgia. June 2000.

34. Giddens, Howard. Response to survey from authors. Macon, Georgia. March 2000.

35. Fanning, J. W., Jr. Personal taped interview by author. Madison County, Georgia. 28 August 2000.

36. Jenks, Sibyle Frances Cook. Taped interview by Sherry LaBoon. Athens, Georgia. 17 June 1997.

37. Fanning, J. W. Jr. Personal taped interview by author. Madison County, Georgia. 28 August 2000.

38. Fanning, J. W. Jr. Personal taped interview by author. Madison County, Georgia. 28 August 2000.

39. Jenks, Sibyle Frances Cook. Taped interview by Sherry LaBoon. Athens, Georgia. 17 June 1997.

40. Fanning, J. W. Jr. Personal taped interview by author. Madison County, Georgia. 28 August 2000.

41. Jenks, Sibyle Frances Cook. Taped interview by Sherry LaBoon. Athens, Georgia. 17 June 1997.

42. Fanning, J. W., Jr. Personal taped interview by author. Madison County, Georgia. 28 August 2000.

43. Fanning, J. W., Jr. Personal taped interview by author. Madison County, Georgia. 28 August 2000.

44. Fanning, J. W., Jr. Personal taped interview by author. Madison County, Georgia. 28 August 2000.

45. Jenks, Sibyle Frances Cook. Taped interview by Sherry LaBoon. Athens, Georgia. 17 June 1997.

46. Fanning, J. W., Jr. Personal taped interview by author. Madison County, Georgia. 28 August 2000.

47. Fanning, J. W., Jr. Personal taped interview by author. Madison County, Georgia. 28 August 2000.

48. NeSmith, Dink. Communication from J. W. Fanning. Ca. 1988.

49. Davison, Fred C. Personal interview by author. Augusta, Georgia. 22 May 2000.

50. JWF/SLB. Athens, Georgia. 5 May 1997.

51. Fanning, J. W. Personal communication with author. Athens, Georgia. 1990.

52. Fanning, J. W. Personal communication with author. Athens, Georgia. 1990.

53. Davison, Fred C. Personal interview by author. Augusta, Georgia. 22 May 2000.

54. Jenks, Sibyle Frances Cook. Taped interview by Sherry LaBoon. Athens, Georgia. 17 June 1997.

55. Younts, S. E. Collection of J. W. Fanning quotes. Unpublished. December 2000.

56. Fanning, J. W. Communication to Cora Lee on her eighty-seventh birthday. May 1992.

57. Jenks, Sibyle Frances Cook. Taped interview by Sherry LaBoon. Athens, Georgia. 17 June 1997.

58. Fanning, J. W. Jr. Personal taped interview by author. Madison County, Georgia. 28 August 2000.

59. Greene, John. Personal communication to author. Anderson, South Carolina. December 2000.

60. Dowdy, Mary. Taped interview by Sherry LaBoon. 18 August 1997.

61. Greer, William, Jr. Response to survey from authors. Norfolk Virginia. March 2000.

62. Hammock, Joseph C. Personal communication with author. Athens, Georgia. 25 May 2001.

63. Dowdy, Mary. Taped interview by Sherry LaBoon. 19 August 1997.

64. Giddens, Joel. Response to survey from authors. Athens, Georgia. March 2000.

65. Hunter, Lucy Lowe. Letter to J. W.'s nurse Mary Dowdy. August 1997.

66. Fanning, J. W. Poem written for the ninety-third birthday of Lucy Lowe Hunter. Decatur, Georgia. 26 July 1997.

67. Chin, Edward. Personal communication to author. Athens, Georgia. Date unknown.

68. Giddens, Joel. Personal communication to authors. Athens, Georgia. August 2000.

69. Fanning, J. W. Personal communication to Fred Birchmore. Athens, Georgia. 23 July 1997.

70. JWF/SLB. Athens, Georgia. 12 July 1997.

Chapter Seven: Leadership Georgia

This chapter is from the notes of contributor Dink NeSmith and from interviews conducted in person, by phone or facsimile machine, or by electronic mail.

Chapter Eight: The J. W. Fanning Institute for Leadership

1. Reed, Norma Q. Interview by editor Melinda D. Hawley. Athens, Georgia. April 2001.

2. Reed, Norma Q. Interview by editor Melinda D. Hawley. Athens, Georgia. April 2001.

3. Reed, Norma Q. Interview by editor Melinda D. Hawley. Athens, Georgia. April 2001.

4. Reed, Norma Q. Interview by editor Melinda D. Hawley. Athens, Georgia. April 2001.

5. Reed, Norma Q. Interview by editor Melinda D. Hawley. Athens, Georgia. April 2001.

6. Meadows, Laura. Response to telephone inquiry by author. Dublin, Georgia. February 2001.

7. Maund, Tim. Reply to survey from authors. Augusta, Georgia. March 2000.

8. Appropriations Legislation. Georgia General Assembly. Atlanta, Georgia. 1998.

9. Pattillo, H. G. Speech at groundbreaking for J. W. Fanning Building. Athens, Georgia. 14 August 1999.

10. Cooper, Melba G. Personal communication with author. 17 September 2001.

11. Reed, Norma Q. Interview by editor Melinda D. Hawley. Athens, Georgia. April 2001.

Index